Today's Deer Hunting Handbook

Today's Deer Hunting Handbook

The Complete Illustrated Guide for New and Experienced Hunters

Robert Amendola

Acclaim Press
MORLEY, MISSOURI

Acclaim Press
— Your Next Great Book —
P.O. Box 238
Morley, MO 63767
(573) 472-9800
www.acclaimpress.com

Book and Cover Design: M. Frene Melton
Front cover photography: Larry Ditto
Illustrations: Terry Staton

Library of Congress Cataloging-in-Publication Data

Amendola, Robert.
Today's deer hunting handbook : the complete illustrated guide for new and experienced hunters / by Robert Amendola.
p. cm.
ISBN 978-1-935001-21-8 (alk. paper) -- ISBN 1-935001-21-3 (alk. paper)
1. White-tailed deer hunting--Handbooks, manuals, etc. 2. Deer hunting--Handbooks, manuals, etc. I. Title.
SK301.A475 2009
799.2'7652--dc22
2009019837

First Printing: 2013
Printed in the United States of America
10 9 8 7 6 5 4 3 2 1

This publication was produced using available information.
The publisher regrets it cannot assume responsibility for errors or omissions.

Contents

I Dedicate This Book

to my wife, Mary, who continuously encouraged me to write about the sport I know, hunting the whitetail deer, and complete this book for new and experienced hunters.

Many people have influenced the hunter I am today.

I would like to mention everyone who has helped me along the way; however, I would need a separate chapter to list them all.

My father, Frank J. Amendola,
instilled in me my love for the outdoors.

Tony Mauro, know as "The Moose,"
taught me the basics and was a great mentor.

Gene Barnicott, a good friend,
picked up where others left off.

If there is a special place for hunters after this life,
all three will be there helping others in a way that meant so much to me.

Thank you from the heart;
you will always be remembered.

– Bob Amendola –

Foreword

"Buzzzzzzz! Buzzzzzzz! Buzzzzzzz! Click."

It's 4:30 am; how the time has flown by. I feel like my head just touched the pillow, and the alarm has already gone off. Zip, my Border Collie who is lying on the floor by my side, just lifted his head a bit and laid it back down. Casey, my Brittany Spaniel, wouldn't stir unless you picked her up and tried to carry her off. She is a good dog, but as a bird dog has no clue. Then there is Possum, a beagle that adopted us a year or so ago, that has a big dog attitude if awakened before his time. Yes, we have three dogs, two of which think that the king size bed on which they are allowed to rest is theirs, and I am allowed to sleep with them. Then there is our cat, CoCo, but she is a whole other story.

My wife stirred, but luckily I can see she is not awake. Not a good way to start a hunting season—waking the Mrs. "Well, I had better get up and start the coffee," I think before I doze back to sleep in the contorted position I am lying in. Anyone who is a dog owner will know what I mean. Another five minutes would feel really nice about now. Another hunting season has begun, and all the thought and preparation won't be worth a hoot unless I get going. Luckily, I laid out all my things last night.

As I get out of bed, Zip is thinking he is going with me again, and I have to tell him to lie back down and be good as not to wake the Mrs. I stumble to the kitchen, where the coffee pot stands as my redemption to the real world, and start fixing it to brew. Making my way to the shower, I am trying to be quiet but determined to get things going.

Now at 4:45 a.m., I am in the shower and wondering if getting up this early is needed or just a custom that should be well thought about for the future. Who was it that said, "You have to be in the woods a half hour before sunrise to allow the woods to calm down"? Must have been said by the Hunting God somewhere, or did I read that? Just about now I am also wondering if the character who said that really does get up at this time himself. My shower is about over, and I am convinced that washing with a no-scent soap has left me without a trace of humanity, so to speak. My camouflage clothes have hung in the garage after being washed with the same sort of manmade concoction, which has left them odor-free as well. I slip into my hunting outfit, socks and boots, and I am ready for the taste of my wake-me-up coffee, which I drink with all haste, wondering if my scent-free clothes will now smell like coffee beans.

A last-minute check has reassured me that my backpack is full of everything I might need in the woods. I put on my camo hat and stick my gloves and head net in one pocket with my razor-edge buck knife in the other. With an assortment of all the necessary tags in my shirt pocket, I am just about ready to leave the house.

Have I forgotten anything? I scramble to look on the shelf for my boot cover scent, which I hurriedly stick into my other shirt pocket. Taking a bottle of water from the counter, I am off. Not bad at all, I think. Just after 5:15 a.m. and with a fifteen-minute trip to my deer stand, I should be in the stand by 5:30, which will give the woods a good thirty minutes to calm down before daylight.

I load my pack and bow together with a full quiver of new arrows topped with the latest sure-fire broadheads into my Workhorse four-wheeler, and I am off. Trying to remember if I had unplugged the coffee pot and remembered to put Zip out before leaving (or did I unplug Zip and put out the coffee pot) runs through my head as I try to avoid the chug holes on the gravel road. I cut across the lower field and park the Workhorse next to the timberline and access road that leads to my freshly tilled and managed food plots. Putting the keys in the cup holder to remember where they are later, I am ready for the stealthy movements that will bring me to my stand.

I spray the bottom of my boots with a cover scent that will make any animal think I am a 178-pound fox, slip on my pack and grab my bow. The bank of low lights attached to my hat illuminates the access road as I slip through the woods in cat-like fashion, like a fox with a flashlight attached to its head. It could happen!

I reach the edge of the food plot after stumbling over a tree root that I swore wasn't there a few days earlier and wonder if my cat-like stealth movements were noticed by anything. Making my way to the left and through a small pine thicket, my light decides it needed a rest, and the illumination ceases. How could this be? It worked fine yesterday. No worry, I am near the opening that will bring me to my stand. Resuming the cat-like stance I was trained to imitate, I direct my attention to the task at hand and remember that my stand is only a short distance ahead. I really don't remember all these low branches, but I am sure they were always there. Slowly making my way in the dark, I reach a familiar area, and my stand is just ahead. The rope I attached to the top of my stand is now visible, and I quickly tie my bow to the end and begin the ascent.

I have a tri-pod hunting stand that I have modified into a four-sided enclosed stand, together with a roof. I am completely enclosed, which serves the dual purpose of concealment and weather barrier. Having sides that are open enough to allow a comfortable archery or rifle shot, I feel more at ease than in an open stand. After I climb into the stand and close the hinged door, I remove my small pack and lay it to one side and pull up my bow.

It is now 5:45 a.m., later than I expected to be getting settled in my stand. I am sitting in the dark and wonder if I have offended the Hunting God. Have I made so much noise with my transformed movements to alert every animal in the woods that my stealthy movements could have been in actuality a meat-eating dinosaur? Here I am, quietly sitting in the dark, fifteen feet in the air, as my mind thinks of many different things. The quiet sounds of the night are around me, and I am now one with nature at last.

I think about how many other hunters are sitting in their stands at this very moment. Maybe we can get a game of cards going by headset; no—who would shuffle the cards, let alone cut the deck? I think of past hunting trips and the time I flushed a turkey from a tree as I was climbing to get into my stand. I remember it sounded like a winged Pterodactyl. Man, was my heart pounding then. I also think of the times I walked through the woods and flushed a rough grouse or two; that set me back a bit. It's funny how your mind starts to wander while you are sitting in your deer stand, waiting for sunrise to show its waking glaze of the new glinting sunlight. You know, one of these days I am going to write a book about hunting. Not your average book, but one that could be a practical guide for both new and seasoned hunters, a book that answers all the questions and takes all the guesswork out of it. An illustrated and easy to read guide, and book all in one. One of these days…

Today's Deer Hunting Handbook

The Complete Illustrated Guide
for New and Experienced Hunters

Chapter One

The Story of Hunting

Hunting is the practice of pursuing an animal for food, use of their hide for trade or one's own need, and for sport. If you trace back to a time before human civilization in the early ancestry of our forefathers, and even further back to an era that sustained primitive man, you would see that hunting was a way of life.

Focusing our attention on the whitetail deer, one would have to begin *The Story of Hunting* with our American Woodland Indians, whose survival depended greatly on their skilled ability and strategies to hunt. While hunting, the Woodland Indian learned to position himself within a relatively close distance of a deer and then harvested his quarry, using the entire animal for sustenance, shelter and clothing. Using a self-constructed bow and arrows made of wood, the American Indian was able to effectively place a shot with amazing accuracy. Their stealthy movements and knowledge of pursuit has given the hunter of today examples that are often copied and closely compared.

The preparation for a hunt was a culmination of several different practices that an Indian brave would do. Fasting for several days, abstaining from tobacco and alcohol, followed by sitting in a sweat lodge to cleanse his body of impurities and odor, the Indian hunter would effectively control his human scent. After leaving the sweat lodge, the brave would next paint his face and body for camouflage as the final composition for the upcoming hunt. The iterative procedures incorporated by the Indians have truly lead many an industry to the art of concealment and scent control.

Practices and strategies of the American Indian spearheaded the archery industry of today, evolving from the wooden bow to the later longbow and recurve bows. Modifications and technology gave rise to the compound bow and further development to the current and highly accurate crossbow.

But our story does not end here. The use of the firearm came into play with the explorers and early settlers who ventured their way and traveled to the Indian land, bringing with them the flintlocks and later the muzzle-loading guns.

As time went on, hunting became easier, and what first started with a bow gave rise to the firearm.

Deer could now be harvested more easily and at farther distances. As firearms improved, emphasis was placed on faster and improved rifles and ammunition, which could shoot longer distances, delivering greater speed and accuracy. The way and time of the Indian moved aside, and the dawn of meat hunting for market approached. Whitetails were slaughtered in record numbers to fulfill the demand of fresh and easily obtained meat.

Seen as an unlimited supply, meat hunting for market all but brought about the extinction of the whitetail deer in some states. Many people spoke out about the plight of the deer including Theodore Roosevelt, who was one of our greatest presidents and protectors of wildlife. In 1916, Theodore Roosevelt stated, "Defenders of the short-sighted men who in their greed and selfishness will, if permitted, rob our country of half its charm by their reckless extermination of all useful and beautiful wild things sometimes seek to champion them by saying 'the game belongs to the people.' So it does; and not merely to the people now alive, but to the unborn people."

The deer herds of yesteryear were lessened considerably, triggering the need for management through the organization of state game departments. The deer herds that remained were now under the protection and control of an organized body with the help of trained agents, known today as Conservation Officers.

The need to limit the taking of whitetail deer was apparent. Rules and regulations to harvest deer were enacted stemming from the concerns of many during the years of hunting for markets. Many big bucks were taken in the beginning, because the average buck lived long enough to grow a big rack. Hunting was different in that hunters often camped in groups for an entire season. At the end of the hunt, sometimes eight to more than a dozen big bucks could be seen hanging from meat poles. Today's custom of hunting for only a few days at a time to sometimes a week long cannot compare to the hunts of years past. That is not to say all the big bucks are gone. With

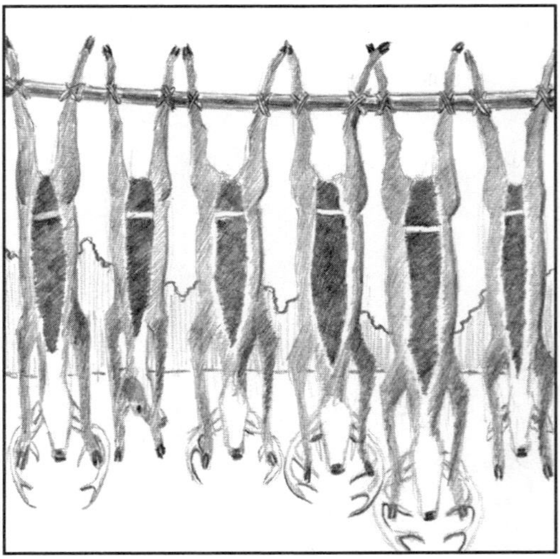

today's game management, many areas produce big bucks and many of trophy size can be harvested.

The story of hunting continues, as the future of hunting has yet to be written. With you as our new or experienced hunter, this story lives on. Your actions and the actions of millions of other whitetail hunters across this nation will carve the future in the annals that follow.

Whitetail deer management has been taken to new levels as landowners and individuals came together with the foresight and knowledge that more had to be done to ensure not just survival, but a healthier whitetail deer by instituting select agricultural plantings on both state owned and private property.

A new and different call to arms has been enacted as long-time adversaries and supporters of hunting have unknowingly joined together, each believing with their separate ideas to come to the defense of the whitetail deer today. Both anti-hunting people and the present-day hunter agree on the promotion of the form of the natural order as an integral part of this picture; differing only is the harvesting of the species. One believes that nature will survive and the predator in nature will control the carrying capacity of the land, which is the amount of deer that can survive in a particular area. State and local officials believe that due to the lack of sufficient numbers of the predator species, hunting will fill in the gap. Both groups feel that management on some level is necessary to keep a natural balance.

As part of the future, your aid is the important counterbalance on this scale, forming the outcome that will be written at a later date. Stepping back and looking as an observer, I see more change coming that will allow future generations the same enjoyment that you are about to encounter and add to the story of hunting for tomorrow.

Their future depends on you.

Chapter Two

Knowing the Whitetail Deer

Much has been written concerning the whitetail deer. Whitetails can be viewed on many of the hunting shows seen on TV, and when hunters generally talk about hunting, the topic usually turns to these masters of the woods. You can read about deer in outdoor magazines, and extensive, elaborate books have been written that cover their genealogy, if you can stay awake long enough to read those books. I know I can't, so I am going to give you what you need to know as a hunter. Not to say all those other writings are misguiding, but I feel you should have the hunter's version and in *Knowing the Whitetail Deer* will discuss thing of which you should be aware, and will do my best not to put you to sleep.

Whitetail deer are inhabitants of the woods. Their uncanny knack to elude a hunter, keen senses and agility in movement are sometimes compared to mythical creatures by those who have hunted them. They can spot movement at incredible distances. Though they are color blind, that is about as far as their blindness goes,

having eyesight that is far superior to human standards. Moving at dawn and dusk in semi-darkness and in the evenings when they feed the most, the whitetail deer can see astonishingly well. Their hearing is excellent to the point that a deer will hear hunters who are not careful in their approach through the woods, alerting deer long before they can be spotted, but a whitetail's hearing is only second to their eyesight. Another defense mechanism is the whitetail deer's acute sense of smell, which is 100 times greater than a human. Deer will lift their nose in a breeze to smell an unnatural scent coming in their direction, yet some hunters think that their ability to smell is their best defense. I have seen deer from hunting stands lift their nose, stamp one foot and bound off seconds later. On the other hand, I also have a trophy eight-point buck on my wall that I took one afternoon in the Catskill mountains while sitting in an large elevated wooden tree stand about ten feet off the ground. I was with a hunting companion at the time, and smoking my pipe.

It was a foggy day as I recall, and you could barely see the end of your rifle barrel, let alone any distance. It was the type of day that is perfect for either hunting with a buddy or staying back in the cabin under the warm covers on your bed, hoping it wasn't your turn to get up to put another log on the fire. I was whispering to my friend that we probably wouldn't see a thing for a while or until the fog lifted some, so I lit my pipe, deciding to relax for a while and get back to hunting a few hours later in another location. Just about forty-five minutes to an hour later as I recollect, of jawing about old times, past hunts and puffing on my pipe, I glanced outside of the stand at what might be a small break in the fog. I remember it was hard to see through the mass of cloudy mist, and I wondered if my mind was playing tricks on me. As the cover started to break, I saw what appeared to be the brownish part of a downed tree at first. Curiously looking again, to my surprise I saw the outline of what looked to be a deer. Taken back, I began focusing with more intent and said to my friend, "I think I see a deer." As we both looked, the fog eased up a bit; I saw a mature buck standing about forty yards away from the stand. Putting my pipe down and raising my rifle, since I saw the deer first, I dropped the deer where he stood. Now did that deer have a stuffed up nose, or did he just like the smell of my pipe tobacco? I don't rightly know, but it does make one think a bit.

Whitetail deer can remain motionless for long periods of time to observe or remain hidden, allowing hunters to walk within feet of them if they think they have not been seen. Their speed is incredible. While in full flight, whitetail deer have been clocked at 30 to 40 miles per hour. Another ability of the whitetail is their ability to jump. A normal whitetail deer can easily jump an eight-foot fence from a standstill without taking a preliminary step, and broad jumps of 25 to 30 feet are common.

Whitetail deer are also great swimmers. During the fall hunting season when they wear their hollow haired winter coats, the whitetail can maintain buoyancy and swim for long distances. It has been noted that deer can swim up to ten miles per hour. If living by a swamp or pond, a deer would not hesitate to escape what they perceive as danger by swimming, if the deer thinks it is a way out. In cold weather conditions, in frigid water temperatures that humans could not survive, deer could swim with no ill effects at all.

But to truly know the deer, one would have to start their look in the springtime when they begin to migrate from their wintering area, depending upon the climate and geographic location, and begin their journey to their summertime home range. In the southern areas, their migration might only be measured from one lowland fir bottom to a nearby mountainside or secluded meadow. In a northern wintering range, deer may spend days or possibly weeks migrating considerable distances to reach their summertime boundaries. Yes, deer do migrate, contrary to what hunters think. Young deer rely upon the older matriarchal females in the clan for guidance, just as they must be guided when they were fawns and leave their summer habitat. The older deer, as most deer in general, are extremely traditional in their ways and possess a strong attachment to their ranges, returning year after year and often following the same routes. Where deer live is generally determined through social experiences learned at early ages and carried through the rearing cycle. Does and fawns will generally occupy an area where there is the greatest abundance of nutritious choice foods, while bucks tend to occupy areas in the summertime secluded from the does and fawns in poorer quality habitat. However, during a brief period of time before the new fawns are born, both bucks and does are together in search of choice foods in overlapping ranges with little conflict. As summer proceeds the bucks and does separate, forming select bands that travel mostly together.

Beginning around the end of May to early April, bucks will show new antler growth. Depending on the buck's intake of nutritious food, his antlers can grow up to one half inch per day. Antler growth is determined mainly by nutrition, vitamin and mineral intake and the consumption of an adequate diet. There is a large variety in shape and structure in whitetail deer's antlers, which are purely physical characteristics and often passed down to buck's offspring. Age cannot be solely determined by antler development, which some think is true. By late July bucks can display full-size antlers in velvet. Velvet is a soft membrane that surrounds newly grown antlers filled with blood vessels and sensory hairs. They can run through the wood lots easily with their newly grown set of antlers. You might wonder why they don't get them all tangled as they move through the woods. Bucks have a unique sense with which they can judge their own rack size and together with the sensory hairs in their velvet warn them of a collision. Later, as they lose and rub off their velvet on saplings and trees, their antlers harden as the cool weather approaches, and they gracefully move through dense cover.

Does that have been bred in the fall enter into a 200-day gestation period, having their fawns usually around the end of May to early June depending upon geographic location. Towards the end of a doe's gestation period, the doe will restrict some of her foraging activity and isolate herself, often by going to her choice area. Once there she will drive away other deer if they approach, remaining secretive to have her young.

Does usually have two fawns during ideal conditions. Once the fawns are born, a doe will generally display continued territorial behavior and defensive postures to protect her young around other deer, which generally lasts six to eight weeks. The isolation of the mother with her fawns imprints the mother and infant bond. Any significant interference during this isolation period can lead to the breakdown of this imprinting process, which could contribute to the abandonment and possible death of the newborn deer.

Fawns nurse almost immediately, and in the beginning, when the mother lies on her side. Up and walking within thirty minutes, the newborn fawn, with white spots on a reddish brown body, remains at its mother's side as its protector and nutritious source of food. Young fawns spend much of their time hiding in the beginning, but are quickly introduced to their mother's range. Learning from its mother's encouragement, a new fawn can travel up to several hundred yards within hours of being born. When a fawn is only a few days old, it begins to nibble on vegetation but does not start to ruminate until about two to three weeks.

Predators looking to prey on young fawns maintain a vigilant search. Coyotes, bobcats, bears, mountain lions and even a turned out and unmanaged domestic dog will hunt out a fawn. Those that survive the elements grow rapidly, generally doubling their weight within two weeks. Traveling with their mothers, the fawns mature and lose their spots mid-to-late September in the warmer climates, and later in cooler locations and become yearling deer. Though these yearlings look like a small deer to a hunter, they are still dependant on their mother for nutrition and survival. Mature does that have young yearlings with them should not be harvested. Harvesting mature does that have yearlings dependant can result in the death of these yearlings by winter's end.

In the summertime, when deer are in their feeding ranges, food resources are normally adequate for the whitetail deer's summer diet. Deer have been known to eat mushrooms and lichens to green leafy browse. In farmland, deer supplement their diet with nutritious farm crops such as corn, sugar beets, soybeans and rye. A deer's range generally has a diversity and wide variety of grasses and shrubs, and their feeding habits change in response to changes in forage availability. Deer usually adapt, and if their range couples with an area that has houses, they have been known to feast on ornamentals and some planted flowers such as roses and tulips. An average deer will spend about 75 percent of its time foraging.

As fall readily approaches, it triggers several behaviors. Mature does and young yearlings increase their feeding, to develop a fat reserve that will be needed in the winter. As woods feeders in the fall, deer will generally consume a lot of browse, feasting on buds, twigs, acorns and nuts; for dessert they will go to the fully ripe fruit on persimmon and apple trees. If there are farms with either wheat or soybean fields, you will generally see deer feeding heavily there in the late afternoon. In some areas winter can arrive early, making it important that fawns reach their full potential in their final stage of growth. Generally, the young yearlings that are long-legged and fat have the best chance to survive winter weather. Bucks start the fattening process as well, but also begin to show aggression, often

Your local Conservation Officer can assist you. They know deer ranges.

sparring with one another, and rubs can be see on different saplings. As their sex hormone levels begin rising, they tend to break off from traditional boundaries, seeking out new ranges that will put them in closer contact with the does. As the rut draws near, the neck of a breeding buck begins to swell, and he can often be seen in the same area feeding with the does prior to courtship. Feeding continues, and often a higher number of deer will congregate in one area, unlike other times of the year.

As the deer herds expand, natural herbage can be consumed to the point of severely damaging the deer's feeding area. In a time when predators were abundant, nature was able to work out the carrying capacity of the land. To maintain a system of checks and balances today, hunting adjusts the carrying capacity of the land occupied by deer. Without hunting by responsible individuals, a whitetail deer herd could easily expand to the point of starvation.

Chapter Three

Signs to Be Familiar With

Now that you have decided to hunt, you have entered into the select and prestigious club together with millions of other hunters who like yourself, flock to the woods each year, wanting to bring home one of the most cunning of all the big game animals, the whitetail deer. The enjoyment you will have, the sights you will see, and the feeling of being one with nature cannot be measured as you enter the wonderful world of hunting. By now you are trying to learn as much as you can about the subject to make you more successful, which puts you in a different class from the hunter who thinks he can simply enter the woods, have a seat on a stump and a deer will sooner or later pass in his direction. I won't say it can't happen, but if you know the *Signs to Be Familiar With*, you won't have to leave bringing home a deer to chance.

Whitetail deer leave signs during each of the different and changing seasons. By knowing what to look for and when, you can figure the location of deer, which will give you an advantage when the fall hunt approaches. Success in the field is measured in time—not only the time you spend hunting, but also the time you take reading and knowing the signs of deer during the off-season when scouting areas to hunt. This is critical part of hunting, and I can't stress this enough; average hunters who may scout areas only days or a week before their hunt often overlook it. Though some of these hunters will bring home a deer, the majority will not. It is estimated that only one out of seven hunters will be successful in bringing home a deer. If you look at all the number of hunters in your state and the published results of deer harvested at the end of the year by the conservation department, by doing the math you will clearly see that often the number of unsuccessful hunters is even higher at times than the average I have just told you. While you are looking up the stats, check to see what counties are consistently posted as counties that prove to have more deer killed each season. If you keep past conservation journals, the stats will be recorded every year at the end of the hunting season. These high-kill counties are a good place to start scouting in.

Scouting for areas to hunt and reading the signs is a vital preparation that must begin long before the approach of fall. If you are a new or experienced hunter, entering the woods in the late spring and summer is a refreshing time to be in the woods. If you are married and have children, it is the perfect way of allowing your family to be part of your hunt and an introduction of your children to what hunting is all about. Hunting is not just shooting a deer. It is the culmination of all that is involved, and the end result, if you have done your homework, is the successful harvest of a whitetail deer.

Too many hunters leave their family at home and go away each year, isolating their loved ones from an activity that they could become involved in. By involving your family in the scouting process, the upcoming hunt could become a family achievement by their participation. I do hope you think about this, as I feel it is important to you as a family man or woman who would like to be a successful hunter or huntress.

The late spring to early summer is when you should begin your first scouting trip. This is the trip when you will be looking for places that contain the favorite foods deer crave this time of year. After deer have left their holdup in the winter yards, they seek lush, herbaceous growth that is easily digestible for their energy needs, containing vitamins and minerals in plants like adder's tongue, violets, trilliums and assorted spring flora. They will feed on fresh, new, young grasses that show in patches in the woods, staying close to cover and avoiding openings that reveal too little cover. The deer are leery at this time of the year, having survived winter and a nutritional shortage in the food they consumed to stay alive in the bleak, dense winter yard they remained in through winter's end. Upon leaving their winter yard to go to their spring and summer range, deer tend to feed heavily to regain lost weight. It is also the time of the year that deer show that they are not all browsers as most hunters think. As summer approaches, the whitetails will begin eating mushrooms and green leafy browse for the first time. Since many hunters have not done their homework, they only see whitetails in the fall when deer have changed their eating habits to the fall range food due to the decrease of abundance and the fact that the grasses mature and dry out.

Good relations with local landowners can make the difference when it is time to pick your hunting location.

If you are not hunting on state land and are thinking of hunting on private land, it is a good time of the year to get permission well in advance of the hunting season from the land owner of the property you wish to scout and later hunt. It is also good to be aware that all property, whether it be posted or not, is owned by someone. State land will generally be posted, though sometimes it may not be, and this is also true of private land. If private land is not posted and you hunt on it, you may not get in trouble for hunting, but you could get in trouble for trespassing, possibly losing the right to ever hunt that land again.

When on your scouting trip, look for fresh water in small streams or spring-filled ponds as deer will always return to these areas at least once or twice a day. Look at the grasses and flowers and see if you can see bite marks that will be visible on flower stems. Naturally look for tracks and focus your attention on the cover surrounding these feeding areas as deer will generally want to feed in areas that border thick cover. Once you find their summer feeding area that borders this cover, look for tracks going into and coming out of the cover and make a note of it. Look for deer droppings and make a note of it when they are spotted. Also make a note of what foods for deer you have found in the area. Do not enter the cover on this scouting trip. Remember this, make a note of where it is, and leave it at that for now.

Your next scouting trip should be in mid-summer at the very latest. If you have gotten prior permission from a landowner, you might want to bring along a pie or cake as a good gesture. When on private lands, remember to close all gates that are closed and leave gates that are opened open. If you see any trash, empty pop bottles or cans, be sure to pick them up for the landowner. Courtesy goes a long way and will be remembered.

You don't want to make too frequent trips to one area, but if you like what you see, make note and return to that spot as well as others you have recorded. Depending on the area, this is the time when you will be looking for apple trees that have new apples on them, cherry trees, beech woods with budding nuts, and the different types of oak trees with new acorn growth. Look for this in the area you liked the most when you first started your scouting and then in other areas. These trees can be found in the cover, the thick woods you can now enter. You may be wondering why you can enter the cover now. In the late spring and early summer, whitetails do not go far from their feeding area and will remain in the cover adjoining their feeding area if not disturbed. Once they finish their late spring and early summer feeding range, they go deeper into the cover to find their mid-to-late summer feeding range and will be less likely to be driven off. They will move if disturbed then, but generally they always return to their summer range. Avoid all open areas and fields. One rule of thumb to remember is that if you can see a distance in one direction or another, so can the deer, and deer avoid these areas during the day.

In the thirty years I have been hunting, I have seen many hunters in the woods sitting in a stand that is fairly open. Most of the time when I approach them, making my presence well known in advance, I ask them if they have seen anything. Nine out of ten times they tell me no, and they can't understand it because it is a good spot with loads of tracks.

Keep This In Mind. Deer will only enter these areas on two, and only two, occasions. The first is during the evening hours when they feel safe to move to their feeding range, and the second is when they are driven out of their normal covered location. The open area might be loaded with tracks, but avoid them at all cost. I am not talking about a man-made food plot. That is entirely different, and I will cover that later in this book.

As you look for the trees I have told you to look for, you should also look for thicker cover hardhack; tall, thick tangle brush; a pine grove; a large outcropping or a rock shelf leading to a plateau. Look for these that are adjacent to the tree grove you are scouting and make your notes. Also look for tracks leading to and from these areas. Look for paw marks in the ground as deer will often dig for mineral deposits this time of year. If you find them, make a note. If you have brought your family with you on your scouting trips, you can set up a game where they get points for all the signs you tell them to look for and they find and tell you. Each sign noted and recorded is ten points. Deer droppings are fifteen points. If a deer is seen, that's an automatic twenty-five points. At the end of the day, you add up their points, praise all the children, and you can end the scouting trip with a meal out as a family. Believe me when I tell you, it will be a day and a meal you will always remember.

Deer signs tell you where deer have been and likely to return.

Let us see what we have in your notes. You have looked at areas and found the late spring food ranges, and now you have found where the deer's summer range is. You have looked in several areas and have picked one area that stands out the best. We will call this area your primary target area. Next, select two areas that looked good but not as good as the first. These will be your secondary target areas.

Your next scouting trip should be about three weeks before the start of your hunting trip in the fall. This is not your last scouting trip, as you need to make one other trip. If you have family, this is an important trip for them as well. If you have made a point game of your previous scouting trips, tell them that this trip will have specific signs for them to locate, but they must walk and move quietly. It is a test to see how quiet you all can be and how well the different signs can be located. On this trip you will be looking for half chewed acorns or nuts. Chew marks that can be clearly visible as a (V) indent or bite in an acorn or nut. Apple trees that show deer activity with chew marks or deer tracks under it. Browse that has been nibbled on that is clearly visible by the (V) shaped bite marks. You might see a deer bed, which will be a matted down area in the grass or leaves. If you see that, make a note of it. Look for deer droppings and tracks and make a note of it. Look for a sapling or tree that a deer might have rubbed his antlers on, which is called a rub. This can be seen as a freshly rubbed area of a tree that is generally six to twelve inches up from the ground to an area of about two feet. If you find small saplings rubbed, it could indicate a smaller buck, but I have seen ten-point bucks rub on saplings that were only two inches in diameter and four-pointers rubbing on much larger diameter trees. As a general rule, don't make assumptions because of the size of a tree, other than the fact that a buck has been in the area.

You should also look for coralberry, greenbriers, honey locust, yellow ironweed, sumacs, buck brush (leaves and fruit), wine cup, vetches, white avens, and thorn chokecherries, as these are a deer's favorite foods for this time of year. When you find them and see deer activity, make a note of it. These foods are what keep deer in the area. You need to be aware of these foods and what they look like to identify them at a glance.

If you have taken the family, be sure to praise all who have helped with this scouting trip and tell them how important their input is. Make it a family outing if at all possible so you keep their interest high and remind them there is only one more scouting trip before the hunt. Tell them that this upcoming trip is important as it will be the last scouting trip to determine your hunting location.

Your last scouting trip of the season is important, as your hunting success will be determined by all that you have accomplished to and including this trip. By now you have narrowed down the hunting locations to three possible areas. This will be the last scouting trip prior to stand location. On this trip you are looking for rubs and scrapes, which are pawed-out areas on the ground that bucks make as a calling card to breed. Bucks generally paw out an area on the ground and urinate in it as their calling card to does ready to breed. This is an important sign and should be noted and not disturbed so as not to leave any human scent in the area. As this is your final scouting trip, look for all signs of deer that include tracks

Rubs are a good sign of a buck in the area, either rubbing off velvet, or marking his territory.

coming in and out of the area and make a note. Be familiar where the heavy cover is to know the area they go to bed. Look for escape routes, which are thick areas where deer will go to escape danger. Look for where the feeding areas are in relation to the bedding areas and make a note. Bedding areas will be areas that offer the best cover and are surrounded by thick cover. Be aware of secondary approach areas where the deer may come in if the wind shifts from one direction to the next. Listen to the input from your family and decide if it warrants further investigation and make notes about it. If it has recently rained, it is the best time to look for game trails, or runways, as many veteran hunters call them. A good time to do your last scouting is a day or two after a heavy rain. You can see clearly see if the runways have fresh tracks, which will be helpful in positioning a stand later on. There is no sense in using an unused trail for reference later on.

Once you have your notes compiled and have scouted your primary and secondary areas, leave the areas, as the final scouting trip is now over. You should return home and correlate all your notes to be sure you have selected the best primary and secondary target areas by reading all the signs for which you are now familiar.

Chapter Four

Tips to See More Deer

There are many hunters today who have never gotten a shot off at a buck. Though they say they hunt every year, they claim that they rarely see deer and have never seen a whitetail buck. If you ask them how many times they scouted their hunting area, they will either say that they have been hunting the same area for years or that they checked out the area a week or possibly two weeks prior to the season. They may even say that they saw a lot of tracks and the deer were there before the start of the season.

I often hear stories of how the deer moved or changed their habits after the first few shots were fired. They are partly right, because whitetail deer do change their habits when being pressured, so we will talk about that next.

If you have done your homework and made several scouting trips to determine the primary and secondary target areas, you will have seen tracks leading to the thick cover I spoke of in the previous chapter. That thickest cover is usually the escape route deer will take when pressured. Whitetail deer will seek this type of cover after the first day of the hunting season as their protection.

Remember that whitetails are full-time deer, and you are a part-time hunter. Learn their habits and you'll find their location.

I am going to make a bold statement here that experienced hunters may agree or disagree with. Some will say, "Yeah, it's probably true," but if they think back to past hunts, they will say I am right or scratch their heads wondering before it does sink in. One of the worst days to hunt is the day after the opening of the firearm-hunting season. The second day of the hunting season, after the guns are fired at whitetails by those venison seekers in every area, the whole ball game changes. Unless you position yourself on secondary routes or around the thickest cover and change from your primary hunting position, you will not see deer except if they are pushed to you. Even on my own property, I will hunt opening day of the firearm season and not hunt again for two days after opening day.

After opening day, whitetail deer are shell-shocked and scared. They immediately seek heavy cover from the invasion in their woods and stop using regular trails until the cover of darkness when they feel safe again. If you have a limited time to hunt, you should hunt the heavy cover during the day and in the afternoons; position yourself close to a feeding area near thick cover. Doing drives through the heavy cover will push the deer out to other hunters on a stand. I usually wait two days on my property, and by doing so, the third day is like a second opening day. The deer will again resume their normal pattern, except for the late day feeding when the deer usually move closer to dusk. The land that borders mine on two sides is not hunted, and on one side there is limited pressure. As whitetails are not pushed on my property and the property around me, this allows a period for the deer to calm down and feel relaxed.

I know this as a fact, as I wait until I again see deer again moving through two large fields I have on my property, which generally takes place two days after opening day. I do not do drives on my property, and have found the deer to be relaxed and back to their opening day patterns. If you have your own property or have exclusive permission to hunt another's property, try it and you will see a noticeable difference. If you wish to hunt on the second and third day, pick another location. I guarantee you will have success when you come back to hunt on the fourth day after leaving the property not hunted for two days after opening day.

If the property you own or have permission to hunt on is less than seventy-five acres and the land around you is heavily hunted, this will not work. However, if the deer are not pushed by drives and excessive hunting pressure, you will notice a surprising difference.

The average hunter who has not done his homework has two strikes against him at the very start of their hunting season. The first is that he has no idea of the deer's fall feeding range and protection cover, and second is that he is not familiar with the whitetail's escapes routes to these protected areas.

The thick hardhack fields, tangle brush fields, dense pine groves and swamps are the usual protected areas that whitetail deer will feel safe when pressured. Since one or more border the primary target area you have selected to be your hunting area, you should not be one of the hunters who claim he or she does not see deer.

To see more deer, one has to be in the area deer are in or the area deer will escape to once the pressure starts. This is important in the "Tips to See More Deer" when you are hunting on state land or private land that is not your own. Knowing the location in which to position yourself is an important asset when hunting. It is not the only asset to see more deer, but it ranks in the top five.

The second asset to be aware of is movement. Deer have the keen ability to see movement at a long distance. If you are moving in your stand or hunting location, a whitetail deer will generally pick up that movement and avoid you long before you are able to spot it. If you are in a hunting ground blind, elevated stand, or simply hunting on the ground, it is important that you remain still. Movement is measured in degree, meaning that if you wish to turn, do it in small degrees.

This is a good time to tell you how a hunter moves while hunting. There are two things to remember about movement, and they are stealth and moving slowly whenever you move. Always judge your movement as if a deer is staring right at you and move accordingly. If you are sitting while you are hunting and wish to turn your head do it slowly. If you are walking, do a two-step movement. Keep in mind that deer or any other animal in the woods moves with caution, stealth and slow movements when under pressure, except when they are escaping an imminent threat. Never stop in an open area if you can stop by a tree or brush to break

Deer have keen eyesight and will often remain motionless and unnoticed when they see movement. Stay focused and alert.

up your outline. Also, when you are entering the woods to get to your hunting stand or location, you are hunting. I can't tell you how many times I see hunters going to their stands or favorite locations walking like they are in a race or marathon. The first thing they say is that they want to get to their stand and allow the woods to calm down for a while. Let me tell you, you can't calm the woods down for any purpose if you have scared deer totally out of the area. Yes, the woods will calm down, but the deer will be across the next ridge or meadow when they do. I generally appreciate it because I have killed more deer that were pushed to me by these marathon hunters, trying to get to their stands in haste. Then there are those who drive their vehicle to a spot, park and leave a light on to get ready, then close a vehicle door that can be heard about 200 yards away. When they do start to move, they talk to one another about when they will meet up for lunch or get together for the walk out of the woods. I guess it would be a good time to tell you that most deer are not hard of hearing when it is dark and you are moving to your stand, thinking you can be quiet when you reach your stand and then allow the woods to quiet down.

Now, let's discuss what you may have put in your backpack or fanny pack. Did you remember to pack a sandwich; was it bologna and cheese or are you a liverwurst lover? Did you remember to put on the mustard or mayonnaise? What about that apple to curb your appetite or the candy bar to keep you going till lunch? I know you are a coffee or tea person, so you can't forget that thermos, right?

The question is, are you trying to see deer or simply want to alert them of your presence in the woods? But you are only going to take a few sips or a few bites, right? I guess the whitetail deer, who has a nose 100 times more sensitive than a human's, will cut you a break and have their nose clip on when you do that. When you are in the woods, and even when you take a break from hunting to eat or for a snack, you are still hunting if you are in the woods. Every time you move or crinkle a piece of cellophane or aluminum wrap or bite into that sandwich or open that hot thermos which lets the scent of your drink escape, the potential to be seen or detected by a deer is there, and you have just again reduced your chances of seeing a whitetail.

You may be asking, "What do I do when I get hungry and still want to hunt?" I recommend you leave the woods quietly and slowly, if you are to the point that hunger that has made your hunt unbearable, until such time as you are able to be able to sit still and quiet for the rest of your hunt. If you are planning to be in the woods for several hours or a day, I do not know of any hunter who has died of starvation or lack of a sip of coffee or tea for that amount of time. Though I am not of a nature to give medical advice, I do believe you could possibly survive a few hours without the substance you crave and you might even enjoy it more if you were explaining to another hunter about the deer you just harvested while you were partaking in the snack or feast.

Now that you understand how I feel about lunch or snacks in the woods, let's continue talking about scent. Ah yes, you have done your homework and have washed your clothing with a scent-free liquid or powder. Now where are you going to store those clothes before you put them on? Are they hanging in your hunting cabin or closet? Is there a wood burning stove in your cabin? Are they now in a closet with clothes that were washed with scented soap? Does anyone smoke in the cabin? Is it the night before the hunt and you and your hunting pals are sitting down to a feast before the hunt of Italian food or cooked venison with onions and potatoes? The reason I am asking you these questions is just because you washed your hunting apparel with a scent-free additive does not guarantee they will be scent-free come morning. I generally hang my hunting clothes either outside a hunting cabin under an overhang, or in an area of my garage that has a separate storage closet specifically for my hunting apparel to keep them odor-free at all times. I also will not put them on until right after I have taken a shower and then not be in an area to pick up any scent. This way I ensure my clothes and body are scent-free. Before leaving and well before arriving to my choice location, I have applied cover scent to my boots and an area scent to my pants. I use an area scent, meaning acorn scent if I am hunting an oak grove, pine scent if I am hunting the pines and an odor barrier scent at other times. This will allow me to pass through the woods undetected by an unnatural odor.

You can go out and purchase the new scent barrier clothing that guarantees you will remain scent-free and is claimed to be the only proven way to be scent free. That clothing is fine till next year when something else is developed and you are told that is the only way to go. I have been hunting a number of years, and I think a good rule of thumb is to remember to be practical whenever you can. Enough said about that.

Let's say you are a person who has their own piece of property, and wants to hunt it and wishes to see more deer. There are several things you can do, the first of which that I recommend is to contact the local state game management agent, who will inform you of what is legal for your area. He or she may also put you in contact with other conservation agents who will take a tour of your property, giving you recommendations on the grasses, plants, trees and food plots you can use on your property to attract wildlife. Do not be too quick to put in a food plot by reading an advertisement or seeing a recommendation on TV alone. I recommended you talk to the officials who can better tell you this after they have seen your property. They may recommend what you have seen or read about or offer to furnish you with seed free of charge. In my home state of Missouri, the local Conservation agent supplies me with sacks of seed to plant in the food plots on my property. State Game management offices look to help the landowners, thus help the deer herd as well, by offering the landowners seed with no out-of-pocket expense. Your local Conservation agent may do the same. If not, they will be more than helpful with ideas and suggestions on what to do in your particular area. Food plots on your property will attract more deer and wildlife to your property. Your conservation department will also offer you advice concerning select cutting, canopy raising and trimming areas to attract more wildlife as well. This will help not only deer, but turkeys and all wildlife on your property. Their service is free and their advice invaluable.

To see deer look for the horizontals. Trees grow upright and horizontals are either downed trees or a whitetail deer.

Does the property you are planning to hunt have small patches of thick brushy cover? Has any area been logged with large treetops left behind? These are places for mature bucks and should not be overlooked because of the dense coverage. Many a mature buck has been shot that sprang up from the thickets of brush and snarled tree tops, which offer excellent hiding places for the mature bruisers.

As the season progresses, I often hear that the bucks have disappeared from the area. Mature bucks will often change both their holdup area and their sleeping area seeking the thickest of cover. They will often hold up in small and odd patches of tall brush and grasses that are usually overlooked, and only be stirred from these areas under pressure, quickly returning to them when they feel the pressure has eased. When doing walks in these areas, return for a second walk a few hours later, and you may be surprised to kick out a really nice buck. You may have to squat down on your haunches or be on your knees to study cover. When doing so, look for the legs of deer or a part of a deer. Limit tree stand hunting to early morning and late afternoons and plan on doing slow walks during the day through brush and heavy cover. Walk two steps, and then another two steps, then stop by a tree or brush to break your outline. Look and listen for about ten minutes or longer between steps. Whitetail deer have four legs and take a two-step and then another two steps usually when feeding and walking through the woods. By walking the way I just described, you will sound like a deer walking and feeding by other deer in the distance if you do it slowly. Never rush or feel you have to barrel through cover. Hunters who pace themselves, moving slowly like the turtle, take many large deer. Remember, always that deer have keen senses and can easily see movement. Deer step on branches and twigs, so do not worry if you make a little sound. You don't want to sound like a predator charging forward, but if you step on a branch or twig, remain by a tree a little longer and look without too much body movement. If while standing motionless you see a movement, check it out by standing still and observe until you have fully checked it out.

No matter how slight the movement, it could be the flick or a deer's tail or the twitch of a whitetail's ear. Slowly rotate your head and avoid upper body movement when at all possible. You can walk through dry leaves. You will make a little noise but if you do it slowly as I mentioned earlier, you can go unnoticed from feeding deer. Deer are very curious creatures that often stop and look intently when they hear a noise. If the noise stops, a deer will generally go on feeding unbothered. Usually after the first few days of hunting pressure, deer are skittish from being pushed or shot at, so be aware of this and move accordingly.

Weather has a significant effect on deer and where they will be located. A skillful hunter is aware of this and will know where to look for deer in various kinds of weather. On warm days deer tend to be a bit lazy, seeking shade and often lying down in an area that offers the most shade to cool down. On cold days, deer will bed on the side of a mountain or slope with a southern exposure, where sunlight can filter through the trees to provide warmth. Deer are very much like humans in that when it rains or snows, they will look for cover to hold up in until it passes. On windy days they seek cover in thick pines, lowland pockets or on the lee side of hills. Deer movements are also affected by weather as deer will change from their normal routine in inclement weather and wait it out. Be aware also that not all deer will react the same to given weather conditions, as I have seen some deer feeding in the fields on my property during a heavy rain, while others escaped for cover. Keep in mind one fact about whitetail deer: though deer are predictable, once you think you have figured out all the answers, nature comes along and changes the questions.

Chapter Five

Buying a Rifle or Shotgun

Whether you are new to hunting or a seasoned veteran to the sport and reading this book for the first time, I decided to put this chapter here with your interest at heart. If you are an experienced hunter, some tips I will include might help you in finding a specific rifle or shotgun that would suit your needs also.

Buying a rifle or shotgun is important and should not be looked at lightly or rushed into by either the new or experienced hunter. You should take your time, weigh several options and look in several different gun shops as well as sporting goods stores. Do not allow a sales agent to talk you into buying a firearm of their choice until you feel it is the one for you and your choice.

When you look at different firearms, keep in mind when sales people are telling you what they consider you should own to kill a deer. It's not the rifle that makes the killing shot, it's the person behind the rifle that does it. Think about that before you decide on which firearm to purchase. It takes only one shot placed in the right area to do the job.

While taking trips to scouting different areas, you may pass by a gun shop or another area that you are not accustomed to shopping. I have found that the small local gun shops are excellent for finding deals on guns of all sorts.

For the new hunter seeking his first firearm and wishing to hunt a rifle area, I strongly recommend a used rifle, preferably a bolt-action rifle. I say this because it is a fact that a new hunter will probably go through about three rifles on average before deciding and settling on a rifle he or she is comfortable with using as their permanent rifle of choice. You could also save on the average of $100.00 to $250.00 by purchasing a used rifle as opposed to a new rifle. Later you may decide you want to sell it to purchase a different rifle or simply just get another type of rifle. Why spend top dollar in the beginning until you have used the rifle and decided if you are comfortable with that particular model?

In the years I have been hunting, I have purchased many firearms, and some of the best deals I have ever encountered were from small gun shops I have driven past on scouting trips. I recommend you wait until you have visited a few gun shops before you make any decision on purchasing; you may be surprised on how much money you could save. It is also a great way to meet other hunters, learn about different hunting areas and possibly make new and interesting friends. Another way to purchase a good quality firearm is by going to a gun show. Gun shows are events that generally have as many as fifty or more different gun dealers who bring several of their firearms to the show in the hope to sell or trade them. At a gun show you can speak to many different dealers and gather valuable information about all different action rifles and ammunition. Some of these shows have gun manufacturers present, and you can speak to them directly to ask specific questions about different model firearms.

Then there are hunting seminars and trade shows that are open to the public, usually around hunting season, where you can gather tons of information about firearms. I do hope you will attend as many hunting seminars as you possibly can. I have always found these seminars to be entertaining and filled with all kinds of hunting ideas and a great way to meet other hunters in a relaxed atmosphere. I have conducted many hunting seminars throughout the years and I look forward to meeting you.

I want you to be familiar with several different options so you don't feel that you have to run out to the first shopping center you see to purchase your firearm.

Local gun shows are a great place to find good deals on firearms.

A good used firearm in quality condition and excellent working order, backed by a reputable gun dealer, could be your wisest choice in the beginning or years later. For the hunter seeking a particular model or individual preference, it could also prove to be your best source of locating what you seek and save you some money, which we all like to do.

There are both left-handed and right-handed firearms. If you are left-handed and wish to shoot left-handed, you should be looking for a left-handed firearm; the same is true if you are right-handed and wish to shoot right-handed. There is nothing worse than a left-handed shooter trying to shoot a right-handed gun. You can, but the loading and ejection port for the ammunition is on the opposite side, as well as the proper side for the cheek plate. If you don't know if you want to shoot left-handed or right-handed, go to a local firearms dealer and try holding and looking down the barrel of both types of firearms.

There are many different caliber rifles on the market today, most of which will down a whitetail deer, but you should be mindful that some calibers are better suited than others for hunting whitetail deer. There are hunters who like a lightweight rifle that will down a deer with a skillfully placed shot, while others prefer the knock down power of the heavier calibers. I will try to break the calibers down in the light range and then the heavier ranges. Be aware that just because a caliber can be used for shooting a whitetail deer doesn't mean that it will be right one for you. The lighter calibers like the .223 Remington, .257 Roberts and the .243 Winchester were designed as varmint rifles primarily, but with a hunter who can place an accurate shot at close to midrange, they also can be used for hunting a deer. A big game rifle with a lighter kick when fired would be the 7MM or the .308 Browning rifle. These rifles are excellent for taking a whitetail deer and will not knock you back with recoil when fired or make you hard of hearing with the muzzle blast. With any rifle, when sighting in and firing numerous shots, you should wear both ear and eye protection. The all-around big game rifles would be the .300 Savage, .30-06 Springfield, .270 Winchester and the .338 Winchester. Be mindful that you can also buy these rifles by other manufacturers than I have mentioned here. In order not to fill this book with all the name calibers and manufacturers, I have listed what I feel to be the norm. The magnum rifles are good, and you can use them, but I would consider them overkill for a whitetail deer. But I have seen hunters using a .340 Weatherby and even a .375 H&H while hunting a whitetail deer, even though they are considered calibers that should be used on heavy or dangerous North American Game like an elk or either a brown or grizzly bear. You will take down a deer with them, and if the deer is standing next to a tree, you may even take down part of the tree, as well as feeling a healthy kick to your shoulder that you may remember later on that day.

Every individual has what is called a dominant or master eye. Just as you have a dominant hand either left or right, you also have a dominant eye, and you should aim your firearm using your dominant eye. To determine which of your eyes is dominant, there is a simple test. Form a small triangle with your hands touching your thumbs together and forefingers. Then stretch both of your arms out in front

Forming a triangle like this and bringing it back to your face will show you your dominant or master eye.

of you and focus on an object while looking through the triangle opening you have created with your touching thumbs and forefingers. Next, bring both your hands slowly towards your face while you are still looking at the object through the opening in the triangle, and the triangle will come to your dominant eye.

If you are left-handed, you generally will have a left dominant eye; the same is true if you are right-handed. Do not be alarmed if this is not the case with you. You would simply determine whether you want to shoot left- or right-handed, which will depend on your individual comfort level and practice just the same until you feel comfortable and develop accuracy with the firearm. Practice in either case is a must to be both knowledgeable and consistent with your firearm.

Though there are many different models and manufacturers of rifles and shotguns, as well as many different calibers in each, there are five different types of actions on rifles and four types of actions on shotguns. On rifles there are bolt action, pump action, break or hinge action, lever action and semi-automatic

firearms. On the shotguns there are bolt action, pump action, break action with both single or double barrel, and semi-automatic. The state and the area you intend to hunt will determine if a rifle or shotgun is allowed. Some states allow either but particular areas may require a hunter to use a shotgun only. To be sure, you should check the requirements of the area you wish to hunt.

The bolt action is an excellent firearm and has been around for quite a while. I recommend this firearm to a new or veteran hunter because it is a good, safe rifle. It also requires that the user practice often with the rifle because most of the time in the beginning, you will only get one opportunity as well as only one shot off, which has to be placed accurately. Being an ethical hunter and sportsman or sportswoman requires you to place an accurate shot that will deliver a clean and quick kill. Once you have mastered a firearm and practiced to be consistent with your accuracy, one shot should be all that is necessary. Later in this book we will discuss shot placement, but for now and in "Buying a Rifle or Shotgun" all you need to know that the bolt action rifle is the firearm of choice.

The pump action is a very good firearm, and I myself have several. I do not choose this to be a beginner firearm, as too often knowing that you can make a quick second shot may take away from beginners taking their time to deliver the perfect placement of their first shot. It is a great firearm to own and a safe firearm, but I do not recommend them to a beginner as their first and primary gun.

The lever action firearm has been around for a long time, and the model 30-30 lever action has sold in the millions. I do not consider the older models as safe firearms because an individual has to put the loaded gun on half cock to have this firearm on safety. The newer models that have a traditional slide safety are best, but I do not recommend this gun for the beginner or novice. Accidental discharges have been recorded with this firearm, and I believe this action should be the firearm of choice for a hunter who has been around firearms for longer than the beginner.

The semi-automatic is a splendid firearm and the pinnacle of success for the firearm industry. Using a semi-automatic gun, the hunter can deliver three or four shots rapidly, which you will generally hear in the woods every hunting season. I own a few myself, but I rarely hunt with them, as most of the time I have not found the need for a second shot. I often wonder if many who use them simply aim at a deer and keep pulling the trigger in the hopes that one out of four shots will hit the deer. I will not recommend that a beginner buy this action firearm as their first choice. Once you have fired several firearms in the field though, a semi-automatic gun is a good one to own.

This reminds me of one of my first hunts in South Dakota for whitetail deer with a good friend of mine named Bob several years back when I was but a younker. We were hunting a hog's back slope one afternoon in the late fall. It was bitter cold with about six inches of fresh snow on already frozen ground. We were positioned about half way up a ridge on a shelf, giving us a great field of view. We tried to keep warm in our red plaid insulated hunting outfits. After a little more than an hour, we noticed a few does feeding as they moved up to our position. We also noticed another hunter moving parallel to the deer and below them about seventy five yards. I remember saying to my friend while looking at the deer, "I wonder if that guy sees us up here." Just about that time, the hunter below spotted the deer and opened fire with shots shattering bark and hitting a tree above us. My hunting companion and I dove for cover, hugging the ground behind a rock cluster outcropping. The hunter fired four rapid shots, and about the time we were fixing to get up, he fired another four shots and then four more shots in succession. During the barrage of shots fired, my buddy shouted out, "Hit something, will you?" A few seconds later, in what appeared to be a momentary lapse in the shots fired, my buddy looked at me and said, "I'm not getting up unless you tell me I can shoot back." I looked at him with a laugh and said, "I think he emptied all his clips." We slowly and cautiously got to our feet, keeping some cover between us and the hunter down below. As we got up, we saw the deer bounding off, unharmed. I called out to the hunter, letting him know our exact location if he didn't hear my friend yelling out to him. The hunter came up the ridge to us, but when he got to us the first thing he said was that he didn't see us and just saw the deer moving. We learned he was a new hunter, and this was his first hunting trip with his new semi-automatic rifle.

I told him that we saw the deer in flight with their tails up high and that it didn't look like he hit any of them, but I was curious and asked if he was aiming at the group or just one deer. He said without hesitation that he was aiming at one but if he hit another it would be okay also since he had three clips. I smiled and shook my head, after telling him good luck as he turned to leave. Both my buddy, who was talking to himself now and muttering out loud, and I decided it was time to leave to find another location to hunt.

I do feel that had that hunter been using a bolt action rifle after having spent some time at a firing range getting proficient with his firearm, he might have gotten one of those deer with only one shot and not aged my buddy and me by ten years.

Another point to consider is that more whitetail deer are shot in cover rather then out in an open field. Besides, after the first shot is fired, you will generally be looking at a running deer in the fields.

Chapter Six

Buying a Bow

Hunting with bow and arrow is often considered one of the purest forms of hunting big game animals. Unlike using a rifle or shotgun, the hunter must position himself relatively close to his prey while remaining undetected, matching skill against instinct with a whitetail deer. A bow hunter must be able to shoot an arrow with speed and precision, delivering perfect shot placement in order to bring home a deer. Persistence, determination, hours of practicing and many scouting trips to determine the likeliest of hunting stands must all join together in the bow hunter's quest for success in the field. Considered the sport of kings from long ago, the bow hunter of today is part of a group of dedicated hunters who believe that the harvesting of a whitetail deer in this manner is the ultimate hunting challenge.

There are several different types of bows.

Bow hunting for whitetail deer is unlike hunting with a firearm, as the hunter must not only be able to enter and leave the woods undetected, but also must be able to stand within a close distance without being scented. Mistakes are unforgiving, as only the sight of the flag of a fleeing deer's tail will be seen if you are detected.

As a new or veteran hunter who has decided to take up hunting with a bow just as in buying a firearm, you should take your time and consider all the features of the particular bow you want to use and what is available.

There are four different types of bows that can be used for hunting. The longbow has been around the longest. It is used by hunters who are interested in a more traditional shooting style with very little added attachments. They are available with different weights to be drawn back in order to shoot; the average weight is between 30 and 80 pounds at full draw (pulled completely back). Many states require that bow hunters use a bow with a minimum draw weight of 40 pounds. Well in advance and prior to hunting, a prospective bow hunter should become aware of the state requirement for the area.

The recurve bow, which is similar to the longbow, has the limbs on the end curved away from the middle of the bow. The recurve bow is shorter than the longbow and due to its design can deliver more speed with the same draw weight as the longbow. It fires an arrow quieter and smoother, and is considered the choice of many hunters who seek these features while hunting in a traditional style.

The compound bow is the most popular today for hunting. It can shoot arrows more than 100 yards at speeds to exceed 140 miles per hour. Wheels, pulleys and cables attached to the limbs make it easier for the hunter to hold in position at full draw, propelling an arrow much faster than either the longbow or the recurve bow. The compound bow comes in a variety of styles and is available from many different manufacturers. The compound bow, just as the longbow and recurve bow, is considered a short-range hunting tool, with an average shot of 40 yards or less. This is considered the effective range to penetrate, pass through and deliver a fatal shot to a deer. It is important to know that even at this average range, shot placement is critical for a clean, quick kill. A bow hunter must be consistent in his or her shot placement in a vital area as an error could result in wounding or crippling a deer. Accuracy and performance demands continued practice to be effective.

The crossbow is the combination in design of a compound bow mounted horizontally on a firearm-like stock with a trigger release. Using a crossbow, the hunter is able to draw the bow string back, lock the string in a fixed, fully-drawn position and fire it using a trigger release. Crossbows can propel an arrow, called a bolt, at a distance of more than 200 yards with an effective range of 75 yards at speeds of 250 miles per hour. The crossbow is not allowed in some states. Though different states allow the use of a crossbow for hunting, I recommend you check with the state you wish to hunt for the regulation governing hunting with a crossbow.

Safety should be observed at all times when using any of the different hunting bows. It is important to know and remember: you should never dry fire a bow, which is releasing a bow string while at full or partial draw without an arrow. By dry firing, energy is transferred back through the bow limbs instead of to the arrow. The bow can break apart and shatter, causing serious injury to the shooter or anyone near them.

Similar to buying a firearm, a hunter must use a bow that is suited to them. Longbows are interchangeable for both right- and left-handed shooters, but the same is not true for other bow types. On the recurve bow, you have an arrow rest and sight window when aiming the bow. Because of these features, there are both left- and right-handed recurve bows. Another consideration is your draw length. The draw length is the distance you can pull the bow string back to your anchor point, also known as your nock point, when holding the arrow in a full draw position. Different bows have different draw lengths. If you buy a bow from a reputable archery dealer, they will be able to measure your correct draw length. To find out your own draw length, put a yard stick between both your hands, putting one end to the center of your chest between your arms. Extend your arms and finger tips so they are parallel to the ground and have someone mark the length on the yard stick at the very end of your finger tips, and that is your draw length. Knowing your draw length is important when purchasing a bow or arrows for the

Your local archery dealer can be a wealth of information.

bow. There are also several attachments you can have mounted to your bow to help silence the arrow release and also for aiming. What you want and the size of your pocketbook will determine what is best for you.

Practice, practice and more practice is needed in order to be proficient with a bow and to place an arrow in the perfect location to kill a whitetail deer. Unless you have practiced and are proficient, you should not try to harvest a deer. Many deer can be seen in the woods limping from being hit with a misplaced arrow. Other deer that are hit poorly will be left to travel for several hours or even a day to die unfound and unclaimed by the hunter.

I suggest before buying a bow you visit several archery establishments and talk to the people there and try their bows. Be mindful that if an archery shop only carries one particular type of bow, they will only praise that particular type bow and say theirs is the best on the market. That might be true but only in their eyes. This is why it is important that you visit several archery shops or at least one with several different manufacturer and model bows, so you get a full spectrum of what is available and chose the bow that best suits you. Be mindful that speed is important but that silence is also. The fastest bow might not be the quietest on the market, and the reverse is also true. Be patient and take your time, as hard as it will be for you, and you will do just fine. If you are in a rush to practice, try this as a simple practice exercise.

Get yourself a single red brick. You can find one at any home furnishing center and even at some hardware stores. When you get home, if you are planning to shoot right handed with a bow, hold the brick out with your left hand, fully extended, and then bring your hand back to you three inches until you have a slight bend in your arm holding the brick. This will be about the position you will be holding your bow while shooting, and the brick will be about the same weight as your average bow with all the attachments you will have on it. Practice till you are able to hold that brick in that position for 5 minutes. Think it is easy? Try it. It is an excellent exercise for all the times you are holding the bow at full draw and

Strengthening your bow arm is just as important as practicing with your bow.

can't move as a deer is watching you. The first time it happens, and it will happen, you will be glad you practiced with the brick.

On broadheads for hunting, be advised that there are many in all shapes and sizes, from fixed blade heads to the mechanical ones that open upon impact. Some will guarantee to leave you a great blood trail, and some will promise you a dead deer if you use them. Just remember two things when it comes to broadheads. All broadheads kill by cutting blood vessels or cutting a deer's spine, unlike the high energy shock of bullets fired by a firearm. No matter which broadhead you use, if you do not put the arrow in the zone for a kill shot, you won't get the deer. Just as in real estate, the same is true when shooting a bow: location is everything.

I will also give you a hunting tip that most firearm hunters should be aware of. A deer, just like humans, pumps adrenalin when they run or get scared. A deer running when wounded pumps adrenalin through its body if it runs a long distance before death. Ever wonder why some deer meat has a stronger taste when it is cooked the same way as you have been cooking venison in the past? Think about how long that deer ran before it dropped in the woods and the time it took you to find it.

As I mentioned earlier, bow accessories are as numerous as what you can imagine your bow should be equipped with. You can buy silencers for the cables, lighted pin sights to scope like sights, arrows of different weights and compositions, soft bow cases to hardened ones that can withstand accidental run over by a vehicle. You can shoot by holding the string with your fingers to draw back and hold at your anchor point or with a mechanical release. I recommend using a mechanical release, as it allows the shooter to release an arrow with the same pressure each time you shoot. This is important for target shooting as well as hunting. Most attachments aid the delivery of your quick clean shot, but shot placement is entirely up to your continuous practice. No attachment will help you if you can't maintain accuracy with every arrow you release.

I have shot whitetail deer with recurve bows, compound bows and also a crossbow. What is important is not the bow, as a bow type is only the model you choose to use. What is important, and I can't stress this enough to you, is shot placement. When hunting with any bow, it is critical that you remember this: there is no warm-up in the field while hunting. Your first shot is the only shot to be concerned with. In closing, remember whatever bow you choose, practice until every shot is placed perfectly, where you want it to be.

Chapter Seven

Developing Your Skills

Now that you have bought your firearm or bow, you are probably anxious to start practicing as soon as possible. This is good, but there are several things you need to do first that you will appreciate at a later date that is part of developing your skills. The first is to copy down the manufacturer, model number and serial number of either the firearm or bow. After you have written this information down, store it in a safe location with your other important papers. This will help you considerably and give you some peace of mind if they are ever stolen either in your home or away on a hunting trip. There is nothing worse than talking to officials who are trying to help you at this particular time and all you can tell them is a manufacturer and the type action of the firearm or the name of a bow. Several states are now able to send firearm dealers, sport shop owners and pawn broker's electronic reports on stolen firearms and bows to look out for. If you have recorded the information, it will be extremely helpful in getting back your lost item should it be resold or used. If you are a veteran hunter with several firearms, it is well worth your time to do this as soon as possible, if you have not done so already. This information is also needed should you ever decide to hunt outside the U.S., either in Canada or another country. Different countries require this information upon crossing their border. If you plan on driving your car or renting a car, countries such as Canada will need at the border crossing a separate certificate of insurance, which you obtain from your vehicle insurance company showing coverage outside the U.S. Most insurance companies will readily provide this certificate to you, if given prior notice.

Frequent trips to the range will improve your accuracy.

Developing Your Skills encompasses more than just sighting in your firearm and practicing with your bow. It entails being ready and seasoned in several different areas.

For instance, your hunting companion and those you plan on hunting with could be neighbors or your friends from work. Comradeship is an important factor for an enjoyable and memorable hunt, yet another important factor to consider is the safety consciousness of the individual or group you plan on hunting with. Usually by talking about hunting and practicing together before hand, you can easily determine ahead of time if your potential hunting companions are well suited to hunt in a safe and intelligent manner. You may decide to join a hunting club or sportsmen's club that has hunting and fishing as well as a cabin in the area you wish to hunt. There are many of them throughout the country, and it is a real pleasure to be a member of these clubs. The fellowship, meals together, stories around a fireplace and hunts will long be remembered, and some really close friendships can be formed. Deer camps, as most veteran hunters readily call them, can impart to you great times and a feeling of belonging to an important group

Hunting companions and fellowship make every trip memorable.

of individuals who share your interests. Hunting with a safety conscious group is important, and the lives of you and others will depend upon it. Just as there are good hunting camps, there are also bad hunting camps, like the group that wants to stay up late and play cards, drink alcoholic beverages or watch hunting videos till very late hours at night and then wants to sleep in the next morning rather than getting up to go hunting. These are the camps to stay away from. As a general rule of the camps I have been associated with, no drinking of beer or alcohol after dinner the night before is allowed when you are going to hunt the next morning. These are the clubs that are serious about hunting and also believe it is important for everyone to get a good night's sleep to be well-rested for the next day's hunt by having a lights out rule at an early hour in the evening. Clubs that have firm rules in place that are observed by all are the camps you want to be associated with. It is also nice to be part of a group that helps one another after you shoot a deer, making your hunt even more enjoyable.

Another consideration is whether you plan on cutting up a deer yourself or having it processed by a butcher. Later in this book we will cover processing your deer yourself, but in the event you wish to have it done for you, you should know of a few butchers before your hunt and have their phone numbers with you.

If you are hunting with a rifle, shotgun or bow, you need to practice long before hunting season. If you have purchased a firearm, you will need to determine ahead of time if you are going to hunt using open sights on your firearm or a telescopic scope. I strongly recommend a telescopic scope because it offers a great field of vision while looking through it at a deer and also allows you to see clearly what is behind the deer. There are many different types of telescopic scopes; I recommend a variable scope with 3 to 9 lens adjustments. A scope of this kind will allow you to clearly see a deer either at a short distance or further away. It is also helpful when you are sighting in your firearm at a rifle range.

Many people close one eye when they are sighting in their firearm whether looking through open sights or a telescopic scope. For the hunter, this is wrong, and I will explain why. If you are a target shooter, you keep one eye closed because you are only focusing on a paper target for shot placement and not what is next to it, on either side or behind it. As a hunter, you must be concerned with the whole picture. You must focus on the deer's approach, when it stops, what is behind the deer and the direction the deer takes if it does not drop instantly. Closing one eye only allows one half of the picture for the hunter. If you have never fired a firearm before, it will be easy for

A good rifle scope will allow you to focus better for every shot. Practice by keeping both eyes open.

you to practice with both eyes open as you look down the rifle barrel with open sights or while using a scope. For a veteran hunter who has never aimed this way it will take some practice, but once you do it, both aiming at a deer and your accuracy will improve.

When I was young and hunting for several years already, I picked up a new 30-30 lever action rifle. I was staying at a farm in upstate New York after making good friends with a farmer named Paul who I met in a field whose property adjoined the hunting club I belonged to. I fired the new 30-30 several times and could not get it sighted in while using open sights. I mentioned to the farmer that I was thinking of returning the gun to the gun shop because it had to be defective. The farmer asked if he could fire the gun, and I agreed. He leaned up against a tree and put four shots in the bull's eye at 60 yards. He turned and handed the rifle back to me and said, "Yep, there's a defect, but I don't think it's with this gun!" He told me to lean against the tree for support and aim at the target and squeeze it as if I were milking a cow. Well, living in Bronx, NY at the time, I didn't milk too many cows, but I got the general idea. I leaned up against the tree, closed one eye to aim, and Paul yelled out STOP! and hit me in back of the head. He asked, "Who ever taught you how to shoot that way? Why are you closing one eye? You're supposed to look at what you shoot, not wink at it." I tried again, and each and every time I tried to close one eye, I got a smack behind my head. Paul stayed with me until I was able to hit the target keeping both eyes open with the same gun I was going to return. I later found out that several of the other hunters who stayed at Paul's house and hunted with him received the same lesson when they sighted their guns in there. I have been sighting in and shooting this way for over 30 years, and most of the people I hunt with and have come in contact with that are crack shots use the same method also. It works, and if you try it, you're going to do it the same way keeping both eyes open.

It is important if you plan on using a rifle or shotgun when hunting that you sight in your firearm and become proficient with the working order and accurate placement of your shot; this will ensure a quick, clean kill of a whitetail deer. Sighting your rifle and shotgun, continued practice at different times and not waiting until the last day before the hunt will make you more confident in your ability and comfortable with your firearm. Every year rifle ranges are jammed with last-minute hunters all trying to sight in their firearms. Sometimes in their haste, they settle for less than what they should. Several also find out

Practice shooting with a rest and without.

that their firearm is not in the proper working order and scramble to look for a gunsmith who already has a busy workload. If a part needs to be ordered or a major repair has to be done, it could cost you not being able to hunt on opening day of the hunting season. I recommend that you sight in well in advance of the season and practice several times to be proficient, with your final trip to the range two to three weeks prior to the opening of the season. This way you are well-prepared, and it will give you the necessary time if a repair is needed. Do not wait until the last minute. This is the time to think about hunting, enjoy quality time with your family and do other things, like deciding where your trophy that you plan to have mounted will go.

Temperature plays an important part when sighting in your rifle or shotgun and if you plan on using a telescopic scope. After firing a few shots, your barrel will heat up and change where the shot will be placed. You will go to the range and see people sighting in and doing well and then make adjustments that should not be made as their barrel warms up. When a rifle or shotgun barrel warms up after your third shot, you should put your firearm back in the gun rack and allow the barrel to cool down. Shooting with a cold barrel is recommended. The same is true when hunting. Don't place your gun in a gun rack next to a wood burning stove when you get to camp. In the first place, the gun rack should not be near a heater, and by doing so, you could inadvertently change the direction of you shot when you hunt the next morning. Keep your firearm in a cool location, either in the trunk of your car or in another area where it won't be affected by heat or a significant temperature change. Another change that could happen is having your scope fog up when you go outside to hunt, which can happen if it sits in a heated area and then is brought outside in the cold. Even though telescopic scopes are sealed, some of them have been known to fog up on occasion, and this is a cause of it.

Another point to consider is that whitetail deer do not have circular targets affixed to their bodies. On your last two practice sessions at the range, it would be wise if you practiced firing at a target that is a life-like picture of a whitetail deer. You can buy targets of deer standing in different positions at many sporting goods stores. If you are practicing well in advance of the hunting season, the range will not be crowded, and you will have the necessary time to practice shot placement at what you will be seeing in the field. You will also see how different it is to shoot at a life-size image of a deer as opposed to a circular target. By doing so, you will be better prepared and even more comfortable with your shot placement while in the field.

You should also think during the time of your practice sessions about picking up a shoulder strap if the person who sold you the firearm did not recommend it, or if one was not already affixed to your firearm. A shoulder strap will make carrying your firearm in the field much easier and can also be used to steady a firearm while firing.

At this time I will give you a tip that you will thank me for later. If you plan on hunting with a firearm during hunting season and have a coat you plan on using, get it out at this time. If you are planning to buy one, remember this. Since you will have a shoulder strap on your firearm, which makes it easy to carry the firearm, shoulder straps often have a nasty habit of sliding off shoulders while walking. A tip to avoid this is to first decide which shoulder you plan to use when carrying your firearm and then have a tailor or someone handy with a needle and thread sew a medium-size button (about the size of a nickel) on that shoulder end on the coat. This will keep your shoulder strap from sliding off your shoulder and your firearm from possible damage. The same is true if you plan on using a shoulder strap for your bow. Damages can be costly, and you will appreciate this simple tip during the hunting season.

As a bow hunter, your practice sessions are just as important as picking out your bow. The best of equipment will not be worth much if you cannot place an arrow accurately each and every time. Your first shot is just as important as your last shot when you practice archery. In the field, your first shot will probably be the only shot you take at your deer. Don't get into the habit of saying while practicing that you have to warm up first, because there is no warming up in the field. Your first and last shot must be accurate and exact, each and every time. You must get to that point before you can think about hunting a whitetail deer. Arrow placement is not forgiving, and like a marksman, you have to be able to aim and focus your attention on a particular area and not the whole deer. Your practice sessions should be often and not attempted when you are tired to the point that you cannot remain focused. As a new bow hunter, you will have sore muscles as you upper body and shoulder muscles develop. When your muscles become sore, it is time to put the bow down and end your practice session. Your accuracy will improve in time if you practice often. Remember the exercise with the red brick, as this will help you more than you realize in the beginning.

Another consideration for both firearm and bow hunters alike is that while in the field you may not always get a shot at a whitetail deer under perfect conditions. Some shots might have to be taken while you are standing, but there are times when sitting and kneeling shots might be necessary. Do not limit all your practicing to one position. By practicing in several different positions and being able to accurately place either a shot or arrow in these positions, your chance of success will greatly increase.

While talking about accurate shot placement, let me be the first person to tell you that you should never, under any condition, take a shot at a moving deer. I know you may have seen this on TV or heard from other hunters how they took their deer while the deer was walking or in flight. You might even think you can hit a moving target, but take a moment to think about it. Accurate shot placement either with a firearm or bow is important to you as a hunter and sportsman. You owe it to yourself with all your practicing and preparations, and to the deer itself, to place a shot for a quick, clean kill. The chance of wounding or crippling a deer doubles when the deer is moving, leaving shot placement only to probability. A wounded deer might travel for miles before it eventually collapses or lies down to die. I recommend you sit back, enjoy watching the deer, and be comfortable knowing this was not your time, and you might meet up with him at another time and place in the field.

In the beginning as a new hunter, you may find this difficult to watch what you are looking for walk away. I know I did when I was a new hunter in the field. Patience is an important factor in hunting, and for some it will take time to develop. This may sound only like words to you right now, but in the field, you will see for yourself.

I watched a twelve-point buck with trophy mass and body size walk just out of my bow range. Now some of you may say I should have taken the shot, and there are those who understand why I did not shoot. In time, this will happen to every one of you at some time in the field. It may not be a twelve-pointer that walks into your sight, but it will happen to you. At that time, the choice will be yours and yours alone as to what you do. Time, patience, your skill, and your judgment will dictate your actions.

Out of range… Let them walk by. Undisturbed deer often return to the same area.

Chapter Eight

All About Food Plots

Food plots draw the deer in.

Many articles have been written concerning food plots today. You can watch hunting videos that will have sections on how to build one and recommend the seed to be planted. Then there are the TV shows that dedicate an entire show on building and maintaining a food plot. Diverse as the ways to establish a proper food plot are the types of plants that people believe should be planted in one. One seed company will claim their seed is the best, in conflict with other companies who claim the same for their product. There has also been some controversy about the ethical side of planting a food plot, after which a person places a hunting stand next to or in the middle of it to then harvest whitetail deer. Some think it is a form of baiting, and we can sit here and debate all sides, but I feel this is not the place. Food plots are legal and even recommended by Conservation offices throughout the country.

Food plots have been around for a while, ever since the first pilgrim planted his corn field after learning from the Indians and wildlife used them as a secondary food source. Helping all forms of wildlife and as a critical component of wildlife habitat management, the whitetail deer being one of them, I believe that they are necessary to supplement the intake of nutritious vitamins and minerals during the spring, summer and fall seasons. During times of drought or an early freeze that prevents the natural habitat from enduring, food plots are an important aid to wildlife nutrition and can prevent starvation. Planting a food plot can also make a piece of hunting property better by promoting healthier deer herds in areas that lack adequate nutritious food and by holding deer on your property.

How to build a food plot and then what to plant are the concerns of those who decide to have a food plot on their property. So we will discuss several issues in the hope that you will become familiar with both the building procedure as well as what you can plant to both attract and support whitetail deer and know *All about Food Plots.*

We will start off with the assumption that you own property or have a piece of property to hunt and have the owner's permission to plant a food plot.

The first step in the process is to take a soil sample and have it checked to find out the composition of the soil in the area you intend to use. Take a clean plastic sandwich bag and fill it with soil from about six inches deep from two or three places in the area you intend to plant your food plot. This will be important in knowing if the soil needs appropriate fertilizer applications prior to or during tillage and planting, not only to increase the forage production, but also to increase the nutritional value of the forage as well.

Take a soil sample for evaluation.

For a small fee you can take soil sample to the Cooperative Extension office in your area, and they will process the soil samples for you and provide you with a printed readout of the composition of your soil as well as the recommendations of what is needed. Some of the seed companies that specialize in food plots offer a free soil sample testing and will provide you with their own plastic bags and instructions for taking a soil sample as well.

As a tip to remember when planning your food plots, put either mineral blocks or mineral drips, which are minerals you place in a burlap bag, hanging from a tree, which will drip to the ground after a rain shower. This will allow whitetails coming to your food plot to get additional mineral supplements in their diet. In the food plots I have on my property, I use both mineral blocks and also mineral drips several feet in the woods on all four sides of the food plots. I find that this is especially helpful for the deer population in the spring and in the winter months after the deer season has ended, when the whitetail's food source becomes scarce. Most of the people who plant food plots forget that whitetails need as much if not more minerals during the winter months. The food plots will do their part, but additional mineral sources are necessary for adequate maintenance and growth of your deer population. Your will also find that you will be using more mineral blocks in the winter months than in the spring.

Some of the types of seed that you can put into seed plots do not require tillage, and they claim to be a no-till seed. I have tried these, and they do work, but I feel that they would work even better in tilled soil. It is not necessary to buy expensive equipment if you do not own your own in order to build a food plot. Some forestry and conservation offices rent equipment like a seed spreader or a No-till Drill. The No-till Drill is a piece of equipment that has a trailer hitch and can be pulled behind a heavy 4-wheel drive pickup or tractor to spread seed. This equipment discs a small row, drops seed in the row, and then covers the seed. Rental fees are quite reasonable, and I have used this equipment myself. The agents in these offices are extremely helpful and will also explain how the equipment works if you are not familiar with it. Some will come to your property to assist in the settings of the machine if you ask them. Conservation offices encourage food plots as a way of helping wildlife and can be helpful by answering your questions concerning what to plant in your particular area.

If you have an area that you want to dedicate to a particular seed type only and remove the herbage that is there, you can do so with chemical application. I believe that balance is the key, and ideally you should plant a variety of foods that deer prefer. Other wildlife will enjoy them also, as deer and turkey will feed in the same area if there is variety. Some Feed and Seed Stores will come and spread the chemical to remove unwanted herbage for a fee, but if you have the equipment or access to equipment to spray, you can do it yourself easily. Usually only one application of this chemical is necessary with a waiting period of three to six weeks before planting can begin.

If you are going to disc an area, depending if it has ever been turned over before, you may want to disc it several times to loosen the soil. I have found that this can be a chore, but if you keep at it, you will complete the task and have good, loose soil to plant.

Choosing the best planting will have to depend on your location and the area you intend to dedicate to your food plot. Under ideal conditions you would like the area to get enough sunlight, for the soil to be moist to allow proper germination and to be surrounded by thick cover to offer the deer a bedding area and a safe location.

Corn is a really good consideration, which is attractive to deer in the fall and winter if deer can stay out of it until it matures. Depending upon the size of the food plot, it might not be the wisest choice unless you have several food plots of it planted to allow enough stalks to mature. This can prove to be quite hard as deer will begin to eat the green leaves and new stalks during the summertime. By fall, you might not have any stalks left to produce corn if you have a small food plot.

Grain Sorghum is a good food source for deer but has its up and down sides. The up side is that it usually is not touched during the summer and can be used as an early fall food that will bring the deer in to feed. The down side is that sorghum, unlike corn, is less desirable as a carbohydrate source in winter and cannot be counted on to bring the deer in when the temperature drops. Many plant Sorghum for deer, but I do not consider it as a preferable winter crop that deer will readily look for.

Alfalfa is good for attracting deer in the summer time and early fall and has crude protein that deer like. Even though whitetail deer really like alfalfa, the downside is that it turns brown quickly after the first frost and deer will then stop coming into an alfalfa food plot. It is also extremely hard to maintain.

Soybeans are great plants that draw deer during the summer, fall and winter months. The beans provide plenty of protein, and the deer really like its taste. Soybeans are resilient plants that can take a lot of grazing by deer and are good in areas that don't get a lot of rain. But soybeans are not ideal in drought conditions, as they do need some water to survive. Once established, they will survive if planted early so the deer and turkey don't snip off the ends of the plant at the early stages of growth.

Clover is considered a universal deer food that is easy to establish, and every hunting property should have at least one clover plot. It is good for deer and turkey and will provide both protein and substance from summer through fall and will last through the cold months. Frost will put clover in a dormant stage, and it will lose some of its nutritional value. If killing frost occurs in your area, clover flattens and loses its attractiveness for deer, though they will come into a clover field at night to feed.

Brassicas come in many different plants, and when it comes to deer food, there are three that deer really like. Purple-top turnips are great, and deer will eat the leaves and tubers, saving the turnip itself, which is partially above ground for the cold winter months. I enjoy picking a few turnips myself and eat them raw as they taste sweet and pretty good if you get hungry. Forage brassica has high protein, and deer can't resist it when the plant matures. Like the purple-top turnips, you can also take some for making a salad for yourself when you get back home, as I think it tastes pretty good. The next is dwarf rape, which is a plant with big leaves that the deer will feed heavily after the first big freeze and on into the winter.

Then there is winter wheat and rye, which are used in the southern regions that offer deer a good food supply. With sufficient rainfall, these plants will grow and be a good plant for a food plot. They grow aggressively and can be eaten by deer within a relatively short time, often within a few weeks after planting. They also stay green well into the winter and are resilient to frost. In the spring, they are the first plant to green up and a good early food for deer to start the weight gaining process.

You must decide which plant you wish to plant in your food plots. If you have several plots, I would plant several different crops. I would plant a wheat and rye mixture in one and possibly a soybean and clover crop in another. Whichever you decide, a food plot can definitely help your hunting area and bring in the deer and other wildlife.

Take advantage of tree lines when setting a stand.

Keep in mind that hunting near or next to a food plot is legal, but you should be mindful of a few things that you will learn by experience for yourself, but I will give you a heads up now. If you hunt in a stand by your food plot during bow season hard, you may have a problem when rifle season arrives. Now, what do I mean by say "hunting hard", you ask? If you hunt using a permanent stand in a fixed location, hunt every weekend and leave scent in the area, you will train the deer to come into the food plot later and later every time. If you want to hunt the food plot, be extremely careful about your scent possibly alerting deer of your presence. I recommend that you do not hunt the same stand every time but alternate your position. Use adequate scent protection and change locations on the average of only two to three days from the same stand. This way you do not allow the deer to pattern you.

I learned this after I made the mistake of hunting one of my food plots too often and from the same fixed stand. After showering with scent-free soap and wearing my hunting clothes that I washed with scent-free detergent, I would get to my stand at 2:30 in the afternoon. After three days, I noticed the deer coming into my food plot would come in later and later each day. I found that by alternating my hunting stands, I saw more deer, and the deer resumed their normal patterns and came into the food plots shortly after I arrived in the afternoon. Now I know what you are thinking; I probably was not scent free while sitting in my fixed stand. However, that was not the case, as I observed deer in the woods while hunting in an alternate stand, looking at my fixed stand while they stood at the edge of the woods. I hope that you will remember this as a rule.

You will never see all the deer in the woods that can see your stand. You may see many deer, but you will never see all the deer in the area of your stand. There are the ones that though hunting pressure have become nocturnal and travel mainly under the cover of darkness.

Using several stands in tree lines increase your chances when wind direction changes.

Then there are the older does that are skittish all the time and avoid an area with any stand in it, even though it is high in a tree and camouflaged. There are also deer that are in the brush that you cannot see that you alert by movement. You will not see them, but they have seen you move and do not come into the food plot until dark. The more you hunt from one stand in the same location, the more you will train the deer to come in later and later. When hunting any food plot, have and use two to three stands in different locations. Try not to use the same stand for more than three days. You could get lucky and not be spotted, but the chances are that you will without ever being aware of it if you use the same stand in the same location each time you hunt.

Chapter Nine

Picking the Perfect Hunting Site

So, you are ready to go and have made the necessary calculations from your notes derived from your numerous scouting trips. You know the general area you wish to hunt and now all that is left is *Picking the Perfect Hunting Site.*

This is a time when you have to combine your notes to choose the most likely areas. You need to pick the three best sites to hunt from. Why three sites, you ask? You are picking three sites for several reasons. First is wind direction. During the changing days of you hunt, the wind will generally shift direction several times. You want to hunt with the wind in your face if at all possible to reduce the

Picking the right stand location can make the difference.

chance of human scent being detected by approaching deer. Sometimes that is not always possible, as the wind does swirl at different times during each day, but normally that is most likely to happen in the late mornings or early afternoons. In the mornings the wind pretty much remains constant until the thermal currents rise. In the late afternoon the wind will usually settle as dusk approaches. On days where the wind is swirling most of the day, deer are often leery and will stay in heavy cover due to the sounds of the tree branches rustling and leaves on the ground blowing in all directions. Then is a good time to hunker down in a thicket, which will be the likeliest of spots to hunt in. You will want an early morning site and also an afternoon site as well.

Whitetail deer will be leaving their feeding area in pre-dawn and early mornings, going to their bedding areas to rest. At midday deer will again move to browse if not disturbed, moving through cover that offers them protection with an adequate supply of food. Then in the late afternoons, they will move again and return to their regular feeding areas to eat throughout the evening. You will want a stand for times when the hunting pressure is on and the whitetails change from their normal routes to use their secondary or escape routes leading in and out of thicker cover.

I find that most hunters will hunt from first light to about 10 a.m. at the latest and then leave the woods for breakfast or a hot cup of coffee. You can see the diner parking lots full of vehicles, and if you go inside, the general sight looks like a fashion show from a hunting catalog. Counters and tables are filled with what appears to be an army of starving hunters.

Most of the deer I have shot in my thirty-five years of hunting have been between 9:30 a.m. and 3 p.m. I know what you are thinking: then why do I have to go into the woods a half hour before sunrise? You know, I often wonder that myself at times. I have taken a few nice size deer about an hour after sunrise, and I have seen deer right at sunrise. You will probably hear stories how this one or that one got their big buck right after sunrise. I have heard the stories also, but I usually get a nice buck every year, and it rarely happens during the early morning hours. But, it can happen.

Opening day of the season is different as deer are being pushed by the invasion of hunters in the woods, and you can see deer at any given time, most of which will be running. But then again, I have only gotten one deer during opening day of rifle season despite the rumor that it is supposed to be one of the best days to be out in the woods hunting.

I remember one year that I was hunting in a camp I belonged to, and everyone in the camp got up at 4:30 a.m. to get ready, have their coffee, sorting out whose hat was where, packing their sandwiches, snacks, and all. I remained in my bed as I had left a note on the table not to wake me up. I knew a particular buck passed by my stand religiously somewhere between 11 a.m. and noon time, and I was darn if I was going to get up at 4:30 a.m. to sit in my stand by 5:30 a.m. to wait for him. I had told the guys at dinner the night before that I would be late coming in for lunch, telling them about this buck, which was a nice, thick-tine, eight-point buck with good weight to him. I said I'd be in for lunch, but it would be after I shot the buck and loaded him into my truck. A few of them laughed and carried on. One commented, "Do you have this guy on a schedule or just tied to a tree?" I smiled and just said, "don't set a place for me, and I'll see you around 1 p.m. or so."

I remember getting up that day around 7 a.m. and fixing myself a fresh cup of coffee and looking around the cabin for a good length of rope, since I would need it to help drag my buck out of the woods. I was thinking I could also use it to tie him down in the back of the truck to keep him from moving around when I was driving back to the cabin. Those gravel roads were pretty torn up back there where I parked my truck.

Well, I left the cabin after I put my pipe and some tobacco in my backpack to store in the truck. "No sense alerting this guy of my presence in advance," I figured, leaving and heading out around 8 a.m. I got to my stand somewhere around 8:40 a.m. and settled back. I saw a few does and a spike buck wandering by, but that was not the buck I was after. I saw several deer between 10 a.m. and 11 a.m. and waited patiently for the buck I was after. It was getting late and the buck still hadn't shown up. Then about 12:35 the buck I was after walked down the deer trail he usually traveled. I laid the crosshairs of my telescopic scope mounted on my .300 Savage and dropped him where he stood with a neck shot.

I climbed out of my stand to examine him after determining he was dead, and he was just as good looking as when I first spotted him a few weeks earlier when I was patterning him on earlier scouting trips. I loaded him in the back of the truck, which was no easy task, because he was a good 140 lb. deer even after being field dressed. I lit my pipe, settled back in the seat of my truck and began the drive back to camp. It was almost 1 p.m. and I had about a thirty-minute ride back. I got to camp, walked in and headed to the sink to wash up a bit. I dished myself out a bowl of stew that was on the stove, cut myself a large chunk of Italian bread, looked around for the jar of grated cheese and was eating when my friend Butch said, "So, you didn't get your deer, huh?" I said, "Nope, he's outside resting a bit in the back of my truck." A few guys laughed and I finished my stew. Just then two guys came in and said, "Hey Bob, that's a nice buck you got in the back of your truck." Everyone in the cabin sprang to their feet and went outside as I sat back sipping my coffee. Butch was the first to come back in and said, "Hey, you weren't kidding last night, were you?" I said, "No, but he was a little late coming by my stand today or I would have been here by 1 p.m."

Knowing where deer will be will make the difference.

I had seen signs of this buck on a few of my scouting trips and saw large deer tracks next to a rub he had made on a few trees. I decided to place a stand that overlooked a nice deer trail he had been using, being mindful not to position myself too close to the trail but close enough to keep a good eye on it. The trail came out of some good thick cover, and the buck, like several other deer I figure, was eating acorns and beechnuts during the late mornings after all the movement quit in the woods. I had seen the deer on three different occasions and figured the average time he was traveling past my area from these sightings.

A good tip to remember is that deer will generally use the same trails in all types of weather if they are not disturbed too much or alerted of danger. Most deer will often pattern hunters as well. Like I said earlier, the average hunter leaves the woods somewhere between 9 and 10 a.m. Deer see this movement and are pushed a bit sometimes and learn when it is safe with no human presence in the woods. Hunters leaving the woods at regular times often will train the deer in this way. Similar to Pavlov's theory, deer can be taught by repetition.

Whitetails do not only move at sunrise and sunset as many hunters believe. They don't sleep all day and wake up using little deer alarm clocks just before nightfall. Whitetail deer have major movements during mid-day to early afternoon, and very few hunters are in the woods during this time of day. Why wait all year for hunting season and then limit your hunting to only two short periods of the day? I find that I do better when I get up later than sunrise after having gotten a good night sleep and ready to devote the whole day to hunting, not just a few hours. If you have picked a good spot and patterned a few deer, you will have a much better hunt.

In *Picking the Perfect Hunting Site*, you have to first scout an area and have a general idea of where you want to hunt. Your next concern is where to position yourself. You want to hunt where the deer are going to be and not where the deer are. What do I mean by this, you ask? You want to be in an area that deer will pass to get to either their feeding or bedding area. You do not want to disturb their feeding or bedding area where the deer are but rather be in the area that they will pass. In other words, you want to be where the deer are going to be.

Look for three things that determine the presence of deer. Game trails worn into the ground from heavy deer movement and fresh tracks showing they are still being used. Look for fresh rubs on the trees that are newer than the ones you saw when you scouted a few weeks earlier. New rubs late in the season are territorial rubs that bucks make to mark their territory and let other bucks know a buck has staked out this area. Early season rubs are the signs of a buck either removing velvet or starting to feel his oats, so to speak. Look for paw marks on the ground under an overhanging tree; this is called a scrape. A scrape is a pawed-out area on the ground that a deer will stand in and urinate, leaving his calling card for breeding, alerting mating does that he is ready to breed. Does that are in heat will find these scrapes, generally during late day and evening hours, leaving their scent for the buck to follow. Bucks will generally check their scrapes a few times during the day and at night. A scrape is where a buck is going to be.

The perfect hunting site will be a position where you can see a fresh scrape but not so close as to alert a deer of your presence. Scrapes will be in an area that has fresh game trails intersecting, leading to and from the area. It will be in an area that has thick cover that offers deer security and an escape route out of danger.

When danger threatens, a buck doesn't panic, he simply moves through thick cover on a trail to a point that he feels safe. Generally that will not be all that far away from where he was originally. Bucks do not have to travel far in thick cover to feel safe, as most hunters will not enter the thick mass of tangling underbrush a deer has used as his escape route. Quite often the deer will return to the same spot he was spooked from once he feels the danger has passed.

Hunters can be patterned just like deer can be, and the older bucks know this. The first thing some hunters will say if they can't get a shot off and see a buck bounding off into thick brush is, "Well, he's history and will probably won't stop until he is in the next county." Then they will move along to keep looking and try to be quieter, hoping to be luckier the next time. Had they stopped and listened they would have heard a few crashes in the cover and then silence because the deer has stopped and is listening. If the deer hears the hunters moving off, the immediate danger is gone. The deer will generally lie down and wait until he perceives there is no threat and cautiously move around, coming to the same general area he was from a different direction. Deer know where they want to feed. They don't find a feeding spot by accident; they already know where their feeding range is and where they want to be. A deer unalarmed or when threatened will move along game trails to get to where they want to go. This is good to remember, and a good place to hunt is overlooking these game trails. One other thing to be mindful of is that some counties record more deer being taken than others. If you have look up the stats at the end of the year, you know that the conservation department posts the amount of deer killed in each county.

Every hunt starts with planning.

If you have chosen this county to do your homework in during your scouting trips, your chances of success are high. Hunting in a county that has proven to be a large deer kill county is always good, but you should have a thorough knowledge of the area to pick the perfect hunting site that will guarantee a successful hunt. If you are a small game hunter as well, you can take advantage of small game hunts to really get to know the area far in advance of the deer hunting season. Be mindful not to make frequent trips small game hunting in an area that you have found that looks promising for whitetail deer hunting. Too many small game hunters will make the mistake of finding a good deer area while they are in the field and consistently come back to the same area to hunt small game, hurting their chances for the later deer season. Once you observe a good area with good sign, make a note of it and leave it to later scouting trips, using caution to keep the area as undisturbed as possible.

Another point to remember is not to be a hunter who feels that you have to cut shooting lanes in an area large enough to drive a truck through. Whitetail deer are full-time inhabitants of the woods, and you are a part-time hunter. Deer have acute senses and will shy away from an area that has been made to look unnatural like a carved-out intersection in the woods. By taking a branch down here or there as not to deflect an arrow or bullet does not mean you have to cut an area that you can walk through with a buddy side by side. Keep the woods as undisturbed as possible if your quest is to bring home a nice buck or doe. Older bucks are not as gullible as does or young deer. They have gotten older by having sharp instincts, being cautious and having full knowledge of their surroundings. Many hunters who use stands like to have a nice trail leading to their stand, sometimes putting orange ribbons on the trees or using florescent spray paint to mark a trail that they can see easily, making a noticeable way in and out for them to find their stands. I often wonder if I will ever see a nicely paved road one day leading to one of them.

My method is simple and proven to work as I try to leave the woods as undisturbed as possible, even when I use a stand or hunting blind. If you need to find your way in, pick up a few luminescent tacks that glow in the dark and affix them to trees while leaving the way undisturbed if you want to get to your hunting area before first light. Every sporting goods store has these luminescent tacks; they work just fine and don't damage trees. Leave the woods just as they are until you have downed a whitetail deer first. You will need those trees in place to lean against while catching your breath as you are dragging your deer out of the woods.

I don't know about you, but every time I shoot a deer and it does not drop in its tracks, they seem to know where I park my truck, never running in that direction. I find that I am always walking up-hill both ways to get to the deer and back to my truck. Sort of like when I was going to school barefoot through the snow, walking up-hill in both directions!

Talking about snow: if you are in a location where it snows prior to the start of big game season, like South Dakota or Montana, I have found that after a fresh snow is a great time to observe deer movement by looking at the tracks in the snow. I have always liked scouting in fresh snow, as you can tell the amount of deer in an area from the tracks they leave, and generally see if the tracks were made by a buck or a doe.

Whitetail doe tracks will be smaller and closer together, where buck tracks will usually be wider apart and show a drag mark just behind their imprint in the snow. The drag mark is the sign of a mature buck, and often his tracks will be behind the doe tracks. Though approximate age cannot be determined by any sign in tracks, you can get a general idea of the weight of a deer from fresh tracks in the snow as heavier deer leave a more pronounced imprint. Remember that tracks only show where deer have been and what direction they are going.

I remember hunting one particular time with a good friend of mine named Cheech, who came with me on one of my earlier hunting trips to Colorado. He claimed to be part Cherokee Indian, and he told me time and time again how he could determine how fresh a track was by looking at it, saying it was because of his Indian blood. But then again, I saw him trip over a root while walking with me in the woods hunting, hurting his knee and letting out a good yell. Turning I looked down to him and said, "I thought an Indian doesn't feel pain!" He looked up at me sharply and said, "You're right, it's the white man in me that was yelling and feeling the pain."

I always go by this general rule: the only fresh deer tracks are the ones that a deer is standing in. Now if I saw deer droppings in the snow next to some tracks and they were still steaming I could make a good assumption with my Italian blood that a deer was by there not all that long ago.

Luck should not be the determining factor for a successful hunt. By determining where the deer are, the trails they use, their feeding and bedding areas and their primary and secondary holdings area, you can pick the perfect hunting site and leave luck to games of chance. Hunting skill, knowledge, as well as being able to place an accurate shot are the determining factors coming together, that allow success in the field.

Picking the perfect hunting site takes work, patience and determination. It does not happen overnight or in one day. It is governed by the time you spend in the field and knowing what to look for. It takes a hunter who has patterned deer movements, is familiar with their habits, knows the terrain of the area with the combination of all his scouting trips to decide the best possible place offering cover and visibility of a particular area. The only elements left to chance should be the factors the hunter cannot control.

Now let's go back and discuss another factor that I consider to be important, without being too repetitious. Many hunters try to hunt too large of an area when they pick a hunting site. They want to see a long way in one or two directions, thinking they will see every deer in the area. They place a stand that sticks out like a sore thumb, thinking it will blend if they put it up well in advance of the season for the deer to become used to it. They are right about deer getting used to it, but the deer will also get used to avoiding it by traveling around it through thicker cover. Whitetail deer do not adjust to change very well and will avoid something new for a long time, perceiving all change as a threat. Be mindful that you might have the perfect hunting site but ruin it by picking a poor stand location.

Chapter Ten

Types of Hunting Stands

Several factors will come into play to determine the type of stand you will be using: terrain you will be hunting; cover in the area; whether you will be hunting on the side of a slope, the top of a mountain, entrance to a swamp, or looking over a food plot; will you be hunting in a ravine that acts as a funnel, or will you be on a rock ledge overlooking a pine thicket? These are some of the considerations that all come into play for the different *Types of Hunting Stands.*

One of the best methods for seeing more deer and hunting motion-free, to a certain extent, is hunting from a stand. Stand hunting can either break the hunter's outline or hide most of the motions that can be detected by a deer. Keep in mind that whitetail deer have incredible eyesight and are always looking for motion while they are either feeding or when traveling through the woods. This is what they are focused on, together with their keen sense of smell and hearing. A hunter using a stand changes the odds from the whitetails to the hunters, often giving the hunter the necessary edge to catch a deer off guard. This is especially true during the rut, when both buck and doe movements are less guarded than other times of the hunting season. I will discuss the different types of hunting stands, some of which I consider safer than others.

Natural Ground Blinds

One of the first stands to be constructed by hunters was the natural ground blind, which was constructed of foliage in the area where hunters wanted to position themselves. If the area was in the hardwoods of oak and maple, the hunter would first select his site and then form a basic circular frame from downed limbs and branches of brush and tree branches as well, leaving a small opening for the hunter to enter and exit from. The person constructing the blind would try to develop the blind's appearance to look in place, resembling ground brush, as part of the natural look for the area and next to trees. Once the frame was constructed, branches off several of the trees in the area were placed to entwine within the frame. The middle of the blind was left open for the hunter to sit, usually with the aid of a portable chair that was set, with all ground leaves brushed aside so the hunter would remain quiet if they moved their feet. Some ground blinds were quite elaborate and tightly woven to block all movement and outline of a hunter. Ground blinds such as these worked well for short time use and could be constructed in less than an hour. The height of the blind was determined by the condition of the hunt, whether it was with bow or gun and if the hunter needed to sit or stand. Areas that provided fir trees were more desirable, as the needles and thickness of the brush acted as a windbreak as well. Some hunters used the same ground blinds year after year and added to the branches of foliage that were needed in spots that appeared to be bare from time and weather conditions.

I remember constructing blinds such as these while hunting both on Long Island, NY, with the bow, and out west in Colorado while rifle hunting for whitetail deer. The ground blinds were a successful additive that allowed me to take a good buck on both hunts.

Concealment and patience are two factors to consider while hunting from any stand. The stand must be constructed in a way to hide your appearance, and you have to be able to either sit or stand comfortably while in the stand. You may be there for some time, and having a few comforts (like a comfortable chair) helps. I know some hunters who use lawn chairs in their stands, but I have found that going to a marine supply and picking up a square swivel mount to affix to the bottom of a slope-back heavy poly chair, like the ones used in john boats, offer maximum comfort. I also buy a two-foot pedestal and mount the pedestal to a wooden frame on the bottom for stability. This will allow you to both sit and turn easily with your feet and with little body movement. It is also a lot more comfortable than sitting on a stump or other hard surface for any length of time. I also bring a plastic bag with me to cover the chair when I leave the stand to keep the seat nice and dry. Sitting on a wet or damp seat can be quite uncomfortable, and limits your patience. Stand hunting can become a test of time. You may see a driven deer at any time, but if you are in a secluded area and deer are moving naturally, you may be there a while. Stay alert and focused because the action can happen at any time.

While hunting on state land or an area with other hunters, a ground blind is not the safest stand to be sitting in. The direction of other hunters and the traveling of a discharged bullet cannot be predicted. To help as a safety feature, I often flag the tree next to my ground blind next to with orange ribbons and luminous tacks, which can be seen at a distance by other hunters. It is also a good idea to mark several trees in the area with orange ribbon as well. Deer are colorblind and will not be alerted to the color, but hunters passing by will see the markings. Remember that the hunter who is patient and able to sit quietly in the stand will take home a deer, if the stand is positioned in an area that deer frequent or pass through.

The advantage of using a ground blind is that, if constructed properly, you will get to see deer well in advance to get that first shot off. You will see more deer than if you were sitting in the open with any movement being detected. The disadvantage of the ground blind is that your human scent will be detected if you do not use a good cover scent and take the steps necessary to allow yourself to be scent-free as well. The second disadvantage is that you are susceptible to weather changes with little protection from the wind, rain or snow.

Pop-up Blind

The pop-up blind was developed as the modern-day substitute for the conventional and natural artistically created ground blind. There are several advantages to pop-up blinds, the first being ease of assembly; these stands are easy to assemble in minutes. The pop-up blind can also be purchased in several different camouflage patterns that will blend into different color settings. The inside color of most pop-ups are black, offering the hunter an added state of concealment. Should a deer spot the blind and try to see movement or anything unnatural, the dark inside color aids to block glare from daylight. Sitting in a pop-up will also conceal most leg and lower body movement, but it is recommended that not too much movement be allowed as some movement creates unnatural noise. You can also select blinds of different sizes, which allows more than one person to be in the same blind at the same time. Pop-up blinds are generally waterproof, which will give protection

Pop-up blinds are easy to setup and move.

Pop-up tent blind.

from the elements. Some blinds are better, allowing you 360-degree sight capabilities, but owning them is determined by personal preference and the size of your pocketbook.

The first disadvantage to owning and using a pop-up blind is that it offers no protection from a stray bullet or a shot being fired in your direction, as you are on ground level, even though you can put orange ribbons on them or on tree around them to point them out. The second is theft. I know of hunters who have set these blinds on state land and a few on their own property to come back another day to find the blind missing. With costs that could range from $100 to $500, there is no way to secure these types of stands from unwanted removal unless they are assembled and disassembled during each and every hunt. The pop-up blind does not offer 100% protection from concealing human scent, even though you can purchase blinds that claim to offer scent protection. Human scent should always be an element of consideration.

Wooden Ground Blind

For the hunter who has property of his own and would like additional comforts from home, the construction of a wooden ground blind could be a good choice. I have seen and hunted out of this type of blind and have also seen wooden

Low wooden ground blinds offer a great field of view.

ground blinds with considerable amenities that included carpeted floors, heat, gunracks, and sliding windows set on tracks that offered quiet opening and closing. Some had windows that could be propped open while occupied, while others allowed complete removal for archery. Stands of this type that you construct yourself can be as elaborate and comfortable as you decide to build.

Wooden ground blinds can be built as a whole unit or in sections that allow easy placement and removal. The advantages of this type of blind are obvious, as you decide what you would like to include, from a waterproof roof to all the comforts you would have if you were sitting in your own den. The first disadvantage of this type of ground blind is the weight of the blind, as it is constructed of wood. Even if you build one in sections, you probably will need help in setting one up as well as a good access to the location of placement. Stands of this type are generally not seen in thick woods, not to say it couldn't be done. I did hunt one that was located in cover and next to the entrance of a swamp in a northern region of the country, and I was told the placement of the stand was a considerable task in itself. The second disadvantage of this type of stand is maintenance, as wooden grounds blinds need to be painted annually to preserve them. The possibility of a raccoon, skunk, porcupine or squirrel taking up residence in one during the winter months is also probable, if adequate steps to prevent this are not thought

Camouflage box blinds offer concealment and block the elements.

out during construction and placement. Theft on private property is not likely, but the possibility of a break-in or unwanted use does exist unless locking windows and doors are added.

Elevated Blind

Elevated blinds made of wood can be built and often used in areas where a raised view is necessary such as overlooking a hardhack field, food plot or area of heavy brush cover where a ground blind is not feasible. You can either build your own or purchase one that is pre-constructed of a heavy grade plastic material that arrives in sections to be assembled at home or on site. The pre-constructed stands can be purchased with many options, depending on your needs and the amount you are willing to spend for one. The elevated blind, like the ground blind, is a stand that allows you to have comfort as well as a greater field of view, as most elevated stands are constructed to have a 360-degree field of view at a longer distance.

The advantages of this type of stand is that it can be made of wood by yourself and be quite sturdy while offer you protection from the elements. Elevated enclosed stands also offer you greater protection from dispersing human scent and being winded by a whitetail deer. Your field of view is also better than using

Elevated stands allow comfort and good visibility.

Elevated wooden platform stand.

a ground blind, and elevated stands can be left in place to be used year after year. A major advantage is that deer, while traveling, will not look up under normal conditions, but I have seen deer look up if they think something is out of place or stands out. As with the wooden blind, stands of this type must be constructed and set in place well before the start of the season to allow whitetail deer to accept this structure as part of their territory and feel at ease with its presence. Be aware that even though you place any stand well in advance of the hunting season, the deer were there first and will always recognize it as a new object in their territory. You may even find them looking up at it as they pass, and some of the wiser and older whitetails that tend to be nocturnal might always avoid the area until they don't feel threatened by it.

The disadvantage of this type of stand, like the wooden ground blind, is that yearly maintenance of this stand is necessary. Another disadvantage is that unless this stand is anchored properly to the ground, the chance of wind damage is possible. Proper anchoring and stability is necessary to eliminate a problem or danger while in use. Pre-constructed elevated stands are fairly new to the hunting scene today, thus the elevated cost. I imagine when new materials are incorporated to construct these stands or when it becomes feasible to mass-produce them, a more desirable cost will be passed on to the consumer. I have not heard of any of these stands reported as stolen after being assembled on site, but one can never completely rule out the possibility.

Ladder Stand

Ladder stands are made for the hunter who seeks an elevated position as well as having a stand that offers mobility and ease of assembly. They can be constructed by a creative individual using wood as a ladder and platform, offering the hunter a basic elevated stand, although wooden ladder stands are not recommended due to the weight of the material. I recommend that one purchase a pre-constructed stand of coated metal that comes boxed and requires the assembly of

Ladder stands are easy to setup and put into position.

a seat and, if included, a foot rest prior to on-site assembly of the ladder and the careful securing of the stand to a tree. Most of the simpler ladder stands can be assembled and handled without help, but the larger and newer model two-man stands are heavier and awkward to handle alone. With this type of stand, a good safety harness is recommended, as accidents can happen while the user is in an elevated position. Stands of this type come in different heights and extensions to the ladder sections can be purchased to offer a higher stand.

The advantages of these stands are the basic variety offered, ease of assembly and movement, as well as an elevated view. They can be assembled, and secured to a tree using cargo straps that often come with the stand to provide a sturdy elevated position. Depending on the height of the stand, a hunter will be stationed above the normal sight level of traveling whitetail deer, but a motionless position is needed as these stands are usually open. Some models offer a blind-like attachment that normally is an added option at an additional cost.

The disadvantage to this type of stand is the possibility of falling while climbing up the ladder or when positioning the user in place on the open type stand that does not have a fixed railing. The larger stands are recommended for comfort, but one must have help for onsite assembly. Ladder stands do not protect you from the elements and movement can be detected if the hunter turns or changes position.

Tripod Stand

Tripod stands have been around for a few years and were the innovation for hunters who wanted an elevated position in an open area just above cover, or in a high brush area, that camouflages its presence. These stands were made for areas you wish to hunt that have trees that are too small to mount regular tree stands or areas with no trees. The tripod stand has a coated, welded steel platform, with a swivel chair mounted in the middle. A three-sided rail base supports the platform, having the appearance of a triangle with a pod-like top, thus the name tripod stand. The legs of this stand usually have several positions that allow you to adjust the legs to make the stand level in either even or uneven terrain. This stand usually comes with a narrow metal railing that is bolted to the base of the platform, which acts more as a guide rail or support for shooting a firearm.

I have one of these stands on my property in a row of trees separating two food plots. Tripod stands work well in areas where an elevated stand is needed for one hunter to use. Manufacturers of these stands do offer attachments for concealment and protection from the elements as well. A tripod stand works well for one hunter in a sitting position, as it allows 360-degree movement.

This stand does have good advantages, as it can be placed between pine trees, making the stand blend in perfectly and hard to see by traveling deer. Since the legs of the stand are made of a green-coated metal rails, I have seen whitetails come within a foot of the stand and not detect its presence. Placing this stand in the middle of a high hardhack field, the platform will stand just above the cover, allowing the stand to blend in where other stands will stick out and be noticeable.

Tripod stands offer an elevated position when trees are not available.

This is also a quiet stand from which to hunt, as the mounted chair swivels without a sound or the squeaks of other stands.

The disadvantages of this stand include not being able to stand, as there is little room between the edge of the platform and the swivel chair mounted square in the middle of the platform. Standing is possible, but I do not recommend this as it offers a safety hazard to a standing hunter using this stand. Another disadvantage is the side rails of this stand. A safety strap can be attached to the side rails, but the rails are designed for shooting support rather than the support of the weight of a hunter. These stands are usually between 12-feet and 15-feet, and falling can cause a potential problem. I would like to add that if a hunter climbs into this stand and remains sitting to hunt, it is a good hunting stand.

In the future, I hope these stands will be constructed with larger and stronger side rails, and with wider and heavier platforms. Since this stand should be constructed on site due to its size and height, I believe this would be a good modification and an added advantage.

Climbing Tree Stand

The climbing tree stand is a stand that allows the hunter to use his legs to lift it up a tree. A person using this stand does not have to exert any physical strength in order to climb a tree. The method of climbing uses a cantilever design with two separate attachments for climbing. The upper attachment locks onto the tree, allowing the user to sit securely facing the tree. You then raise the bottom attachment with your feet and lock it into place with your weight as you stand up. The bottom section has fixed parallel foot straps that you put your feet into that allow you to hold the bottom section in place as you stand. You then raise the top section and repeat the process until you are at the desired height on the tree. Once at the height preferred, you then use locking straps to secure both the upper and lower sections of the stand in place to prevent slippage. Climbing tree stands use a cable, belt material or chain that wraps around the tree to lock the stand to the tree while climbing.

Climbing tree stands have been modified in style and locking devices more than any other type of tree stand and are built by several different manufacturers. You can purchase these stands in a number of different designs with several add-on attachments.

Earlier models of the climbing tree stand did not securely lock the climbing stand to the tree as current models do. As a result of this error in design, many recorded accidents and close calls were attributed to this type of hunting stand.

I remember hunting in the Adirondack Mountains in New York State using an earlier model climbing tree stand. Practicing a number of times with this stand before my hunting trip, I felt quite comfortable in being able to climb a tree and lock the stand into place safely. It was about 6 a.m. when I arrived at the area I wanted to hunt, I attached both sections of the stand to the tree I wanted to climb. I laid my unloaded rifle away from the bottom of the tree, attaching a rope to the rifle barrel and shoulder strap, giving myself 35 feet of rope, and then tied the other end to the top attachment of my stand. This way after I reached my desired height and locked both sections of the stand in place, I would pull up my rifle safely. Putting on a safety strap and attaching the other end to the tree, I was ready to climb the tree.

Climbing tree stands are both easy to transport and can give you an elevated advantage.

I started up the tree and was doing fine, getting up to about 28 feet, which I felt was a comfortable height, matching the canopy of the trees around me as well as having a good field of view. I made sure my safety strap was firmly attached to myself and the tree and that the height of the strap allowed security as well as a comfortable range of movement. Once deciding that all safety precautions were in place, I stood up on the lower level of the stand to put a locking type strap around the tree and upper attachment. After accomplishing this, I then sat down in the seat on the upper attachment and took my feet out of the foot straps on the lower level so I could squat down to secure the lower attachment in the same fashion as the upper attachment. When I removed my feet from the foot straps, the lower attachment slid all the way down the tree. In shock and with eyes that were now twice their usual size at that point, I think I might have alerted every deer within half a mile radius as I yelled out something that sound like a loud frantic and extended version of the word, "NO!"

Here I was, 28-feet up and facing the tree, and the lower attachment was down at the base of the tree; I forgot to tie a piece of rope to attach the upper and lower sections.

Let me tell you something: the feeling I had at this point can only be compared as being a one-legged man in a butt-kicking contest! You cannot imagine the feeling of stupidity, mixed with helplessness and shock all in one at that point in time. Well, my view was pretty good from up there, but my immediate thoughts were not on deer hunting. My mind was racing in between my mouth verbally chastising myself for what I had just done and wondering how many hunters have had this happen to them. Was I the number one and only individual this ever happened to? I also remember wondering if someone up above was watching this and laughing hysterically at the time; I did hear that God has a sense of humor. Another thought that might be even worse was if someone in my group of hunting companions, which included my saintly and forgiving wife, would pass by me, look up, and shake their head. Could this have been a pre-planned plot for the possibility of someone taking a picture for a hunting magazine or the TV series *Ripley's Believe It Or Not?* It's funny what you think about when you are sitting up a tree.

I might have had about a hundred different ideas of how to get a hold of the lower part of my tree stand and get it back into place. I did have thirty-five feet of rope that was still attached to the upper part of the stand, but my rifle was attached to the other end on the ground. All I had to do is bring up my rifle, untie it, cut a small piece of rope and secure the rifle to the upper part of the stand, get a hook and tie it to the end and catch the lower part and pull it up the tree. Yeah right, where do I get the hook? I did have a fanny pack, and I started looking through it. I had everything a hunter would want to carry, but no hook. "This is going to be a long day," I thought when I looked down and realized I had a compass that was attached to my hunting shirt with a four-inch metal band made out of a soft metal. The compass band was designed to slip into a shirt pocket and clip in place with the compass end outside the pocket. I immediately removed the compass from the metal band, took my hunting knife from my pocket and worked a hole into one end of the soft metal band. I took a plastic locking tie strap that I always keep in my fanny pack to secure tags to deer after I shoot one to affix the conservation tag. Using the locking strap, I put it into the hole in the metal band, clamped the strap end together and made a ring. I then tied it to the end of the rope and lowered it down the tree. After a number of tries, I was able to catch a siderail on the lower part of the stand and slowly pull it up the tree.

I immediately tied the upper part of the climbing stand to the lower part, lowered my rifle down the tree and climbed to the ground. I wasn't on the ground ten minutes when my wife approached me, asking if I had seen anything, as it was now about 10:30 a.m. I told her I saw a few birds and that was it. After a while I told my loving and saintly wife what happened while looking intently at her for the next few minutes, expecting all out laughter. But that did not happen, as she simply happened to mention it in passing to my other hunting companions later on, which faithfully reminded me of this episode for several years to follow. Do you know that after checking, nowhere in the assembly instructions did the manufacturer ever mention to secure the lower and upper levels together prior to climbing? Actually from that point on, I really never needed another reminder to do this simple step prior to using any climbing tree stand.

There are several advantages to using a climbing tree stand. The first is being able to position yourself above the eyesight of moving deer without alerting them of your presence. The second is that you are able to hunt without disturbing the area you are hunting in. These hunting stands are now affordable to the average safety-conscious hunter who follows all the manufacturer recommendations for using this type of hunting stand. As well as the many advantages of this type of hunting stand, there are also several disadvantages to consider. The first is height and the possibility of falling out of this type of hunting stand. The next is the chance of the user not securing and locking the stand to a tree correctly and having the stand slide down the tree unexpectedly. Then there is a chance that this could happen and the safety strap would hold you in place and not allow you to climb down the tree, forcing you to wait for help.

Climbing tree stands have accounted for many hunting accidents, but I do feel that they are safe if used properly by someone who has practiced with one well in advance of the hunting season and follows all safety precautions. I also recommend that the user of any climbing tree stand use an **Approved Safety Harness** each and every time they use an elevated stand of this type, which will distribute the user's weight evenly in the event of an accidental fall. Another reminder is that all users of climbing tree stands take their time when ascending and descending.

Know what tree you wish to climb in advance, so you can determine if this is the right tree to climb using this type of stand. Trees with loose or flaking bark are not recommended for climbing with this type of stand, since the teeth that clamp to the tree cannot lock the stand securely. I know of a hunter in one of the hunting clubs where I was a member who tried climbing a tree with loose bark one morning. It was before sunrise, and the hunter had a Mini Maglite® in his mouth as he ascended the tree. As he stood with the metallic flashlight in his mouth, fifteen feet in the air, the lower portion became loose, sliding down the tree and hitting the ground hard. The impact broke seven teeth in the hunter's mouth as he bit into the Maglite®; he suffered a broken leg as well. It was later learned that the hunter was wearing a safety harness, but he failed to secure the end to the tree while ascending. The hunter made two mistakes. The first, that he failed to recognize an improper tree to climb, and the second was the improper use of a safety harness. When questioned about the accident, the hunter told authorities that he was late getting to his stand and was in a hurry. In haste while in the dark, he picked the wrong tree from the one he had previously planned to climb. He also said he was going to lock the safety strap when he got to the height he was going to hunt. I have heard several stories like this and others that show what can happen when a hunter is in a hurry and is negligent with his or her safety precautions. Some stories result in close calls, while others do not. I cannot overemphasize caution while using this type of stand and for hunters to be constantly aware of what they are doing at all times. There are several factors that come into play and determine whether your use of a climbing stand will be safe. Weather conditions for that day and the day before you climb, the tree you plan to climb and condition of the bark, your physical attributes of health and age, the condition of the stand you own and also the fall restraint system you intend to use.

Lock-On Tree Stand

The lock-on tree stand, compared to the climbing tree stand, is relatively safe. With this type of stand, after picking the desired tree that will hold the stand, you first attach a ladder to the tree securely, then climb up and put the stand in place, locking the stand securely to the tree. This can be done well in advance of the season, after which occasional safety checks to determine that the stand remains secure will insure against unwanted surprises. As with the climbing tree stand, the user must have and use an approved safety system. The full-body harness is the best fall restraint system currently on the market. Care must be given as hunters must remain aware that they are in an elevated stand. When seeing deer and after the shot when excitement is high, a knowledgeable hunter must maintain a safe and mindful attitude. As in other tree stands, ascending and descending can be the critical periods to be alert. The lock-on tree stand has a short base platform to stand on, and some stands are equipped with a seat for added comfort and allows the hunter to sit while hunting.

The lock-on tree stand has several advantages. Most hunters who own these lock-on stands have several; you can put these stands in many different locations to handle changes in climate, wind direction and change of deer movement patterns. These stands are also very easy to set up, allowing the hunter using only one stand to change locations. Another advantage of this type of stand is that since you do not climb using this stand, branches do not become a problem or get in the way. The hunter only needs to know the desired height and lock the stand to the tree, using a ladder to climb in and out of the stand.

Lock-on stands can be placed into position well before the season starts.

The disadvantage of this type of stand is the safety factor, as the hunter is in an elevated position while using the stand, and the factor of falling does exist. As with all stands of this type, a safety harness is recommended. Another consideration is the small platform the hunter will be standing on while using this type of stand.

In conclusion, I would like to add that there are several types of hunting stands from which to choose. Whether you decide to hunt from the ground or from an elevated position, there is a wide selection and many types of hunting stands that suit all terrains and locations. No matter what stand you decide to use, remember that even in an enclosed stand that blocks much of your body movement, if the stand has a window that you look out of, you can be seen, and all precautions should be made to prevent this. I recommend either a head net or facemask that breaks up your outline of the face. Though deer are color blind, they can still see movement in a window. All precautions should be taken to remain quiet and control any unnecessary movement.

Chapter Eleven

Why Tree Stands Double Your Chances

You're on the ground at a location you've scouted a number of times, deciding this to be the perfect place to shoot a record-book whitetail deer. It's 5:30 a.m. and the woods are quiet as you wait for sunrise on opening day. As you sit and wait, you hear the call of a barred owl in the distance, letting his presence be known to one and all. The wind is coming from the north, filling your face with the cold reminder that fall has awakened once again. You have positioned yourself on the north side of a ridge facing a hollow that acts like a funnel for deer to move through as they leave their feeding area to go to a heavily covered thicket, which is their regular bedding area. All tracks show that the deer move down this ravine leading to hardhack on the left and a cedar swamp on the right. Logically, your way of thinking tells you that if the deer are relaxed, they bed to the left in the heavy brush; if chased, they head for the swamp. You already know that the best and most likely hunting areas are locations near or adjacent to feeding and bedding areas, positions that contain both scrapes and rubs, which are not far from watering areas and close to the game trails connecting these areas.

Only a few minutes remain to go as you listen for sounds of movement and try to see if anything is stirring. You have waited all year for this, and in your mind, you are going over a checklist of all that was done to get ready for this moment. Your 30-06 rifle is sighted in, and you know you are accurate to the mark at 100 yards or better.

Time passes slowly now as you look at your watch, trying to make as little movement as possible. You think you are concealed the best you possibly can as you wait for the deer you have been thinking about all year to step out and make his presence known to you. Crows are beginning to call and just then, you hear movement behind you. You turn to see a grey squirrel rustling through the leaves looking for acorns and turn back to your position facing the area you think deer will be approaching from. As the sun begins to show its shining face, awakening from a night of peaceful rest, other squirrels move about, and you turn to make sure it is only these small inhabitants of the woods. A red squirrel catches your movement and begins to chatter, alerting all of your presence as you sit wondering when he will quiet down and resume feeding.

You turn back, and out of the corner of your eye, you see a heavy-rack buck running back to cover. You never heard him come in, and he watched your every movement; you've been busted.

Well, welcome to the club. You've now been initiated and have something in common with 98 percent of the whitetail hunters today. The question is, do you want that to happen again, or would you like to correct this by lessening the odds of being spotted by a whitetail deer in the future? I can't promise you that you'll never be busted again, but if you follow what I am about to tell you, you'll know the steps to take to help you avoid this from happening on you next hunt.

Movement alerts a deer as much as scent.

Whitetail deer are full-time residents of the woods with senses far superior to yours, having the odds in their favor right from the start. I can show you how to reverse the odds in your favor and before long you will see *Why Tree Stands Double Your Chances.*

Hunting on ground level has been done for a number of years and quite efficiently, I may add, by those select few who perfected the art and are familiar with all the eccentricity involved for total concealment. I say "art" because you have to be quite talented and artistic to make a stand on ground level and not be detected by a deer. The ground-level, trail-watching hunter must be able to beat a deer at his own game, matching the whitetail's eyes, nose and ears, which by human standards are far superior. That in itself is a challenge, not to mention being able to fatally shoot the whitetail deer while remaining undetected. Now you have two challenges. Want to go for three? What about the time it takes for deer to accept the ground stand you have constructed as a new addition to their home? While you are trying to meet all these challenges that come as questions to your abilities that you have to answer, the whitetail deer is changing all the questions.

Think about it? Will they always come in the same direction and use the trail you are watching? Can you see in all directions, should Mr. Whitetail decide once he has awakened, he is going to be different and travel just off the main trail about 20 to 30 yards away? Ah yes, decisions, decisions and more decisions. You can narrow all this down by using one stand that will alleviate most of the guesswork. Actually, you can use this stand to put the odds in your favor in a number of different ways.

I know you are sitting there wondering, panting, wagging your tail, and waiting for me to throw you the bone, so I won't keep you in suspense any longer; the answer is a tree stand.

A hunter on a stand usually will not spook a deer if the hunter remains calm and avoids motion, especially in an open tree stand. I recommend all tree stands to be enclosed to hide movement from the waist down. I say this also because I feel that while in any tree stand a hunter should be sitting, and not standing. For one, you will be more comfortable when sitting and for another, you will break your silhouette, which could give you away depending on the position of the sun. More hunters are noticed in tree stands while they are standing because they are silhouetted by the sun, causing deer to look up at them. Whitetail deer do not normally go through the woods looking up, but they will if something appears unnatural or stands out during the deer's approach. A hunter sitting cuts his image in half and will blend in better.

I know, I know, you are saying you have seen on TV how hunters dressed in camouflage are standing in their tree stands. I guess if I wanted to sell you camouflage, I would have hunters standing on TV also, but if you are going to hunt and want to break your image, sit. You should be able to shoot a firearm or bow in a sitting position, and you can stand slowly at the last minute if you absolutely cannot make the shot while sitting. I, for one, have shot only two whitetail deer from a standing position. I feel this is important to bring out, because I see too many hunters standing while in their stands. This is definitely wrong, and you should know all the reasons why you should be sitting.

An elevated stand can give you an edge and block movement.

If you are standing, you have to turn your whole body to shoot, and that movement can cause you to be detected. If you are sitting, you can either draw back your bow or focus your firearm at a whitetail with barely any visible movement from the ground. While sitting and having your back to a tree, you can't be detected, even with the sun in front of you. The stand itself blocks your shadow from reaching the ground. There are limited exceptions to this rule, such as a limb in the way, but you should have seen this and removed it before getting set in your stand.

Many hunters develop leg cramps if they sit in one position for a long period of time; having the ability to move your legs for comfort is important. If you are in an elevated stand and it is enclosed, this will enable you to move and still remain undetected.

Concealment of a hunter while on a stand has been a debate for a number of years. Some hunters believe a tree stand should not have camouflaged sides, as it will not blend in with the surroundings. The hunter should only be wearing camouflage clothing to blend in naturally. I disagree with this line of thought, because even though there are camouflage outfits that look natural, they are artificially made and are not as natural looking as claimed to be. I feel that a tree stand or elevated stand can be camouflaged and made to look natural and not stick out if the user of the stand incorporates branches and leaves of the tree or trees in the area. Not to say that if you are in an oak tree with pine trees near you, that you use pine bows as camouflage, but with some creativity, a hunter can camouflage a stand for adequate concealment. With a tree stand, the hunter is working to cut down the deer's odds by first contending with one of a whitetail's defenses, which is his eyesight. I do recommend that hunters wear full camouflage on different occasions when using different techniques of hunting. I usually hunt out of my tree stands wearing jeans and a camouflage shirt and have never had a problem.

I know I will hear flack from this, but I hunt differently than most, and that may be the reason why I never have a problem. I also do not feel that I have to look like a hunter who is posing for a clothing ad in order to shoot a whitetail deer. If you are in a tree stand and have the sides enclosed, a camouflage shirt and jacket are fine. Unless you plan on coming down from the tree stand to stalk or do a still hunt—and we will get into that later on in another chapter—I do not feel that whitetail deer care what you are wearing. Think about this, now that we are on the subject: all deer are color blind. So if a deer is colorblind, why are there so many different camouflage patterns with different colors? The answer is that you, the hunter, can see the difference, but deer cannot to an extent. Whether the camouflage is green, or red, or orange or pretty pink polka dots makes no difference in what you wear if a whitetail is colorblind. Camouflage must break an outline only. Whitetails do not see as you see, and I hope you remember this when looking at camouflage for a stand or clothing. What is perceived and seen to be the best by humans is not what the whitetails actually see, even though industries have been built on convincing you of something entirely different. Just think that before all these companies came about, hunters shot trophy whitetail deer and the hunters who dress as they did twenty years ago are still shooting trophy whitetail deer. I will say that if you need a hunting outfit for bow hunting, pick the best camo outfit you can afford that will wear well, and remember that sometimes you will have to hunt from a visible stand or area where you may want full camouflage. Enough said about that.

I remember one day in late fall I was hunting with a friend named Larry in Nemo, South Dakota. I got to Larry's house, and I was dressed in my regular bow hunting outfit, which was a heavy plaid green shirt and black denim jeans. When Larry answered the door, I saw he was dressed in a red plaid shirt and pants. I said, "Hey Larry, I thought you said we were going to go bow hunting today; did you forget?"

He looked at me casually and said, "No, I have been sitting here and waiting on you."

I looked at him and said, "Well, when are you going to get dressed to hunt?"

Larry looked and said, "I am dressed; don't tell me you think I have to wear green or something else to get a deer?"

I shrugged my shoulders, because I knew from past experience and hunting with Larry that silence was best at this point to avoid a long lecture. Larry was about sixty-seven years old, and I was an aspiring youth, thirty years younger, and an accomplished bow hunter at the time.

We hunted a thicket in a pocket of the woods he owned and he positioned me in a stand, which was about twenty-five feet high and overlooking a runway that Larry said the deer had been using regularly. Larry was in a stand about fifteen yards away overlooking another runway in a stand that was about ten feet off the ground. I wondered if the deer would spot his red outfit from a distance because I sure could, but I didn't say a word. We hunted that morning about three hours with little success, and when I got up and was about to climb down from the stand, I looked over and Larry was motioning me to sit; he was pointing to my right. I looked and saw a nice buck coming through the woods. The deer was coming to Larry's stand and not mine, so I remained still. When the deer got to within thirty paces from the stand, he looked up at Larry, who was sitting motionless. After what appeared to be a long time—but in actuality was only a minute or two—the buck eased on and stopped to lower his head to feed. Larry drew back, made a perfect shot, and killed the buck. I climbed down the tree and congratulated my friend for getting this buck, telling him that I thought he would never get a deer bow hunting in a red outfit.

He looked at me and said, "What do you mean?"

I said, "Didn't you see that buck stop and look at you?"

Larry looked at me and said, "Yeah, he stopped and looked at me after I spit my chewing tobacco at him, trying to get him to go your way. When he stopped and looked up, it was because I swallowed my tobacco and darn near choked. Guess he was wondering if he had to do that CPR thing, or just run for help. Well, when he lowered his head to think it over, I made the shot."

I looked at him and said, "You don't think he spotted you in red?"

Larry looked at me and said, "Bob, deer see in only two or so colors. What spooks them is not what they can see, but what they can't see."

I have never forgotten hunting with Larry and what he taught me about bow hunting and whitetail deer hunting. It is not the color of your clothing that you have to be concerned with, but the pattern on your clothing. A green-checkered shirt has always worked well for me. As years went on, I picked up some camouflage shirts and jackets, some lightweight, some heavier, and I have the same outfits for the past twenty years.

Hunting from a tree stand doubles your chances for both seeing whitetail deer and taking shots at deer also, because it puts you in an elevated stand above their eyesight if you are high enough to blend in with the tree canopy in the immediate area and not stick out to look unnatural. Many hunters who hunt from a tree stand forget the idea that their stand has to be hidden by blending in with the canopy of the trees in the area they are hunting. I have seen hunters in stands fifteen feet up while the tree canopy is twenty-five feet. There they are, up in their stand and sticking out, looking unnatural and out of place. If they would go up another ten feet, they would have a better view for one, and more important, they would blend in naturally. That is another reason why deer look up at hunters. A lot of hunters ask if deer look up. Yes, if you stick out, they will, because you are giving them something to look at. If you are nervous about height, don't use an elevated stand until you are comfortable with height. You should also be aware of your limitations and comfort level with a tree stand.

Many people are willing to sell you a tree stand, whether it is a climbing tree stand, ladder stand or a lock-on stand. You are the one who has to use it. Just because you own one, don't get caught in the trap that as long as you are off the ground you are okay from deer spotting you. I cannot tell you this enough; you have to blend in naturally. Be willing to put the time in to feel comfortable with your stand at different height levels.

Ever notice the TV shows about hunting? Sometimes you see them up high and wonder why they are up so high. At times they show you a camera angle from the ground to a tree stand, and you see how high their stands are. Next time you see a tree stand from that angle, notice where the tree canopy is also, and you will see that the pro's stands match the canopy height. Some people ask, "How high do I have to place my stand?" The answer is simple: have it as high as the tree canopy in the area. If the canopy is fifteen feet, stop at fifteen feet and when your stand blends in. If it is thirty feet, go thirty feet. This is important and a good reason why many hunters who use tree stands have trouble seeing deer. The whitetails are seeing the hunters before the hunters see the deer. If your stand is so low that it sticks out, it does not matter how you camouflage it, you will stick out.

We have covered camouflage and movement, which has taken care of two of the whitetail's defenses, a deer's eyes and ears; so let's move to scent for a while.

The whitetail's nose is far superior to yours. They can be alerted to an unnatural scent in the wind at over 100 yards; how's that for a nose? So you still think that bologna sandwich with cheese and mustard you have in your fanny pack will go unnoticed, or the snacks you have in a plastic bag that you open ever so slowly won't be detected? How about the thermos of coffee or tea for those really cold days?

You're twenty feet up and are blending in like a 185 lb. squirrel in a nest. You're mindful to keep your movements slow and to a minimum. What do you do next? You are having a picnic in a tree and think it is okay. Even if you get the sandwich out without making a sound or the thermos opened, scent just busted you for about a 100-yard distance in every direction. On a day with a little wind, I would say you can about double that distance. Oh, you don't drink coffee or tea and just drink soda? I have a news flash for you: sugar can be detected even further away. Did you know that a black bear can smell honey in a beehive at more than a mile? Whitetail deer are known to have better noses than bears.

You go through the process of picking a perfect location, put up a tree stand to blend in naturally, are cautious about movement, wear camouflaged clothing, and forget about scent because someone once told you that if you are up high, scent will go over a deer's head, and you bought that, right? Well, there are a lot of hunters who do the very same thing and shake their heads wondering why they didn't see a deer that day and blame it on being just a bad day. In actuality, they are right, but the reason for the bad day was because they made it a bad day themselves. Scent does not go in a straight line. If you are up fifteen feet, scent doesn't stay up at fifteen feet. Scent rides on the direction of the breeze or wind currents, and from what I observe, leaves on the ground blow around from a breeze, which tells me something about direction and air currents. Scent moves the same way, with the wind. Whitetail deer will detect scent, even if it comes from thirty feet above them.

So keep the snacks, candy bars, sandwiches, thermoses and soda pop back in your vehicle, unless you are willing to share them with the whitetails. You will have to settle for eating alone, because the deer will know from a distance that you have them and probably won't want to spoil your snack by showing up, unless that is okay with you. No, you won't starve or die from dehydration or malnutrition. I am by no means trying to give you medical advice, just sound hunting advice.

By doing what I have said, you now have eliminated the three defenses the whitetail deer have as their primary protection, and in doing so you have doubled your chances while using a tree stand.

Chapter Twelve

Stand Location That Guarantees Success

In the years I have been involved with both hunting whitetail deer and teaching others how to hunt, one of the first questions I am usually asked is how to select stand locations. On the TV shows you see about hunting whitetail deer, the articles you read in the hunting magazines, and in most hunting seminars you go to, no one ever covers this topic sufficiently, informing you where to put your stand. The hunting books on the market today do not cover the subject in depth, leaving the reader in doubt. You will read what signs to look for and will be told how the hunters are looking over this or that, but when it comes down to actually picking the right place to be, you are left wondering and waiting for more information.

I will make a promise to you here and now. I will show you how to pick a *Stand Location that Guarantees Success* and will not leave it up to any guesswork on your part. Now, I cannot guarantee you will shoot a 12-point buck, especially if you are hunting an area that has not produced any record whitetails in the past. I will say that if you listen closely, are willing to do some work yourself, and follow the steps I will lay out for you, you will not only see deer but also have the good chance for a shot. Whether or not you take the shot will be totally up to you.

There are several things that hunters do wrong unconsciously from the start without ever realizing it. One of the biggest mistakes I have seen in the field are hunters placing their stands in the wrong locations. They are in the right general area, but not where they should be sitting.

I remember one hunt in particular while I was hunting upstate New York with my friend, Gene. I was staying at his house for two weeks after having already taken a nice eight-point buck on the fifth day of the season. I had another week left to fill a doe tag, and I was relaxing more than hunting. The property across from Gene's house was open for hunting, and I decided I was going to get my doe in that location. Gene was busy this day, and I went onto the property after having decided I was going to hunt with a portable climbing tree stand.

Getting up early that day around 8 a.m., I set out to pick my stand location. I had hunted this piece of property the year before with Gene and was familiar with several good stand sites, having scouted well in advance for this hunting season with Gene. I started out packing the stand on my back with my rifle in hand. I got to the top of the ridge and wanted to have the stand facing the west side about half way down one end of a plateau, which was on top of the ridge. There was a large CRP (Conservation Reserve Program) field below, and I knew deer traveled from the field, which was a great bedding area to feed on acorns and hickory nuts that were abundant that year and covered the ground.

Location... Location... Location.

When I got to the plateau, I noticed another hunter in a stand and stopped to chat after he waved me to come to him. When I got to his stand, I saw that he had placed his climbing stand just about in the middle of the plateau about six feet off the ground. I asked him if he had seen anything, and he said no, but his uncle said this was a good location, telling me his uncle had always seen deer moving up the ridge to this plateau.

He was a young lad, and I asked him if he had been hunting long. He said this was his second year hunting and he had not shot a deer so far. Not wanting to interfere with what his uncle had told him or crowd him either, I told him where I was going to hunt, which was about a good quarter mile away. I also told him that he might want to climb the tree a bit higher and to attach his safety harness to the tree once he got up about fifteen feet more, since I saw he had one on, but the other end wasn't attached to the tree. His uncle told him to get off the ground and that he did not have to climb too high since he could see deer coming in any direction after sunup.

I arrived at my location and laid the rifle down after making sure there was no bullet in the chamber and attached a rope to the sling and barrel and the other end to the top part of the climber, making sure both parts of the climbing stand were connected by a three-foot cord. I climbed up the tree to about twenty-eight feet to blend in well with the canopy of the tree and surrounding trees in the area. I was not in the stand a half hour when two large does came out of the CRP field and walked to my stand. I waited until they were about ten yards from my stand and dropped the larger one with a neck shot.

Seeing the doe drop in her tracks, I then opened the chamber to put the empty shell in my pocket, closing the action of my .270 Remington without inserting a new bullet into the chamber. I slowly lowered my rifle down to the ground and climbed down the tree. I walked up to the doe after seeing she was dead, filled out my tag and attached it to her leg, then started to field dress her. After I was done and cleaned up a bit with alcohol wipes I had in my fanny pack, I began to remove the sections of my climbing stand from the tree to secure them together for the slow trip back. I looked up, and the young hunter I had seen earlier was walking to me.

He was excited and congratulated me, saying I was lucky and reminding me he was in his stand for two days without seeing a deer. I asked him if he wanted to hunt a different location other than where he was, and I told him he would have a good chance of seeing deer that afternoon. He immediately said yes, so I told him to hunt the same tree I climbed and used for a stand location. I told him I filled my last tag and this was a good location to see deer and told him why. I told him that I did not want to contradict what his uncle told him, and that his uncle was right in that deer did run up to the plateau, but usually after someone spooks them. The lad offered to help drag the deer to his stand, and I was not about to turn him down since he was about twenty years younger than I was. I also told him how high his stand should be in the tree, and he asked me why. I told him that in this location, if he didn't place his stand at that height to blend in with the canopy, he would stick out and be seen by any deer moving up the ridge, and that the deer might see him before he got a chance to see them. After we got to his stand, I told him where I was staying and asked him to let me know if he got anything that afternoon or the following day. I then took hold of my drag rope and went down to Gene's house with the doe.

I got to Gene's house about forty-five minutes later and saw he was there after running some errands. Together, Gene and I hung the deer by throwing a rope over a limb on a tree that was behind the house, high enough off the ground so the coyotes would not bother it that night. I told Gene about the young hunter I met on the plateau, and he knew his uncle well, telling me that his uncle lived nearby and was up in years, seldom hunting any more.

That evening about 9 p.m., the young hunter and his uncle came to Gene's house, and Gene formally introduced me to the lad's uncle. I learned that the young hunter, named Tim, got his first buck, a small four pointer. His uncle told me he hunted those woods for a number of years on opening day and other days; he usually got a doe and sometimes a nice buck, always seeing deer running up the ridge. We talked a bit and found out that the uncle always hunted in a group who hunted the lower CRP fields regularly doing drives through the field.

Since there was no food for deer on the plateau, the deer his uncle got were chased from the CRP field and up the ridge by other hunters. The uncle usually hunted in or just outside the CRP fields with his friends. I told him, as there were no other hunters hunting during the day from what I could see, I knew deer would not move to the plateau, and that is why the lad was not seeing any deer. The plateau was part of an escape route for deer and not their normal place to travel. Deer would only use that route when they were driven.

My good friend Gene has passed away, but I remember all the hunts we did together, the good times we had in and out of the field, his family, and the memories, which will last a lifetime.

If you stay in a stand long enough, the law of averages predicts you may eventually see a deer, as whitetails constantly move. The question is, do you want to see deer intentionally or by accident? I place hunting stands not where deer were said to be, but rather where deer are going to be. In your experiences, you will hear from different hunters where they have seen deer. A few might even say where they took shots at deer. Since I can't be there hunting with you, I will tell you where to place your stand to see deer; the rest will be up to you.

The first thing I want you to remember—in all the years you intend to hunt, keep this in your mind as rule number 1—you never want to hunt where the deer are but rather where the deer are going to be. You want to place your stand where deer will travel and have to pass by your location. You do not want to disturb their bedding location at any time.

The reason for this is that if you disturb a deer's bedding area and force the deer to change their normal pattern, your stand location has to change also. Whitetail deer will always come back to the same feeding area, but if you change where they bed, you will change the direction they enter their feeding location. Know where their bedding location is and then leave it undisturbed.

Now how do I find their bedding location, you ask? Think back to your scouting trips you made earlier and refer to Chapters 3 and 4 for information on what to look for. A good tip to remember is wait until a good rain and look for fresh tracks on deer trails or runways. After a good rain, you can clearly see footprints on a deer trail and can determine if the footprints are fresh, indicating that the trail is active. There is nothing worse than setting up on a deer trail that hasn't been used in weeks. Follow the game trail, being sure not to walk on the trail itself, as older deer using these trails will detect your imprints and scent your presence.

Rule number two, you never want your presence detected. See if the deer trail leads to heavy cover from a feeding area. If you are hunting in snow, these trails will have good noticeable imprints that you can determine if the footprints are both buck and doe. Deer trails will cross at some point, like an intersection. Make a note after seeing if the intersecting deer trail is being used and has fresh tracks. If the intersecting trail is being used, see if it also goes to the feeding area. Remember the rule not to walk on the deer trail, keeping a six-foot distance from the trail. If you see other intersecting trails in the same area that are fresh also, do the same to determine if they are being used and where they lead to and come from. I say this because a buck will usually follow a primary trail during the rut, which is a deer's breeding time. When bucks have their nose to the ground, they are following does in heat. When you are hunting the rut, you can rely on one primary trail with fresh tracks. On all other times while hunting, you want to know where the intersecting trails are, making a note of them. Look for rubs on trees just off or on a deer trail. If the rubs are on trees on a trail that is being used but not a trail that is worn down showing a lot of traffic by several deer, this is usually a trail made by a buck.

There is an old saying that if the tree being rubbed is wide in diameter, a large rack buck is making the rub. This is partially true, but do not make a note of this as being a fact for all deer, as it is only a general rule. I have watched six-point bucks with small basket racks rub on trees that have a twenty-four inch diameter. On one fall morning, I had a good show from my stand watching a twelve-point buck tear apart a sapling with what appeared to be a buck with an attitude problem. I would have corrected his attitude problem with an arrow, but he was just out of my bow range. I firmly believe and hope you will do the same if a deer is just out

While in your stand SIT STILL. A deer may be looking for movement.

of your range where you can place a quick clean killing shot, do not make the shot. For one, you will take the chance of wounding or crippling the deer, and for another, you will probably get a shot another time when the deer is closer if the whitetail has not been disturbed. Sit back and enjoy watching the deer, and you very well might see the deer again.

On one bow hunt on my property, I watched twenty-three deer that were in my food plot. I sat and watched them for forty minutes. I had more fun watching the youngsters running and fighting than I would have gotten by taking one of them with my bow. By watching them and not taking a shot, I was later able to take a seven-pointer in that same stand a few hours later. Not all hunting has to be what I call, "See and Shoot." Sit back, relax, and have some enjoyment whenever you can. Shots will always be there for you to take if you are in the right area and in the right stand.

Rule number three: always pick a stand site with a lot of cover. When you are selecting the tree to use for your tree stand, pick a tree that either has a big pine tree next to it or has cover branches that will block you from deer walking nearby

Wait for your perfect shot.

or toward your location. This is a common mistake by many hunters who want to pick a site to see too much territory, wanting to see every deer they possibly can. This is completely wrong, as the object is not to see every deer but to see good size deer that do not see you. This is how you are able to get a good shot at a nice size deer. If you blend in with the woods, deer will walk past you as they normally travel without feeling uneasy or cautious about passing by something that appears to be unnatural. Older deer did not get to that stage in life by walking through open woods or passing through areas that make them nervous for one reason or another. Covers are essential; leave the open areas for those who want to shoot a deer by chance. This is also the main reason why deer look up. They do this because something caught their attention. You do not want to catch their attention at any time, except to stop them for a broadside shot, and only when you want to catch their attention. For you ground hunters who wish to find a good location, keep this rule in mind with one addition. Always place your position behind something. You want your image to be blocked; you want to be sitting to block your silhouette. Have you ever came home and thought something was out of place? It bothered you because you felt uneasy; you later learned your wife or girlfriend moved a chair or the couch to a different location in the room. whitetails feel the same when they see or feel something is wrong and out of place in their home, also. If you upset and try to change what I call the natural order of things, whitetails, just as you, feel the difference, and it is unsettling to them. Keep this in mind when you select a stand site, and then try to conceal your presence. When you make a ground blind out of brush, make sure there is ground brush in the area so it does not look out of place. You want it as natural as you possibly can make it and have freedom of movement. Do not make a ground blind that restricts your movement when you are sitting inside. For tree stands, this is very important also, as you must be able to aim a firearm or draw a bow without detection. This goes hand-in-hand with rule number two, but I list it as a separate rule because it encompasses other facets. This is why I feel that all tree stands must have cover on the three open sides to block movement from observation on the ground.

Now I know there are those who will say, "So what do I do, make a ball around my tree stand that will look out of order?" The answer is no, and when you put the camouflage around the sides, have branches going up, down and out, just as the trees around you have branches that extend in every direction. Remember that you need cover as well as freedom of movement; make the stand look natural and not stand out from ground level.

Rule number four, and this is important for every hunter who wants a *Stand Location that Guarantees Success:* Never put in place only one tree stand or one ground blind. Always have two stands, even if you only pick one area to hunt. This is important for a new hunter as well as an experienced hunter. Once a whitetail detects a possible change to the landscape or to their home and you see them walking looking up, change to the alternate stand for the next hunt. They can look up for any reason, but the most common is because you have constructed a stand that looks out of place or they detected your scent. Once that happens, they will always look up as they pass that stand, and you want to be in another location so they will feel at ease. You may not have deer look up at you and take a nice whitetail from your first stand. In this case, you can alternate stands, which is a good idea anyway as you do not want to leave scent in one area by hunting the same stand day after day, especially if you are seeking a particular deer. Trophy hunters who have seen the deer they want to shoot will usually have two and sometimes three stands in the same area but in different locations that offer different views. This way if the whitetail they are after changes patterns and uses an alternate game trail, they are prepared for the change. This is also true for bow hunters.

You have the four basic rules to guarantee success. No, I did not forget about scrapes. I did not mention scrapes earlier because there are several important things to bear in mind when placing a stand next to a scrape. The first thing to avoid—this usually happens to new or inexperienced hunters who see a scrape for the first time—don't try to see it up close. This is about as wrong as sneaking up on a skunk to see if you could get a good whiff or sticking a bobby pin into a light socket. You will only do it once before you learn that some things you should not do. Nevertheless, you go ahead and look closely at the scrape, but do the two other things I mentioned first to see if you could learn from your mistakes. Once you notice a scrape, which is the calling card of a breeding buck, you know two things right off. The first is that there is a breeding buck in the area, and second is that eventually he is going to return to check his scrape for a receptive doe. Be mindful of the second, as most bucks check their scrapes during the night, especially if a good size-breeding buck made the scrape. The young bucks will make a scrape and check it during the mid-day to late afternoon, but that old monster did not get that way from being short on knowledge and quick on barging right in. He will check that scrape under the cover of darkness or just after you can make a legal shot. That old boy has added senses that you will have to be able to match, and you will not just happen to get a shot at him by parking next to his scrape.

Scrapes tell you where deer have been and will be returning.

Scrape hunting is an art, as you cannot set up a stand close to a scrape or you are sure to be seen. You need to see what trails that character is using to get to his scrape and work from that angle. This goes along with the premise of hunting for a trophy or just one particular deer by the use of several stands. There will surely to be at least two, possibly three trails leading to and from his scrape. You also have to be able to determine his trails from the trails of a receptive doe. Most venison-seeking scrape hunters will hunt a scrape after a buck first has built it to be sure the buck, rather than the does, have made the trails to it. You have to hunt the trail and not the scrape to be successful, unless a young buck made the scrape. Shooting a young buck at his scrape takes patience and skill, as all bucks approaching their scrapes are on the alert, with senses in high gear. I recommend hunting the trails, as your chances are better than by sitting overlooking the scrape itself. I do know hunters who have taken bucks by scrapes, but it is doubtful if the whitetail bucks killed by scrape sites are in fact the bucks that actually made the scrape.

As much patience and practice that goes into the hunt is also needed to pick your stand location. It takes several trips to the field in order to know just the area to hunt. The same amount of time is needed to pick the exact location of your stand. Do not rush into your selection, as you must determine without guesswork the right position based on signs and not predictions. Do not estimate but rather know the location and all the signs of whitetail behavior before making your decision. Guesswork on any level should not be a determining factor. It takes me longer to pick the location and exact position of my stand than it takes me to harvest my whitetail deer.

Some hunters will use the same stand year after year and shoot a whitetail deer from that stand every year. This can only accomplished if the area they chose continually shows the same signs and behavior patterns year after year, and they have not disturbed the area.

I have a good friend, one of my long time hunting companions named Steve, who is a retired police detective. Steve hunted the same stand in the same area for years and usually got an eight-point buck out of the same stand. Results such as this are not based on luck but sound reasoning to determine stand location. Steve is a fanatic when it comes to not disturbing an area he is hunting. I firmly believe if he could be lowered to his stand by helicopter rather than walking, he would do so every year so as not to leave footprints or scent in the area. We hunted in a small deer camp that had a cabin and sleeping area, which in itself was just a step just above cave dwelling in creature comforts. It was rough in every sense of the word but a good deer camp in the years we were first members. Steve would hang his hunting clothing outside to reduce the chance of smoke or human scent near his apparel. When on his stand, he was like a pole sitter on a marathon, remaining in place from forty minutes to one hour, before sunrise to evening, waiting in all types of weather to harvest his whitetail.

I remember on one hunt it snowed during the day, and the temperature dropped thirty-three degrees from morning to afternoon. Steve, my other hunting companion named Lenny, a retired high school gym teacher who also scores high on my list of who I consider a true hunter, and myself were the only hunters who remained hunting. I had shot a nice size doe after already taking a good six-pointer the day before. I met up with Lenny, who was dragging a large doe also. We stopped to catch our breath and compare notes, and I asked Lenny if he had seen Steve, since they went into the woods together well before sunrise. Now if you want to meet two hunters who believe you have to be in the woods, sitting, an hour before sunrise, it is them. They are two of a kind, yet as different as can be at the same time but are the best of friends. I asked him if he had seen Steve. He commented that they split at the fork on a trail they took to their separate stands. One trail led to Steve's stand, and the other went in the general direction of Lenny's stand, which, by the way, you had to be a trailblazer with a compass and part Indian to find on your own.

We decided to bring the deer back to the camp and then go to look for Steve, as the temperature was bitter cold. We dropped off the deer and made our way to about a hundred yards or so from Steve's stand. We stopped to catch our wind; and Lenny looked around and asked to borrow my binoculars. He looked and saw Steve sitting in his stand with four inches of snow on his hat, coat, and hunting clothing.

I said, "Len what do you see?"

He said, "I see Steve, but he is not moving at all and looks frozen."

My eyes popped wide open and my mouth dropped after hearing this; I took the binoculars to look. Steve was sitting in his hunting stand, his rifle laid on his

lap, he was covered in snow and was not moving an inch. I looked for a while, but he never moved, and to this day, I still think he was holding his breath. We walked up to him and got within a foot of his stand, expecting the worst. Steve just looked down and said, "Why are you here?"

I said, "I don't know; it could be because it is cold enough to deep freeze hell out here, or maybe we just wanted to see a live snowman. What do you think, with weather this cold?"

Looking down to us all he said was, "go back to the cabin, and I will see you at dark, and do not make any more footprints in the snow!"

I looked at Lenny, he looked at me, and we both walked away, talking and blaming each other for the decision to walk up to his stand to make sure Steve was okay. We walked back to the cabin trying to decide which one of us would take his rifle and hunting stand if Steve froze to death while sitting in his stand. We never had to act on that decision because Steve came back to the cabin with a nice eight-point buck that night. Looking like a Eskimo that got caught out in a blizzard, he muttered how he was lucky he got the deer after some people walked up on him during prime hunting time, as he stared at Lenny and me for a while. After that day, which by the way was five below zero on our camp thermometer, we never walked up on Steve again. I think he would remain motionless if struck by lightning on his stand if there was still light enough to hunt. Just to let you know, I was supposed to get Steve's rifle, and Lenny was to inherit his stand and hunting location.

Steve is a true hunter and can pick a stand location with the best of them, choosing the perfect hunting site and using it year after year. You can be as well, if you take the time and follow the steps I have laid out for you.

Chapter Thirteen

Other Hunting Methods

There are several good hunting techniques involving practice, time in the field, education, and later skill that will allow a hunter to take a whitetail deer. Stand hunting, like any other technique, takes a hunter who is willing to sit in a stand patiently while remaining motionless; this is a good way to see and shoot a whitetail. However, not all hunters are able to sit and remain motionless for long periods and wish to hunt matching their individual talents to the keen senses of a deer. Just as the Indians and their ancestors did many years ago while hunting, they seek to get close to a whitetail and not sit and wait for a deer to come to them.

These hunters would rather test their abilities and skills and participate in a more physical challenge, following the signs of an animal, considered the master of the woods. For them, a foot pursuit becomes their test, with the answer resulting from the methods they have chosen to close the distance effectively in order to shoot a whitetail deer.

However, before any on-foot challenge begins and you take up one of the *Other Hunting Methods*, one has to be aware of all the signs and interpret the meaning for each one a whitetail deer demonstrates. In doing so, you will have the knowledge and an added edge on your side from the start.

Just as deer use different vocal patterns to express different meanings, so do the signs they make. Each sign performed by a whitetail deer in the woods demonstrates if the deer is at ease, tense, uncomfortable, suspicious, or ready to flee. Familiarity with these signs while in your pursuit can change the ultimate outcome of your hunt.

Foot stamping is an important sign to know. If in your pursuit you see a deer, whether it is a buck or doe, and they appear frozen in place while stamping one foot, this tells you that the deer is uncertain about what they have seen or heard. By stamping one foot in an erect posture, the deer is attempting to make a possible threat reveal itself by either moving or making their position known to the deer. The deer has not detected human presence at this point but knows something is out there, and it worries him. The only thing you can do after seeing this sign is to freeze in place and not move at all. The deer will call the next shot by either doing one of three things. They will take a tense feeding stance, resume their relaxed posture, or flee. This foot stamping by a deer can last up to five minutes if the deer has not detected your scent and you remain motionless. Any attempt to raise your firearm or bow for a quick shot will be in vain, as the deer will immediately flee.

Once the deer has made its decision and does not flee but returns to feeding, you may see the whitetail raise its head quickly and stare in this direction several times while remaining with its feet firmly planted in one position. This is the sign that the deer is less alarmed, but still leery. If you notice the deer's tail, and it is not moving from side to side, continue your frozen position until the deer lowers its head and moves its front feet. Once the deer moves its front feet and does not quickly jerk its head up and stare in your direction, the deer is relaxed once again.

Another stance that whitetails display is taking several steps with slow, deliberate stamping steps. During this stance, the deer will move its head from side to side with each step. This means that the deer is on the alert, but does not know where the danger is coming from. The deer is attempting to do a false challenge to position the threat. The deer is trying to make the threat become visible. As with the previous stance, remain motionless.

Movement of a deer's tail can also give you a good idea of the stance of a deer. Relaxed deer will move their tails from side to side when they are at ease and not tense or on the alert. A whitetail with its tail stretched straight out is signaling it is about to flee but hesitant for the moment. A whitetail with its tail standing upright is the sign it is going to flee.

A whitetail deer standing erect with its head up high is on the alert but has not spotted you yet. As soon as you see the deer lift its head up high on the alert, freeze. The deer will then move its head sharply from side to side, looking for you. He will continue this movement until he has pinpointed your location. If you remain motionless, there is a good possibility the deer will not locate your position. Notice the ears of the deer in this stance. They will always be cupped and will turn to hear any unnatural sound. Once the deer's stance changes, so will the position of the whitetail's ears to a more relaxed position.

Still Hunting

The adventure of the hunt, the art of concealment, and the match between hunter and animal can be a hunt you will never forget. Contrary to what the name implies, still hunting is the art of slowly walking through the woods, taking well planned and deliberate steps and never leaving your outline exposed in your search for one of the most cunning and well sought-after animals in North America, the whitetail deer.

One step at a time and always stop by some form of cover to break your image.

I would first like to address the issue about clothing and what a still hunter should wear. Since you will be walking, you should be wearing a rubber-soled boot or high shoe that is both water proof, and most important, comfortable. State laws concerning what a hunter should wear while hunting with a firearm will determine if your jacket or coat should be blaze orange or not. Most states do require a firearm hunter to wear blaze orange to be visible to other hunters, and I do believe this is excellent. All deer are colorblind. It is not the color of your outfit that alerts a deer or makes a deer flee, it is the hunter's movement and scent, which does it every time. You can have the best camouflage outfit on the market, but movement and scent are the only ways a deer will know of your presence and send them fleeing out of the area and for cover. I hope you will remember this for your hunts, as I have repeated this to make you understand. A good pattern is what is necessary and seen by deer, not the color. I do recommend camouflage when still hunting, but I have still hunted successfully with using partial camouflage at times, like when moving through heavy tangling brush.

There are many different ways to still hunt in the woods, and the hunter must develop a style that he feels comfortable using that proves to be a successful way for him to get close enough to a deer and then deliver a fatal shot. I can give you the basics here, but it comes down to the individual hunter learning the basics and then perfecting it by using his or her own style. The basic concept of still hunting has a hunter walking slowly and as quietly as possible while scanning the woods for deer. Many hunters decide to still hunt during the mid-morning hours after they have sat on a stand from first light until about 10:00 a.m. At this time, hunters leave their stands to walk slowly through the woods in search of whitetails bedded or standing in heavy cover. I disagree with still hunting this way, and I will tell you why. If you have sat on your stand for four hours and have not seen a deer, what makes you think you will see them by still hunting the same general area? First off, your stand is probably in the wrong area if you have not seen a deer while you were sitting, and second, you should only still hunt in an area where you know there are deer. I believe that a dedicated still hunter will first scout an area well in advance to know that the area to hunt is a prime location that deer inhabit. I also believe that a hunter who wants to develop their skills in still hunting should be in the woods before sunup and begin still hunting as soon as they are able to see. I say this because at first light, whitetails are moving on trails and are expecting to hear movement in the woods, as all other animals are moving, also. Whitetails expect to hear rustling of leaves from squirrels, turkeys and other animals walking and feeding. Deer will lift their heads to observe when they hear a noise, but generally will not be as alerted as they would when the woods tend to quiet down during the late mornings and early afternoons. No, I am not saying that squirrels, turkeys, and other animals stop feeding during that time, but their feeding activity is more active at sunup and right before dusk. A dedicated still hunter will not devote his method of hunting to be an alternative way to hunt, but will hunt in this manner from first light to increase their chances.

To still hunt properly, the hunter first knows the area he intends to hunt, just as the deer living there do. They know the location of the brush, the streams that run through the area, any natural ponds, and where deer may hold up to bed or feed. They will be familiar with the terrain and the direction they must take while hunting. The hunter is mindful of the wind direction, keeping the wind in their face, to reduce the chance of scent reaching the whitetails before they do.

Once the hunt begins, each step made is deliberate and planned. The hunter is conscious not to step on a branch or twig that can snap to make any unnatural sound that will carry to alert any animal of the approach of possible danger, taking sometimes only one or a few steps and always stopping next to a tree or brush that will conceal their presence. During each stop, the hunter looks straight ahead, then slowly moving their head to the left for a long detailed search and then slowly to the right to see any horizontal image that can resemble the shape or part of a deer. You may not see a whole deer, but the moving of an ear, the flick of a tail, a small brown patch between trees to alert a hunter of the location of a deer. Seeing deer in the woods takes time, patience and practice before mastered. The first thing I do when I teach a new hunter how to see deer is tell them that they have to remember that most objects in the woods are vertical. Trees, plants and bushes grow and stand vertically, while deer are horizontal. When you look through the woods, scan and look for objects that appear to be horizontal. You can practice well before hunting season if you are the passenger in a vehicle that is slowly driving on a country road or through a state park. I trained my wife in this way, and after a short time, she was able to spot deer that she never saw before. Horizontal objects could be either a downed tree or a whitetail deer. Look for the horizontals and you will see more deer; that is the key in seeing them.

Do not be alarmed if during your hunt you make a sound, as moving animals also make sounds while they are walking through the woods. After making a sound, continue and stop next to a tree or bush to conceal your presence and look. If a deer is there, the idea is to see the deer before the deer sees you. This way you can observe the deer to see its stance and determine what you do next. Many times, you may come across deer that are aware of your presence or a possible threat. When this happens, it is time to slow down and think how your movements alerted them to correct and modify your style of still hunting. Are you walking too fast or stopping for too short of a time? If a still hunter covers more than a quarter mile in an hour, the hunter is moving too quickly and not still hunting properly. You are not in a race to cover ground, but in a test of ability and patience. The word still in still hunting means devoid of or abstaining from motion, silence, to remain quiet. In still hunting a hunter approaches by the definition of still and by the manner of stealth. The hunter who has perfected their style of still hunting becomes a ghost, without disclosing their presence, never to be heard, and invisible to the deer. You cannot become a still hunter by deciding you are going to do this every now and then. Still hunting is an art, and like all arts, needs time to be developed.

Weather can play an important role when still hunting. Walking through the woods can be noisy, and it is close to impossible to muffle all noise. Do not be alarmed by making noise. A good time to still hunt is during a light rain or right after a rain shower, as it will wet the leaves and ground and help you to walk quietly. Another good time is the beginning of a snowfall or right afterwards, as deer will move readily in the snow to look for food. Snow does not bother a deer as much as rain. You often will see deer feeding actively during a snowstorm and take shelter under the pines when it rains. My theory, which has worked for me, is to head for the pines in inclement weather—you will not go wrong.

Stalking

Hunters often confuse this form of hunting with still hunting. While the movements are the same as still hunting to some degree, stalking defines another method of hunting whitetail deer. Stalking is used in the hunt for a particular deer or when deer are located. Once you are still hunting and you locate deer in a distance, your approach then becomes a stalk to close the distance.

During your scouting trips, if you see signs that lead you to believe this is a large buck in that particular area, your pursuit of that deer is a stalk.

I have used this method of hunting several times after I discovered the signs of a nice size buck in the area I was hunting. If you are stalking a buck and it is during the rut, which is the breeding time for whitetail deer, some hunters will use a manufactured scent, thinking it will help to help close the distance between

Slow quiet steps produce results.

the deer and the hunter. I believe this to be wrong as you are looking to close the distance without detection. The use of a scent while stalking, or still hunting for that matter, is alerting the deer of your location, as the buck will then be searching intently for what he believes is the doe producing the scent. You want your approach to be unnoticed.

Once you see the deer, your approach has to be slow and well planned. The closer you are to the deer, the greater the chance for detection. If you can make a clean, accurate shot to kill the deer at a range you feel comfortable, take the shot. Many deer are lost in the last few moments before the shot by hunters seeking to get closer and accidentally alerting the deer. I have had the pleasure to know and hunt with hunters who had the ability of getting unbelievably close to deer without detection.

Paul was one of these hunters. I remember one fall morning while staying at Paul's house, I got up to begin an early hunt. I asked Paul if he wanted to join me hunting. He said he would meet up with me in the woods after he did a few chores. I told him the general location where I would be, as it had just snowed the night before and was a perfect time to be in the woods. I still hunted for a while and then decided to take a break and sit under a fir tree that had branches down to the ground for perfect cover to wait for Paul. There were fresh tracks in several directions, and I figured the area was good to see a deer wandering through the woods. I was sitting there for about twenty minutes when I felt a tap on my shoulders. I jumped a bit, turning to see Paul standing directly behind me.

Paul had walked down a steep ridge and walked right up to me without making a sound. I feel I am pretty darn good at detecting movement, and my hearing is quite good also, but Paul had a knack for moving without making a sound. Paul had lived his whole life on a farm and is referred to as a "ridge runner," someone who has lived and walked the woods all his life. I have seen Paul do a stalk and get within fourteen feet of a buck, which is something very few hunters are able to do. I was very fortunate to have been able to hunt with Paul and to have him as a good friend when I was learning to hunt.

The Two-Man Drive

Like the name, two people who are both hunting do the two-man drive. One person will act as the driver, while the other hunter will be standing or sitting by cover to get a clear shot at approaching deer driven to their direction. Unlike still hunting and stalking, the driver should not try to slip through the woods quietly, as you are trying to drive the deer to the stander or sitter. I usually carry a battery-operated radio and put it on loud so deer will hear human presence and not try to stay and remain hidden. You are trying to get the deer to move. This can be an effective way to hunt.

After opening day, deer take to thick cover to hide, often remaining hidden during hunting pressure and until they feel the threat has ended. Most importantly, by doing a two-man drive, it is possible to drive through small pockets of cover where older bucks tend to lie when pushed. Mature bucks will be the first to seek cover that normally is overlooked by most hunters. These bucks learn from hunters who pass by small patches of cover to hunt what hunters believe to be the likely spots that whitetails will hold up. Older bucks did not get to be old by making mistakes.

I remember one particular hunt with my good friend and hunting partner Lenny. We were bow hunting without success when Lenny had the idea of doing a two-man drive through a small thick patch of rhododendrons. We normally overlooked this patch because of better areas that usually held deer, and we were successful driving through. It was late in the season, and I wanted to take a nice doe since Lenny had already filled his tag and said he would drive. I positioned myself in a likely spot, and Lenny started the drive. Only a few minutes passed and three does bolted out of the rhododendrons, running past me in full flight. Then I heard rustling in the brush, and a large doe walked out and stopped behind several thick trees. The only possible shot I had was a thirty-seven yard neck shot. I drew back my compound bow, shooting the doe right through her neck, and

The driver moves the deer to the sitter.

she dropped instantly. A few minutes later Lenny came from the cover, and we walked over to the doe. He said he had pushed a buck and asked me if I had seen the buck come past me. I told him about the does that went past me at high speed, telling him that the buck never came past me. Lenny looked at the doe, and I told him where I was standing. He asked why I shot the doe in the neck, and I told him what happened. The only shot I had was a neck shot as her body stood behind the trees when she stopped. Her body was completely blocked by the trees, and I could only see her head and neck sticking out. He congratulated me on making one heck of a shot, and I began to field dress the doe.

There were five deer in that patch of rhododendrons that we had passed just about every day for a week and never stopped to hunt. The patch was about sixty by sixty feet, which we took for granted was empty, as it was close to the cabin. We never made that mistake again, and in future hunts, we drove through many other patches that were small and shot a few deer from them.

Some two-man drives can be accidental, as what happened one day while hunting with another good friend and hunting partner named Steve. We had walked through the woods of our hunting club to the back piece of the property to hunt a thicket that we knew held deer. I stopped on a knoll that had a stump I could sit on, with another tree next to it that acted as a perfect backrest. I put a hot seat down to cushion me a bit. Steve walked along the logging road, which went to the end of the property, and was barely out of sight when a large four-point buck bolted from the cover, stopping only ten yards in front of me to look back. I picked up my .300 Savage rifle and dropped him with a quick shot, breaking the buck's backbone and dropping the deer instantly.

Steve quickly came back down the logging road, asking me if I dropped my rifle, as he was barely out of sight when he heard my rifle go off. I pointed to the buck and Steve shook his head, saying it would have been his deer if I walked a little faster to get to the back of the property. We joked about it; as I kept telling him during our walk, hunting does not have to be a marathon race. I said since he thought it was his deer, maybe he should field dress the buck. He declined, but he did help drag the buck back to camp.

Sometimes when you sit in your stand and other hunters are walking through the woods to get to their stands, they will unconsciously push deer past you. Generally, whitetails will not be overly alarmed, making a wide circle around one hunter if they see only one person in their area. Deer are also very curious, avoiding a hunter in this way by keeping an eye on him or knowing the hunter's location by scent. If a hunter spooks a lone deer, he could have a chance at shooting him by backtracking and picking a position, using this pattern of circling. The hunter using this tactic should remain mindful that the approaching whitetail will be on guard, but generally return to the same area that the deer was originally spotted.

The Gang Drive

The gang drive is another effective method of hunting, where from three to a dozen or more hunters act as drivers to move the deer to the awaiting hunters acting as the standers. Gang drives are effective if you have enough hunters to act as standers, and the standers remain in their position until after the drive is completed.

I say this because a curious incident happened one day involving a few of my friends with whom I was hunting who decided to act as drivers with myself, to a lone stander, my wife.

We were hunting one early afternoon after lunch, and I decided to put my wife in a high ladder stand on a knoll, which had been a good location to shoot white-tails. It bordered a swamp on one side and a small thick hardhack field on the other. Behind the stand was a heavy covered pine wooded area. If the swamp and hardhack field were pushed, deer would have no choice but to run past the stand.

My friends quickly volunteered to push the hardhack field, which left the swamp for me to drive. I want you to know that if you never pushed through a swamp to do a drive, it is an experience in itself. All of us drivers agreed to meet

Gang drives are good after the first two days of rifle season.

in a wooded patch where the swamp and hardhack joined, and then push the deer to my wife as she waited in the stand.

All went well until I slipped in the swamp and emerged to join my comrades, looking like a science fiction creature, covered in mud and briers. My other friends had similar experiences as it had snowed a few days earlier and the hardhack field was full of mud, brush and tangling thorn bushes.

We got to the wooded thicket and saw the tracks of several large deer all heading right for the area we wanted them to go. I walked and commented to my friends, "Why isn't she shooting?" We had all jumped several nice deer during the drive, and they were heading right to my wife's stand. We got to the stand, but the stand was empty. The deer tracks were right under her stand, but my wife was nowhere to be found. My friend called me over and showed me tracks in the snow, which led through a field and up to our parked vehicle. When we got to the vehicle, we saw my wife sitting inside and drinking a cup of coffee. I stopped to catch my breath and said, "What are you doing here?" Or something to that effect as calmly as I could. My wife looked up and said, "I got cold."

Being a hunter—wise, kind, considerate and knowledgeable—and a husband, I understood and we left it at that. I did remind her on occasion, it being fourteen years ago this season, that you never, ever, leave a stand when you are a sitter and there are others who are driving to you. That being said, it is also a good policy to alternate positions and allow the hunters who did the drive to be the sitters on the next drive. This way everyone gets to walk and sit.

For safety reasons, it is recommended that the drivers do not shoot at the deer, as they take a chance by wounding a deer that is running. More important, you would not like to create any possible problem by sending a stray bullet in the direction of other drivers or sitters. Drivers can shoot if they know the backstop of where the bullet will go if there is a miss. If the driver knows the exact location of all involved in the drive, and there is no chance of someone being injured with their shot, the driver can shoot without a problem. Gang drives can produce several deer, but caution should be emphasized to know the position of all involved in this method of hunting.

Hunting Using a Boat

This method of hunting is good if you are hunting an area that backs up to a lake, and the other side is not accessible. It is also good while hunting a swamp, which has large pockets of water and land mixed. In areas such as this, whitetails will often hold up in the swamps in clusters of woods feeling safe. Deer are excellent swimmers and will not hesitate to swim across a lake or jump to a swamp to feel safe. Older bucks will stay in wooded areas backing up to water, as deer do not expect danger coming from the water.

I first found this out while hunting in a good outfitting camp in Maine. We had been hunting a heavy wooded area and were seeing only small rack bucks. Wanting to hold out for a thick beam whitetail, my guide told me we were going to take the boat out tomorrow and hunt an area on the other side of the lake by our camp, which was only accessible by boat. We all got up early the next morning, and the guide already had the boat by the shoreline. One of the hunters in camp named Jeff and I were going to hunt in the woods across the lake, as Jeff had also passed on a few smaller bucks.

We got into the boat, reached the opposite shoreline, and anchored the boat to the shoreline so it would not drift. The guide took Jeff to a rock outcropping, telling him to keep a sharp eye since this area was not hunted this season. I was positioned in a small blind that had been constructed several years earlier. There was a swivel chair in the blind, and it actually was quite comfortable. A few hours had passed and I heard a shot, then another coming from the direction Jeff was hunting. Figuring he had already gotten his buck, now it was my turn. About thirty-five minutes later a nice, heavy-tined nine-pointer came past my stand, and I shot the deer through his heart. I waited, and shortly later, the guide came past my stand, and I learned the buck I had shot had passed by Jeff's stand, and he missed him after firing two shots. The buck had passed by Jeff and circled coming by my stand, which was closer to the water. The following day, Jeff got a nice twelve-pointer from the blind I had used the day before.

Whitetail deer will often head to an area either backing up to water or surrounded by water as a safety area to hold up. A wise hunter who has access to a boat should keep this in mind. If there is a swamp in your area and the water is not deep, you can hunt the area wearing a pair of hip boots and warm socks. Some very large bucks are taken out of swamps and areas that back up to water.

Some hunters avoid swamps, thinking deer will not go to a swamp for protection and to keep dry and would rather head for heavy cover. This is a misconception, because not all swamps are very wet. Most swamps have dry land inside with thick cover past the water. The older bucks will head for a swamp when the shooting starts, staying hidden most of the time, especially if there is a food source in the swamp on dry land. Hunters who approach a swamp and walk around the edges will see signs where the deer enter and exit. Many swamps have areas of dry land accessible on one side, and a wise hunter will investigate these areas as a possible stand location. In areas like these, portable tree stands come in handy and are an easy set up for a good stand. Younger deer will follow the older and more mature whitetails who know where the swamps are for protection. Swamps are good areas for seeing other game animals. Black bear, bobcat, wild hogs, and coyotes also favor these protective areas for food and shelter. When driving swamps, do not be surprised if more than deer exit during the drive.

Chapter Fourteen

Hunting Out of State

As a hunter who has traveled most of the country, in many states throughout North America and outside of the United States, I have learned quite a bit about *Hunting Out of State.* In my younger years, I would read in hunting magazine articles about areas that guaranteed a hunter would see and shoot trophy whitetail bucks. I decided one year after reading one such article that I was going to try for a monster buck, selecting Maine as my state of choice for this hunt. An article I read named one area in particular where large whitetail bucks were taken year after year, and recommended this area as a hotspot to hunt that should not be overlooked.

I prepared for the hunt, packed my truck, leaving room for the trophy buck I was sure to return with, and headed for Maine. I drove to the exact area stated in the magazine article. I searched for a motel, since the article said there were several that offered good comfortable accommodations, which actually turned out to be only two motels. One was closed for renovations, and the other had rooms that were far short of what I expected. The room I stayed in was actually on a slant; if you placed a ball on the floor at one end, it would easily roll to the door at the other end. There was hot water, but only if you were the first to get up in the morning to use the shower. The curtains in the room were constructed out of a material that resembled fiberglass, with torn curtains on the windows in the bathroom. There was a bottled water container in the room for drinking water, and the water smelled like sulphur when you ran the shower. No refrigerator or phones were in the room, and no cooking was allowed. For that I paid $70.00 a night.

Nevertheless, since the article stated the area was excellent for producing trophy bucks, I did not complain because I was planning to spend my days in the woods. I later found out from several local people that most of the prime areas were on private land, and the game warden I contacted for information on places to hunt was of very little help. I did manage to get permission to hunt from one land owner who already had several locals hunting his property. The owner only allowed six hunters on his property per day, and they were booked for that day and the next. I did manage to schedule my hunt from Wednesday through Sunday.

Thinking I would not need more than the four days, I was happy knowing I would shoot a nice buck while I was there. Wednesday and Thursday brought heavy driving rains that resembled a monsoon. Friday and Saturday were clear, but I hunted both days without seeing a deer. I did hear of nice deer taken on other properties, but not from the property I was hunting. I hunted Sunday morning and saw a small five-point buck, but let it walk past me since I was interested in a much larger buck. In the end, I left Maine to return home Sunday afternoon, wondering about the article I read and if the author had actually hunted the area at all.

I later read about the large whitetail deer in the Black Hills of South Dakota as well as the mule deer and antelope in the prairie of the Dakotas. I decided I had to try it and set off for a hunt in Nemo, South Dakota. I stayed at a country lodge that had one of the best accommodations I had ever seen. My room was large enough to fit several hunters comfortably. It was a single room that resembled a log cabin. The bed was designed to fit the decor of Amish construction with a view from the window that overlooked a wooded forest. The price of the room included a country breakfast, and the owner, who knew I was hunting, offered to pack me bag lunches, which were waiting for me each morning. The downstairs waiting area had a nice fireplace with couches and end tables filled with magazines of every type. The dining area was large and could easily handle all the people who stayed in a scenic Old World Inn setting.

The owner sat with me when I arrived and told me of several good areas to hunt for whitetails, which I appreciated and made me feel at ease with this trip from the start. I hunted the following morning, but that day ended with me seeing only a few does and one spike buck. I went to the lounge for a drink that evening, and there was an old timer sitting by the bar, who upon my arrival asked me how I did. I told him what I had seen, and he shook his head smiling, shortly after our conversation. The next day I was determined to get a nice buck and hunted an area that looked like a view from a hunting magazine, with thick ground cover, brush and a small stream at the base of a ridge, which led to a small-planted field. I counted twelve separate does and three bucks going into the field, but did not see a buck over seven points. That night I returned to the lodge and the same older man was sitting by the bar. Again, he asked me how I had done, and after I told him of my day, he shook his head again and smiled. After a while, he got up, sat next to me, and said, "Son, what are yer looking for?" I told him that I read of how South Dakota held some of the best whitetail bucks, and I was here to bring one back home. He smiled, finished his drink, and told me if I wanted a nice buck, meet him outside at 6:00 a.m. the next morning, and then left before I could buy him a drink or get his name.

I finished my one glass of beer, which I normally have after a long day of hunting, lit my pipe, and settled back to relax and await my dinner. The next morning, I arrived, and the old man was waiting for me. He rolled down the window and waved for me to get in, so I put my pack and rifle in his pickup truck and we rolled down a few gravel roads without speaking until we got to a small field. He turned in and drove to the end of the field to an opening that led to a larger field surrounded by thick wooded hills on three sides. He then stopped and turned the key off. He said, "By the way, I am Tom, and you're Bob." He told me that the owner of the lodge told him my name, in case I was wondering. He reached down and opened a bag that contained a six-pack of beer, took one out, opened a can, and took a drink. He offered me one, which at this hour I refused.

I said, "I thought we were going to hunt."

He looked at me and said, "We are; you look at the bald ridge to your left through the windshield, and in a little while, tell me what you see."

I figured it was only the third day of my hunt, so I would go along with it and see if the man was pulling my leg or knew something I didn't. About ten minutes later, I looked up and started to see a few deer, then a few more, and after a short time, it looked like there was a herd of deer on the ridge and feeding just below. The man looked at me, and said, "Get your rifle, and open the door quietly. You can lay your gun on the hood of my truck and pick the buck you want." I opened the door and laid my unloaded rifle on the hood. I looked through my scope and saw several nice bucks, but did not want to shoot one this way. I looked back in and told the man I would rather hunt to get my buck, and he said, "We are hunting, shoot one!" I asked him who owned the field, and he told me he did. I got back inside and asked him if I could hunt his property. He shook his head and said it was okay, but could not understand why I wanted to walk around the woods when I could get what I wanted this way. After a while, we went back to the lodge; I bought him breakfast, and we talked. It turned out that he owned 2,600 acres, was retired and living with his wife on a pension. Their children were all grown and lived far from the ranch, and Tom did not hunt anymore due to arthritis in both hands. He told me his hands were painful, cramping at times, and he was supposed to be on medication and not beer. He also told me he was seventy-seven years old, and he enjoyed his beer a lot more than taking pills, and he thought it helped him reduce the pain and made him feel better. Besides which, he commented, no pills were ever going to make him any younger, and he wasn't going to live forever, so he might as well enjoy himself.

I hunted his property and took a nice nine-point buck that afternoon. The following day I took a large doe and gave it to Tom and his wife. I became good friends with him and his wife and returned to Nemo several times to visit them and hunt. To this day, I still like Nemo, South Dakota, considering it one of the best places I've ever visited and hunted.

Through the years, I learned by trial and error what a hunter needs to do to hunt successfully out of state. However, it was not before I had made several more mistakes and a few other unsuccessful drive-away hunting trips until I learned. I found that one of the first things a hunter should do before he makes a hunt out of state or any area unfamiliar to them is to contact a person who is familiar with the area. Someone who knows how to hunt the area, the location of the whitetails during the time you will be there, and the best time to hunt the area. If you cannot find a contact, see if there is a guide in the area and talk to him.

I am not saying that it is necessary to hire a guide, but a guide does know the area, and some will give you some good tips to make your hunt more successful. You could contact the local game warden and see if he will meet with you or give you some help concerning licenses and selecting a good area to hunt. I have found that some game wardens are helpful and can give you good information about prime hunt areas and where large bucks have been checked in. You can also contact the local sporting goods store or gun shops in the area, as their information is excellent, and inquire about comfortable places to stay and maps of the area.

I have come up with the following checklist of questions you should know and decide before starting an out-of-state hunting trip:

1. Are you looking to hunt private land? If the answer is yes, you will need landowner permission well in advance before you travel.

Conservation officers and forestry workers can help you when picking a place to hunt, use their knowledge.

2. Are you going to hunt state land? Do you know the location of the state land? It is helpful to get a map of the area if you cannot do pre-scouting.
3. Where are you going to stay during the hunt? You need to check the local accommodations and reserve a room. Many motels and hotels are booked well in advance of a hunting season, and you should keep this in mind.
4. Do you have a local contact? It is extremely helpful to know someone who knows the area, best time to hunt and conditions of the area.

5. Will your hunt coincide with your vacation time, and will you be able to take additional time if plans change?
6. Will you be using an outfitter or guide? It is helpful to get this information and contact them for advice or plan to meet with them once you have arrived.
7. Are you physically prepared for the hunt? If you are out of shape, do you need to prepare by walking more? Do you need to bring any extra medication you are taking?
8. Are you aware of the season dates, what licenses you will need, and where to get them? Will you have to show your state hunting license or show a hunter safety course certificate to purchase an out-of-state license?
9. Do you know the regulations on firearms in the area? Do you know if the area you plan to hunt requires a rifle or a shotgun?
10. Did you figure out the entire cost of the hunt and how much you may have to spend during your time away from home for lodging and meals?
11. Are you going to fly, rent a car or drive to the area you wish to hunt?
12. Are you familiar with the airlines regulations concerning transporting a firearm if you intend to fly?
13. Is your vehicle in shape for a long, out-of-state drive?
14. Are you going to take meat home with you? Will you bring coolers and know where you can get ice to keep the meat cold?
15. Are you looking for a trophy? Will you be using a local taxidermist or bringing your trophy home?

These are only a few of the questions that you should be aware of, and know the answers to, before you decide on an out-of-state hunt or another location far away from your home.

When I was younger, I was fascinated with hunting camps where you used a wood stove and outhouse and roughed it a bit. Now as I am getting a bit older, I enjoy my creature comforts. I want to stay at a nice motel, hotel or a warm secluded bed and breakfast whenever I can. I like to shower after I get in from my hunt, sit next to a warm fire, light my pipe on occasion, and sit down each night to have a good hot meal. I still enjoy the fellowship of other hunters, but sometimes like to hunt with my favorite hunting partner and loving critic, my wife, Mary. So when I hunt out of state, I tend to look for comfortable accommodations.

There are places you can go for top-notch accommodations and have gourmet meals prepared for you at each sitting. The question is, what is your comfort level, which amenities do you prefer, and what can your pocket book afford?

I like to plan for the unexpected every time I hunt out of state. What do I mean by planning for the unexpected? First, I have my mechanic look at my vehicle (if I am not renting a truck) to make sure it is ready for the trip ahead. A tune-up, a brake job or even a sluggish transmission can cause a serious problem when on the road away from home. I also like to have extra clothing, rain gear, and an extra pair of boots in case the weather turns. Another good idea is to take an extra

Do your homework and plan every detail for a hunt.

firearm. Hunters who bring their favorite rifle but forget to bring a spare firearm with them can spoil an out-of-state hunt. You could drop your rifle, have a scope act up, or have any number of things happen in the field. The answer is to be prepared.

When I go on these hunts, I also have contact phone numbers to call when I get to the area, letting them know where I am and when I will be there. I like to have a plan in mind for my hunt and a backup plan for inclement weather. This is important because not all hunts are under ideal conditions. I also feel it is important for any hunter who hunts either out-of-state or in their home state to make a checklist of all they intend to bring on their hunt, then check it off as you pack it in your vehicle or luggage for the airlines.

I will never forget a hunt I made in my younger years in a hunting camp I was a member of. It was a four-hour drive to get there from where I lived during good weather conditions and a bit of a tail wind, if you know what I mean. Well, opening day was the next day, but I had an event I had to attend the afternoon before. I was able to get out of the affair by 5 p.m., which gave me time to pack my truck and drive upstate. I did well and made good time, arriving at camp by 10 p.m., which would give me time to get a good night's sleep before the hunt. I unpacked the truck and was inside the cabin when I realized that in my haste, I forgot to pack my rifles in the truck. I remembered I brought them out of the house in the hard double case they were in and set them along with my other hunting items next to my driveway. I checked and double-checked and realized my rifles and were not with me. I called back home and spoke to my neighbor, who was a hunter also, but not going to hunt opening day with us. My neighbor was a long-time member of our hunting camp but was trying to get over bronchitis and was planning to join us in a few days. He answered the phone, and I asked him if my hunting case was on the lawn next to my driveway. After a few minutes, he came back to the phone and said yes, asking where I was. I said I was upstate at the hunting camp and asked him to bring the gun case with my rifles inside his house, and I would be there in a few hours. I got back inside my truck, made the four-hour ride back home, picked up my rifles, then made the trip back upstate. Since that day, I always have a checklist and check each item off as I pack it into my vehicle. I cannot tell you how many times I have heard of hunters forgetting to pack their ammunition, hunting tags, or some other items they really need, only to realize it either the night before the hunt or the morning of the hunt. That is no way to start a hunt off, and I can tell you from experience that it does not sit comfortably.

Preparation is a must; with all the different clothing and hunting gear an average hunter brings with them on a hunt, it is necessary to make and keep a checklist. Now I know some of you will say, "It will not happen to me." I know, because I said the very same thing, and it happened to me and several of the people I have hunted with in the past. Hunting tags, doe permits, hot seats and ammunition have a unique way of not winding up with hunters in the field. Now since none of us is absent-minded, it must relate to some sort of magic. So in order to break the spell from ever happening to you, I recommend a checklist of all you need to bring. Maybe one day, you just might be glad you used it and leave the ones who laugh at your organized list to wonder where their hunting items have gone.

Hunting out of state can be an adventure and filled with memories that will last a lifetime. Taking your time to prepare by looking into all aspects of the hunt is the key for a successful hunt. It can mean the difference between wasting your money on a hunt or enjoying the time of your life on the hunt of a lifetime. Remember that because a place advertises as being the best that does not mean it is the best for you. Plan carefully, wisely, take your time, and review all your options. Many of these hunts out of state are costly, but a good hunt is worth its weight in gold.

I have been invited to be a guest at many hunting lodges, and have hunted with many outfitters and a few celebrities across the country. If you would like to know of places that offer both good accommodations and excellent hunts, I invite you to contact me. I will let you know my opinion and recommendations for the area.

Chapter Fifteen

Picking the Right Outfitter

Today's hunter has far more opportunities in selecting a place that holds trophy whitetails than ever before. Many states have outfitting services where you can hunt for two days to two weeks, with accommodations from simple, moderately furnished cabins to extravagant lodges that offer five-star luxuries. If you are looking for a one time memorable hunt or new to selecting the right outfitter, you may find it is no simple task. There are places that offer deluxe accommodations and sing high praises about what they can do for you, when in actuality their services are far from what their brochure looks like when you arrive. Then there are lodges that are quite impressive in areas where excessive hunting took place for years, telling you the old story that you should have been there last week, after you spend a week without seeing a buck. *Picking the Right Outfitter* is important, and knowing what to ask and what to look for can make all the difference.

I will never forget a hunt I booked for black bear when I was quite a bit younger, which was a fortuitous way of picking an outfitter. I was asked if I would like to go with a friend of mine to an outdoor expo at the Coliseum on Long Island, New York, which had manufactures and outfitters in one gathering. Having a Saturday open, I decided to take my wife, Mary, with us, and make it a day of relaxed company to see what was being offered in the way of new hunting products soon to be on the market. I was fascinated to see the number of outfitters all under the same roof and decided I would stop and chat with each. From guides to booking agents, all with photo albums and videos of their services, I made a day of seeing what they all had to offer. I stopped by one booth that offered black bear hunts, stating that many record black bears were shot in his camp. Without looking deeper, I put a deposit on a hunt for that fall season for my wife and me. Deciding on a bear hunt to round my experiences, I wanted to shoot a black bear over 300 pounds to have mounted in my den. Since the outfitter said his clients shot many bears in the 300-pound range and showed me pictures of the bears taken, I thought he would be the right outfitter.

I had little communication with the outfitter prior to the hunt, having a brochure with a map on how to get to his camp in eastern Canada. I loaded the car the Saturday before the hunt, figuring to drive to Canada in two days; and my wife and I would sleep in camp the night before the hunt. We had a little trouble with the map on the brochure as a road ended, and we had to stop several times for better directions once we were in the area of the camp. I felt a little uncomfortable when I mentioned the camp and outfitting service I was looking for and a person in a general store asked me if I was sure I wanted to hunt there. Thinking there may be some rivalry in the area with different camps, I left the comments to idle opinion and continued.

Hunting expos are a great place to talk to different outfitters.

We got to camp, and the lodge was close to the pictures in the catalog, but it was clear that the pictures were the best the lodge had to offer in atmosphere. The rooms were small but adequate, which worked well for the lack of heat in the accommodations provided. Finding out that one large older furnace supplied the heat for the entire lodge, I asked for additional blankets when learning the furnace needed repair.

I spoke to the outfitter, who said he was going to be our guide for the hunt back at the expo, and learned that he was going to have a local guide from the area act as our guide. He stated that he would be overseeing the guide, deciding where we would hunt. There were ten other hunters who were staying at the lodge to hunt that week, and the outfitter stated he needed additional help in guiding. I thought it was odd that an outfitter did not have sufficient guides already on staff for the season, but shrugged it off. I did wonder why there were ten other hunters in camp, since his brochure stated that his hunts were limited to five hunters per week. Without a calculator, I can add ten and two and conclude that twelve hunters were a bit higher than five all by myself. Since we were a couple, my wife and I were given a private room, which did help to give us some privacy.

This being one of the first hunts I took my wife on, I had some concerns. I spoke to the outfitter, who assured me I would be satisfied and my wife and I would return, each with the bear we wanted. We filled out the necessary hunting tags, and after a delicious meal, which was prepared by the outfitter's wife, who by the way was a fantastic person, my wife and I settled in for the night.

The next morning came early, and we awoke with the smell of fresh coffee and bacon being prepared. We dressed and went to the dining area to see the other hunters sitting at a long table, with a smaller table set for my wife and me. Not wanting to be secluded from the other hunters, my wife and I moved our table and sat with the other hunters. At another table sat the outfitter with several others who were the guides. We were introduced to our guide, who said he would be outside in an hour to take us to our stand to hunt. We finished breakfast, dressed for the hunt and were outside in an hour. Our guide was inside and came out about a half hour later, asking us where we would like to hunt. I looked at my wife and turned to the guide and said, "I thought that was your job to tell us where we are going to hunt."

The guide went back inside, then came back fifteen minutes later and told us he was going to take us to our stands. Puzzled, I did not say a word. We drove to a thick wooded area, and my wife was first to be positioned in her stand. When the guide came back to the truck, I told him that this was one of my wife's first hunts, and I would appreciate it if he checked on her to make sure she was okay in an hour or so, and he agreed to see she was okay. He then took me to my stand, which was several miles away. My stand consisted of three trees with a platform about thirty feet high and a wooden ladder, which was 2x4's nailed to two trees to climb, with no rope attached to raise my rifle. This was a set-up that probably took someone every bit of fifteen minutes to prepare with a barrel that was full of bait to entice every bear in the area, I assumed. Since I made it a habit to bring rope with me, I attached one end to my rifle and the other to my belt loop, climbed the makeshift ladder to get to the platform, and raised my rifle. The guide said he would see me at lunchtime, which was noon. There was no chair, no railing, and I had to stand or sit on the platform, which overlooked what was supposed to be a baited 55-gallon drum.

I sat for four hours without any luck or seeing a bear, so I lowered my rifle to the ground and climbed down the ladder. I walked over to see what was in the 55-gallon drum, wondering what they baited to attract bears, and saw that the drum was empty. Just then, the guide came. I talked to him a bit, as we were going in for lunch. I told him the drum was empty and had no bait, and he said he would speak to the outfitter about it. I asked if he baited the stands himself and then learned that my guide was not a licensed guide, but a person from town who was friends with the outfitter and helped him on occasion. I also found out that my guide had never guided a hunt for black bear and was just a hunter himself. I learned that the outfitter lost his guide license the week before due to a drunk driving charge. He ran his pickup off the road into a gully and had to have it towed out. He borrowed a truck from a relative and was operating with a suspended license. We picked up my wife, who did not see a bear either, and returned to camp. Upon arrival at camp, we went to our room, and I let my wife know the situation. I agreed not to say a word to the outfitter and give it a day or so. That afternoon we were positioned in different stands that were baited with bags of old donuts and sugar rolls by our guide once we got to the stand. The afternoon hunt ended without my wife or me seeing a bear. We returned to the lodge and heard of one bear being seen by a hunter's stand, but it was a small bear, and he passed it up.

The following day came, and we had a feast prepared for breakfast. All the hunters were wondering why they had not seen any black bears, and the outfitter stated that you do not see bears every day you hunt. As a hunter, I know this to be true with hunting other wildlife, but I hoped our morning hunt would be different and that my wife would see and shoot her first black bear. We were taken to our stands and hunted the morning without seeing any bears. When we got back to camp, we learned that a hunter had shot a bear, and my wife and I went outside to see. When we got to the area where the bear was lying, we saw that it was an immature cub. I looked at my wife and took her back inside the lodge. I told her to have lunch and relax, as the sight of a cub the size of a small sporting breed dog was upsetting. We sat down to eat lunch, and the outfitter came to the table to ask the hunter who shot the cub if the cub was alone or with another bear. Without hesitation, the hunter said the cub was with another cub and a larger black bear, but he couldn't get a shot at the larger bear. The outfitter then said he was going to position another hunter in his stand to shoot the other cub and another nearby to take the larger bear.

After hearing this, I got up and asked to speak to the outfitter in private. We went to his office, which was just off from the dining room, and with a loud voice, I explained the stupidity of what the outfitter was planning. Being outspoken probably added to my ability to carry my voice and to make it perfectly clear what I thought of the outfitter's ideas. I explained that first off, it was illegal to shoot an immature cub and what his actions would lead to by reducing the black bear population drastically with his plan. I let him know that if one cub was a female and it was killed, he just lost three bears, the cub growing up to be a breeding female and the two cubs she would have had later on. If the other cub was a male and he was shot, there was no telling how many bears he could have sired in the following years. The sow he was planning to kill was a breeding female, and because she had cubs, she should have been off limits to all hunters. On paper, I sketched that by his actions, he was reducing the bear population in his area easily by fourteen bears by taking the two illegal cubs and the sow, and I could not be part of a hunt that had his way of thinking. I also brought up that he was operating with a suspended license and if I had my way, he would not get his license back.

I returned to the table, got my wife, and told her I had enough and we were leaving. A few minutes later, the outfitter said he wanted to speak to me and asked if I would be satisfied with a free hunt for my wife and me at another time, possibly the spring. I said that wasn't necessary and we were leaving after we packed.

The outfitter then gave me a check for what I paid for the hunt, and said my wife and I were welcome to come back for a free hunt in either the spring or the fall, whichever we decided. I never took him up on that and believe even stronger today that this particular outfitter should not have a license to guide others hunting black bear in eastern Canada. He had no clue to wildlife conservation or management and was seriously affecting the bear population in his area, as well as operating illegally. I have since reported him and his outfitting name to the Conservation Department in the hope they would address the problem and his type of hunting. I did learn from this hunt, but it was not until I booked another bad hunt and many successful and rewarding hunts that I learned what was necessary in order to pick the right outfitter.

My wife and I selected an outfitter one year after attending another hunting expo. I actually was not planning on going on another hunt for black bear at the time. I went to the expo to see if the outfitter I used earlier would be there. I walked around looking at all the booths, saw he was not there, and felt quite good knowing he may not have gotten his license back. My wife was standing next to a booth that had a large bear mounted, which was positioned standing straight up, showing its teeth and claws, that stood about six feet and weighed about 465 lbs. when it was shot. I talked to the outfitter who was also from Canada. He knew the outfitter Mary and I went to in the previous year and said he didn't think the outfitter got his license back due to a drinking problem. This outfitter had a camp in a different location and said he could provide me with a list of references, if we liked. My wife said this would be her birthday gift to me, so I agreed, and Mary gave the outfitter a deposit.

My wife and I hunted with this outfitter that fall, but we failed to see bears that were over 150 pounds, let alone anything near what the outfitter claimed his camps produced. We did have an enjoyable hunt and saw black bear every day we went out, but the outfitter fell short of what he claimed, both in his brochure and what we were told. The accommodations were as they were listed, but again, the best pictures were the best he had to offer. He had no website, and I later learned his references came from hunters who were given free hunts to sing his praises. My wife and I did not take a bear, and I am glad we both held out for what we wanted and got on later hunts. I again learned more about picking the right outfitter.

I have gone on several whitetail, mule deer, black tail deer, antelope, and wild boar hunts to name only a few, and have learned over the years what to look for and how to pick the right outfitter. The first thing every hunter should be aware of is that outfitters are in the business of making money. They are running a business and like every other business, they have to make money to stay in business. They also have to provide a service that will keep hunters coming back or recommending them to other hunters to allow their business to grow. The problem is that there are also those in the same business who make money on inexperienced hunters or first-time hunters using an outfitter who will only hunt once whether they get what they seek or not. A bad outfitter stays in business by offering the sky to attract new hunters, then filling the new hunter's heads with excuses and poor service during their stay in camp. There are more bad outfitters today than ever before because the demand for outfitters has skyrocketed due to television coverage of trophy whitetail deer being taken in many states across the country. Many ranches are turning to hunting as a rising business, incorporating deer hunting as a way of added revenue, seeing the big business potential through advertising and booking agents that act as the go-between the ranch owner and the client.

Even if you have decided on the hunt you want and know what state you will hunt, get your license, book an airline and hotel, you still have to pick the right outfitter operating in the area you wish to hunt. You also have to do a lot of planning, like how you will transport your firearm? What is required from the airlines so far as a hard and locking gun case? Will there be any connecting flights, and how will your firearm arrive? Will it arrive when you do? Then you have to decide how you will have to pack your hunting gear? What is the weight requirement you are allowed by the airlines? Will you have to box and send your equipment

Communication is the key to planning a successful hunt. Don't be afraid to ask questions.

in advance? Who will be there to pick it up for you if it gets there before you do? Then there is the consideration of how you will get your venison back to where you live. Who will butcher your deer, pack and freeze the meat? Will you be doing the field dressing and trophy preparation? Do the airlines ship freezer meat? What about your antlers; how will they be shipped and by whom? These are some considerations you might want to think about. How about clothes; if you have never hunted this area before, do you know what clothes you will need and what you will not? Will you need heavy boots for snow or hiking boots to get to your stand? Will you need a sleeping bag and air mattress, or will you be sleeping on a cot or bed? Will you need a backpack, and will you be carrying it or will someone else? Do you know the best time to book the hunt? Will your hunt coincide with the rut?

These are some additional questions you might want to consider in your preparation. Notice I have said nothing yet about picking an outfitter. The reason for this is that you have to know these questions before you can look for the person to answer them. A good outfitter will have all the answers to these and many more that will come up before and during the hunt.

Will you be hunting alone or with a hunting friend, your wife or your girlfriend or boyfriend? Do they offer accommodations for couples? Do you wish simple or deluxe accommodations? Do you want a cold camp or hot camp if you are packing it in by horseback? Do you want all preparations made by an outfitter? Transportation to and from, or do you wish to make transportation plans on your own?

Remember, there are many different types of outfitters as well as the good and the bad. Some will do it all for you; all you need to do is pack what they tell you and show up. Many others have stores in their lodge that have what you forgot to pack, while some might be remote, and what you forget can't be replaced during the hunt.

Now you should know something right from the start. No matter what is promised in a brochure or what an outfitter claims, it is impossible for an outfitter to continually produce results that are guaranteed. Because of the sheer nature of hunting itself and the many different hunters using a lodge, results vary. Not to say you will not see a trophy whitetail in areas that claim trophy whitetails on a hunt, but you still have to contend with the weather and the whitetail itself, with all their senses and the timing of your hunt. Some outfitters offer a guaranteed hunt and will offer their clients a return hunt at a reduced rate. This is an important option to consider carefully. Is the outfitter offering a return hunt as a consideration if you do not get what you want, or is it a way to get additional income knowing you will not see a trophy right from the start? To know this you have to look further.

Any person looking to book an outfitter must first see all that is being offered and what is being guaranteed, if anything. An outfitter cannot control many contributing factors. Will your hunt be guaranteed no matter what, or only under certain circumstances? Bad weather cannot be controlled by the outfitter, so if that is the contributing factor, the guarantee may not be honored. Do you know what

hunting pressure is being applied in the area you will be hunting? Many outfitters are aware of all the factors involved and know both the good and bad effects that could determine their client's opportunities to shoot a trophy deer. The outfitters know that they will get some clients who either cannot hunt as hard as you have to, or shoot as you have to, in order to bring home a trophy. As a general rule a good outfitter will tell you how long they are in business and that they will do everything possible to make your hunt as comfortable as they can and as rewarding as possible. This is the sign of an honest outfitter who knows he cannot make promises he cannot keep right from the start. As a rule, try to avoid outfitters who offer guarantees. Guarantees are for hunting in preserves that have the land and the trophies that cannot leave their property.

Now do not get me wrong, I am not trying to put a knock on hunting preserves. Preserve hunting in the right preserve with adequate land and amenities can be fun, but remember, it is a preserve. Hunting open land is different, and it is hard for a good outfitter to make a guarantee for each hunter. I believe in fair chase and in hunting open land. Open lands are areas that outfitters lease for hunting, state-owned lands or reservations without fences. It generally will be areas that the outfitter has permission to hunt exclusively where he knows the area and deer population.

You should inquire with several outfitters in the area to determine the best one for you and the hunt you wish to plan. Once you make a contact with an outfitter, you should ask specific questions and be sure to get answers to all the questions you ask:

1. Ask for a list of references from out-of-state hunters who used the outfitter. A good outfitter will have current lists and provide them upon request. Be sure to contact everyone on the list and ask for their honest opinion about the outfitter and their hunt using the outfitter. Ask each contact on the list what was taken when they were in camp to decide if the odds are in your favor for your hunt. Ask how they felt about the accommodations and the guides in camp. Be sure to ask if there were things that were expected and not provided as well as the general atmosphere in the camp. This can prove to be important in a comfortable hunt.
2. Know from the start what is provided to the guests as far as sleeping and dining. Do you have specific requests? State them to the outfitter to see if you both agree.
3. Ask the outfitter if he has a list of clothing you should bring, and if not, ask what he recommends. Ask if you will need waterproof boots and hiking boots. Many a hunt can be spoiled with cold, wet feet.
4. Be sure to ask what average range you will be shooting at deer, so you can go to the range and practice and have your rifle or bow set accordingly.
5. Make sure you know the sleeping arrangements. If you are hunting as a couple, make the outfitter aware of this to see if he has adequate accommodations.
6. Inquire about bathroom facilities, showers and other amenities for your comfort. Know what is included and what is considered extra, if anything.
7. Check about dining facilities and meals, and see what is included in the price of the hunt.
8. Ask the outfitter if he supplies the hunting tags or if you need to make other arrangements.
9. Will you be picked up at an airport by the outfitter or will you be driving? Make sure the outfitter knows your plans and see if he recommends other options. Some outfitters meet their hunters in town, while others prefer you drive to the camp or be picked up in a certain location at a designated time.
10. Inquire about guide services, if you will have a separate licensed guide or the outfitter himself as the guide.
11. Check with the outfitter if Blaze Orange is a requirement. Some states require their hunters to wear Blaze Orange as a rule while other states do not. This could save you from having to run around at the last minute to get ready for the hunt.

12. Make sure you ask the outfitter about the hunting stands used at their camps. Are they ladder stands, tripod stands, elevated platform stands or wooden stands? This is important, and as a rule, I always bring a climbing stand with me on a hunt as an added precaution.

Be sure to ask your outfitter about the stands he uses.

I have been on a few hunts with outfitters that had stands less than desirable. One hunt in particular in Indiana comes to mind. The outfitter had a beautiful lodge, three star accommodations, and a top notch setup, except a few of his hunting stands. I remember one stand my guide took me to the fourth afternoon of the hunt. When we got to the stand, it was a wooden stand built into the tree and was at least ten years old and coming apart. One railing had fallen off, and it squeaked with a mild wind that day. I looked at the guide, and he looked at me and I asked him, "When was the last time you looked at this stand?"

He said, "This is the first time this year."

As I looked up at the stand, I asked, "Who was the last person to hunt out of this stand, Teddy Roosevelt?"

The guide laughed and agreed the stand was in bad shape. I said, "Bad shape? A dozen termites, all holding hands, are holding this stand together." I shook my head and told the guide I would use my climbing tree stand for the afternoon hunt. I did get a nice buck out of the area and was glad I had brought my own climbing stand with me.

As well as the above questions, be aware that many things come as extras or unforeseen on a guided hunt that you would not have to worry about at home. As an out-of-state hunter, be sure to bring extra money with you, and make sure you have a source such as a bankcard or credit card with you on a guided hunt. I remember one hunt for a whitetail buck when I was in South Dakota. I had completed a five-day hunt successfully and was planning on leaving the following day, That night we had a twenty-eight inch snowfall, and I had to remain in camp three extra days. This changed all my departure plans as well as my flight out. Extra money can come in handy for the unexpected.

Butchering and processing your meat, freezer wrapping it, as well as taxidermy fees are always extra and not figured into an outfitter fee. If you plan on flying, know the rules for the particular airlines you are using. If you are driving, have several coolers and a supply of dry ice to keep the meat frozen. If you intend to use a processing plant in the area you wish to hunt, contact them in advance to give them some notice. Many butchers who process wild game and processing plants, especially the ones out west, cannot be expected to make room for you on short notices as they are usually filled with hanging deer from other outfitters and hunters. In the Midwest and southern areas, it may be difficult to find a butcher. It would be wise to prepare well in advance and ask the outfitter who he recommends to process your meat. Waiting to the last minute could be a disaster if you do not have a butcher nearby that will cut-up your meat. Ask the butcher or processing plant to pack your meat in sturdy boxes that can hold dry ice or boxes acceptable for the airlines to ship. If the butcher does not know already, let him know not to pack the meat in boxes that weigh more than fifty pounds. Most airlines have a fifty-pound weight limit on boxes being shipped. Also, make sure the boxes are clearly labeled frozen meat. The last thing you need is to have the boxes stored next to a heater or warm surface to begin the defrosting process before you get home. Two good friends of mine returned home after they both shot nice size elks in Colorado on a seven-day pack horse hunt to find all their meat had gone bad by carelessness; someone did not follow all the necessary precautions with handling frozen meat. It was a hard and expensive lesson to learn.

In today's age of airline security, be sure to find out in advance what is required for transporting firearms. Years ago, I would never transport my firearm as cargo baggage for fear of it being damaged or winding up in Seattle when I was hunting in Colorado. With modern hard gun cases, rifles do not damage as easily as in years past, and all firearms must go in cargo on all airlines. Some require serial numbers and other proof of ownership, the name of the outfitter or place you plan to hunt, or reason for transporting a firearm. A good rule is to check early and be prepared.

Call the airlines well in advance for rules and restrictions concerning transporting firearms or bows.

It is customary to tip the guide at the end of your hunt. I say this because I have seen many hunters pack up, leave camp, and forget to tip the guide, thinking the outfitter is paying him. This is true, but an average guide does a lot for a hunter, and the better guides do even more. The guide is the one who is in the field with you and positions you in the best spot to take a good buck. The guide usually carries all the equipment except your rifle, field dresses your buck, and prepares the rack for taxidermy. He is the one with you all the time and takes care of whatever you need for the hunt in the field. I generally tip the guide a minimum of 10% of the cost of the hunt. If the guide is good, 20% is customary. If you ever plan to use the outfitter again, this will go a long way and be appreciated by the guide. Even if you do not plan to return, this is a good policy.

By following the instructions in this chapter, you should have a good understanding of the questions to ask when selecting the right outfitter for you. It is always helpful to use an outfitter that has been recommended by someone you know and trust, but that always cannot be the case. Be open-minded and listen to all the outfitter has to say. Carry a pen and paper; be sure to write your questions down that you want to ask and make a note of the answers the outfitter gives you to refer back when making your decision. Do not rush into picking an outfitter or be talked into leaving a deposit before you are sure you have the right outfitter for you. Picking the right outfitter is important for an enjoyable and memorable hunt. I have used many outfitters over the years I have been hunting. If you take your time and follow what I have said, you will do fine.

Chapter Sixteen

Hunting Equipment

Hunting today has grown from the time of the simple bow and arrow, or later, the primitive flintlock with ball and powder, sitting on a stump in the forest and waiting to shoot. You could sneak along a forest trail, blending in with Mother Nature in your hunting quest with bow or firearm in hand. Using an old shirt and sturdy jeans that will tackle any briers, your methods were simple. You went out and took your chances against whatever the outdoors threw at you.

Today we have high-powered rifles, high tech compound bows and crossbows, modern 4-wheel drive trucks, campers, SUVs and ATVs, to make a hunter's dream of taking a nice whitetail deer a reality. There are aircraft, jets, high-speed transportation, buses, motorboats of all sorts and ways to travel that your ancestors never dreamed possible. We have outfitters, guides and the Internet that joins everyone together. Television shows bring us to places in small capsules of time, telling us where we should go and who we should ask for. You can hunt your own state, and in some places, your own backyard. You can travel to the top of the Rockies or down below to the Everglades in Florida. You can go to Canada, Mexico or Africa, and just about any county you can imagine hunting.

All you need is an unlimited supply of money, being your own boss, an understanding wife who will put up with your desirable passion, and a small plane at your disposal for transportation wherever you want to go. Let's see, your own pilot, a chauffer, maybe a butler, or how about a short-skirted maid. Okay, okay… forget the maid, but a separate cook would be nice and even come in real handy.

Oh…you don't have all that? Okay, then you are like most of us in our current society, working in some sort of a job, and having to live with today's cultural ideas and reality.

That being said, let's begin our journey by selecting equipment that the average hunter should have in their quest for the elusive whitetail deer.

You do know that if you selected all the items that were on the market today for hunting, you would need a separate truck to haul behind you in order to have everything that people say you need. Now if you wish to buy everything, go ahead, but if you want to know what you really need, I have composed a list and broken it down into categories. Today you have portable tree stands, which are a godsend from years earlier where hunting from the ground was the only option unless you built your own tree stand on location. Hunting has changed over the years, and with change comes new equipment on the market. From lean-tos, we went to tents on camp out and from tents to campers. With many people hunting away from home, the equipment needed by an average hunter grew for necessity of the hunt as well as creature comforts.

If you are hunting with an outfitter, most will have the camp equipment in camp and set up, depending whether you are in a cold or hot camp. The guides usually will have your place ready, but it is wise to check to see what you would need to bring with you. Some camps using tents have heaters, while some outfitters ask you to bring your own heater and sleeping bag. There are a variety of heaters that you can bring to keep a tent warm besides a sleeping bag. In the old days, there was a fire outside in camp, and you slept on a cot or in a sleeping bag. Today there are tents with wooden floors, and you may find a few that have heaters.

You can also purchase propane heaters, propane lights, and propane stoves for cooking. There is a big difference between cooking over a campfire than cooking on a stove. The campfire might be more traditional, but it also could be 12 degrees outside. Then there is the chance of rain and trying to keep a fire going while it is pouring rain outside. Using a portable propane stove will work well, even in the rain. You can cook inside the tent with an opening to let the smoke escape while you stay dry. That in itself is a big plus.

You don't need to bring everything. Be selective.

A heater and above ground cot will keep you warm and dry.

Tent camping is okay and at times enjoyable, but I would rather have a camper with a bed, shower, stove and table. Roughing it is fine during a dry summer day or evening, but as I get a bit older, I do like my creature comforts. I enjoy a warm chair to sit on and being out of the cold when I wish to relax and eat or after a day hunt. I like a hot shower when I am done hunting for the day, as well as changing out of my hunting clothes into warm clothes. I have listed as follows a few items you might want to consider bringing on a hunt.

Portable Boot Dryers

You can find both electric boot dryers and battery-operated boot dryers. I have found the electric boot dryers to be an important item to have on any hunt, whether you are hunting from an outdoor camp or an indoor lodge. Warm, dry boots are necessary to begin any hunt. Wet or damp boots generally will dry within two to three hours, and if left overnight, they will be completely dry and warm.

Putting your feet into warm boots in the morning can make the difference between a comfortable hunt and a hunt you cannot wait to be over. A good portable boot dryer will cost around $35 at most of the large sporting goods stores like Bass Pro or Cabela's. Every day you put your feet into warm boots, you will be glad you spent the money for it.

Hand Warmers or Muffs

You can generally go to any sporting goods store or department in a general store to buy hand warmers. If I am going to be hunting for one week, I usually buy enough that I have two for a morning hunt and two for an afternoon hunt totaling four for one day of hunting. They generally say they last four hours, but I find that if they last two hours, it is good. You can also buy smaller warmers for your boots that keep your toes toasty warm.

I will tell you another tip to keep your feet warm. Bring two small plastic bags with you. When you get to where you want to hunt, take off your boot and put your stocking-covered foot in the plastic bag, then put your foot back into the boot. If your socks are dry, your feet will stay warm inside the plastic covering in your boot. Do not walk with your feet in the plastic bags in your boots, as you will perspire, and your socks will become wet and cold. I learned this while hunting northern Canada, and it does work if you are prone to cold feet while on a stand.

Muffs are hand warmers that can be attached to the front buttons of your coat to put your hands in to keep warm. They are good, except in rain or wet snow, as the outside will get wet if the material is not waterproof and then make your hands damp and cold. I try to stock up on hand warmers a month or so before the season; they cost around $1.00 for a package of two. You can store them for a long time, and they will stay good if not opened from their plastic bag they come in. Remember not to discard the plastic bag in the woods. What you carry in, carry out.

Thermos Bottle

You can buy vacuum thermos bottles for hot drinks that are built strong. They are made of steel that will not rust or change the flavor of the drink inside. If you want a hot drink to stay hot for hours, all you need to do it put boiling water inside for about fifteen minutes before you put your hot drink into the thermos. The same holds true for cold drinks by adding cold water for the same time before adding your drink.

Be mindful to leave this in your car or vehicle and not in your stand to drink, as deer do have a good nose as one of their senses. You can pick up storage canisters for a sandwich, but I strongly recommend that you do not pack sandwiches, drinks, candy, chewing gum or the like into your stand, unless you want to have a picnic and not be there hunting. Trust me, you will survive the hunt for the few hours you will be on your stand. The good thermos bottles cost about $29.99 and are well worth the price.

Emergency Kit

You never know when there will be an emergency, and I did not learn to keep an emergency kit available on every outdoor trip until my wife, Mary, and I went fishing and she got a hook stuck into her hand. We were fishing with our good friends and their son when my wife got a hook stuck in her hand. I held my wife's hand from moving as my friend used a pair of small pliers to pull the hook out. We were not far from home and wrapped her hand in a handkerchief until we put ointment on it.

An emergency can happen at any time, and I recommend on every outdoor outing that you have an emergency kit. I also recommend a signaling device of some sort, such as flares. You want to be able to signal for help as well as handle an emergency. We will discuss this more in later chapters. A good emergency kit with antibacterial ointment and several size gauze bandages are needed equipment. A good emergency kit will run under $50.00. It is good to have, but I hope you will never need it.

Hot Seat

You will not know how much you miss having a hot seat until you use one on a cold damp day. I generally bring two hot seats with me, one that is a cushion seat and the other a regular hot seat with filler that radiates heat. These seats are great to have with you, and I do not go hunting without mine. They are fairly inexpensive and cost somewhere around $6.00, depending where you buy them.

Portable Sewing Kit

I never used to carry a portable sewing kit until I hunted a trip to Canada and needed to have pants sewn and didn't have one. It is like an emergency kit, good to have and hope you never need it. A good portable sewing kit cost about $10.00 on average. Make sure it has a few different size needles, thread and a few different size buttons. Don't worry, they come with instructions.

Four-Wheel Drive Vehicle

This is a fairly new piece of equipment that hunters are using. Years ago when I started hunting, there were no 4-wheel drive vehicles; you parked your car and hiked into the woods. Today, you not only have 4-wheel drive trucks and SUVs, you also have ATVs that are popular. They are even making silent and electric models that you can drive into the woods by stealth, with attachments of all sorts. The problem I see with ATVs is that they can tear up a logging road or leave ruts by hunters not being careful, especially on wet days.

Some areas in states do not allow ATVs to be used in many areas while hunting. Some of the state forest lands do not permit the use of ATVs at all on their land. It is good to check the area you intend to hunt, to see if ATVs are allowed if you plan to use one on your hunt. On my own property I have a few logging roads, and I allow ATVs on them, but only to the select few who hunt my property, as they can cause damage to roads.

With all the modern equipment available to hunters on the market today, I feel some areas should be limited to walk-in hunting and bow hunting only to preserve as many areas as possible in its natural state. If much of this equipment were available to our forefathers, I wonder what wildlife would be around today.

I have enclosed a Hunter's Checklist for you to use as a reference and guide. You can make your own or use what you think you should have by looking at this list. The type and amount of the equipment you will need will depend primarily on the area and region in the country where you intend to hunt. It will also depend on whether you are going to be hunting one day or a week.

If you are camping out and do not already have a camper, a good quality tent is advisable. A good quality tent will have a floor made of a durable, heavy plastic, which will act as a shield from the ground and dampness. You will also need other items for convenience, like a small axe to chop wood and to hammer stakes. I cannot possibly cover every situation, but this is a good list of hunting equipment. As I said earlier, you can copy this list or modify one of your own to cover your individual needs.

If you are allergic to dog or cat hair, you may be allergic to the hair on deer. Be sure to bring your allergy medication with you. You can use the field dressing gloves to help, and this should take care of the problem. As on any trip away from home, be sure to tell someone where you will be. Do not say, "I am going hunting," and leave it at that.

Hunting Equipment List

Firearm Hunting Equipment

- ❍ Rifle
- ❍ Spare Rifle
- ❍ Pistol
- ❍ Ammunitions
- ❍ Belt Cartridge Holder
- ❍ Slings
- ❍ Rifle Cases – Hard & Soft
- ❍ Pistol Cases
- ❍ Binoculars
- ❍ Spotting Scope
- ❍ Range Finder
- ❍ Rifle/Pistol Cleaning Kits
- ❍ Knife
- ❍ Climbing Tree Stand
- ❍ Ladder Tree Stand
- ❍ Portable Branch Saw
- ❍ Screw-in Tree Hooks
- ❍ 2 Lengths of Rope
- ❍ Plastic Ties for Tags
- ❍ Hunting License
- ❍ Any Special Tags
- ❍ Hunting Regulations
- ❍ Several Pens
- ❍ Compass
- ❍ Maps & Topos
- ❍ Deer Calls
- ❍ Scents
- ❍ Large & Small Flashlight
- ❍ Batteries for Each
- ❍ 2-Way Radios & Chargers
- ❍ Safety Harness
- ❍ Flourescent Tape/Marking
- ❍ Luminous Head Tacks
- ❍ Boot Dryer
- ❍ Drag Sling
- ❍ Hot Seat
- ❍ Field Dressing Gloves
- ❍ Disposable Gloves
- ❍ Bone Saw
- ❍ Camera/Extra Film
- ❍ Plastic Bags – all sizes
- ❍ Butcher Phone Number
- ❍ Emergency Kit
- ❍ Cell Phone/Charger
- ❍ Wallet & Extra Money
- ❍ Medications Needed

Archery Hunting Equipment

- ❍ Hunting Bow
- ❍ Spare Hunting Bow
- ❍ Spare Bow String
- ❍ Spare Bow Cable
- ❍ Bow Vise
- ❍ Hunting Arrows
- ❍ Extra Arrows
- ❍ Practice Arrows
- ❍ Broadheads
- ❍ Extra Broadheads
- ❍ Broadhead Tightner
- ❍ Arrow Cement
- ❍ Broadhead File/Sharpener
- ❍ Field Tips
- ❍ Bow Wax
- ❍ Vasoline
- ❍ Extra Nicks
- ❍ Nick Cement
- ❍ Extra Arrow Shaft Inserts
- ❍ Spare Fletching/Cock & Hen
- ❍ Extra Sight
- ❍ Armguard
- ❍ Shooting Glove/Release
- ❍ Portable Tree Stand
- ❍ Safety Harness
- ❍ Allen Wrenches/Bow Tools
- ❍ Bow Case – Hard & Soft
- ❍ Camouflage Bow Tape
- ❍ Archery License
- ❍ Any Special Tags
- ❍ Archery Regulations
- ❍ Tag Holder
- ❍ Binoculars
- ❍ Range Finder
- ❍ 2 Lengths Rope
- ❍ Knife
- ❍ Drag Sling
- ❍ Hot Seat
- ❍ Field Dressing Gloves
- ❍ Camera/Extra Film
- ❍ Plastic Bags – all sizes
- ❍ Butcher Phone Number
- ❍ Cell Phone/Charger
- ❍ Wallet & Extra Money
- ❍ Medications Needed

Camping Equipment

- ❍ Camper
- ❍ Tent
- ❍ Tarpaulin
- ❍ Stakes
- ❍ Hammer
- ❍ Axe
- ❍ Wood Saw
- ❍ Tent Stitcher Material
- ❍ Tent Stitcher Kit
- ❍ Sleeping Bag
- ❍ Cot
- ❍ Air Mattress
- ❍ Blankets
- ❍ Sheets
- ❍ Pillows
- ❍ Portable Heater
- ❍ Propane Stove
- ❍ Propane Lights
- ❍ Extra Mantles
- ❍ Extra Fuel
- ❍ 2 Lengths of Rope
- ❍ Twine
- ❍ Plastic Ties – 12 inch
- ❍ Cooking Utensils
- ❍ Eating Utensils
- ❍ Glasses & Cups
- ❍ Coolers
- ❍ Drinking Water Bottles
- ❍ Table & Chairs
- ❍ Waterproof Matches
- ❍ Can Opener
- ❍ Bottle Opener
- ❍ Firewood
- ❍ Large Camp Knife
- ❍ Towels
- ❍ Flashlights
- ❍ Extra Batteries
- ❍ Shovel
- ❍ Tools
- ❍ Buckets
- ❍ Camping Permits
- ❍ Portable Latrine
- ❍ Toiletries
- ❍ Emergency Kit/Flares
- ❍ Cell Phone/Charger
- ❍ Wallet & Extra Money
- ❍ Medications Needed

Other Items To Consider

- ❍ Rain Gear
- ❍ Boots
- ❍ Extra Pair of Boots
- ❍ Boot Waterproofing
- ❍ Boot Silicone Waterproofing
- ❍ Spare Boot Laces
- ❍ Alarm Clock
- ❍ Sewing Kit
- ❍ Extra Pair of Glases
- ❍ Backpacks
- ❍ Sharpening Stones
- ❍ Fire Extinguisher
- ❍ Generator
- ❍ Fuel for Generator
- ❍ Extension Cords
- ❍ Food
- ❍ Coffee Pot
- ❍ Coffee & Tea
- ❍ Cold Drinks
- ❍ Soups
- ❍ Ice
- ❍ Survival Kit
- ❍ Safety Pins
- ❍ Skillet to Cook
- ❍ Insect Repellant
- ❍ Suntan Lotion
- ❍ Tweezers
- ❍ Handkerchiefs
- ❍ Extra Belt
- ❍ Bult Salt (hide preparation)
- ❍ Eye Drops
- ❍ Dutch Oven
- ❍ Wire
- ❍ Tools
- ❍ Reading Material
- ❍ Aluminum Foil
- ❍ Plastic Wrap
- ❍ Food Canisters
- ❍ Maps & Directions
- ❍ Phone Book
- ❍ Spare Gas Cans
- ❍ Permits to Federal Lands
- ❍ Emergency Kit
- ❍ Medications Needed

Chapter Seventeen

The Truth About Calling Whitetail Deer

I have found in my years of hunting that there seems to be a general misconception among hunters concerning the use of whitetail deer calls. Some will tell you that you can call a buck only during the rut, so why bother carrying a deer call if it is early bow season or any time prior to the rut or after the rut has ended? Then there are those who do not believe a deer call will work at all because they have heard this from other hunters or possibly have tried a deer call that they bought at a sporting goods store, blew it a couple of times, and a buck never came running to them.

To be honest, in my early days of hunting, I was a skeptic myself. I did learn through time, practice, trial and error, and experience that one of the best tools a hunter can have in his arsenal of weapons is a deer call. But knowing how and when to use a deer call is one aspect of whitetail deer hunting that is seldom taught to young hunters first starting out. Generally, a young hunter will be taught what to look for when purchasing a firearm or bow. They will be shown the different types of rifles, shotguns, muzzleloaders, and bows, the safe method of handling a firearm or bow and how to sight in and shoot properly. They will be taught how to pick a stand and what they should look for as far as deer signs and the conditions that will determine a successful hunt. Then, the teaching process ends, and the new hunter is left to test his abilities in the woods. To me, this process of educating a new hunter is like giving a hunter a gun, sending him into the field and not providing him with ammunition.

I guess if you are teaching a new hunter who is your son or daughter about hunting and you yourself do not use a deer call or never had any luck with them because you were not shown how to use them effectively, you could not pass on any information about them. I am going to explain in this chapter the different types of whitetail deer calls, the ones I have found to be the most effective, and at what time to use them. I will explain how to use whitetail deer calls correctly and when to stop calling.

It is my desire to teach new and experienced hunters about a tool that every whitetail hunter needs to carry every time they go into the woods hunting and how to use this tool properly. You may be an experienced hunter reading this and saying, "I have gotten several bucks and have not used a deer call, so why should I bother?" My question to you is, do you shoot or see a nice buck every time you are in the field? Have you taken a trophy whitetail buck? Have you gone a season or a few days without seeing a buck? Have you had a doe permit and never filled the tag? If the answer is yes to any of these questions, you need to learn how to make the change, and using a deer call will make that change happen.

The first thing a hunter has to know is that all whitetail deer communicate. They vocalize to one another by sounds to express interest, intent, desire, help, fear, and trouble. If you are a new hunter who has spent time hunting or a veteran hunter with many years under your belt, you have heard one of a whitetail deer's messages spoken directly to you, with their ability to communicate. Have you ever heard a deer *Blow*? Now why are you smiling? You have heard it in the woods; it is the sound you know already, and you know what it means. It means you were seen, identified, winded, or busted. All animals communicate. Just because they do not run around speaking English does not mean they cannot communicate and get their message across to other animals in the woods. You know other animals can communicate because you have heard them. Ever sit on a stand, hear a grey or red squirrel bark, and wonder when that squirrel is going to stop? What was the squirrel doing? Come on, you know the answer as well as I do. That squirrel was letting everyone in the woods know something is

Calling deer does work.

not right. Look out and be cautious, take cover. Ever see how a deer reacts when it hears a squirrel bark, or have you ever had a deer walk in to you relaxed and at ease while a squirrel is barking? You know as well as I that the answer is no. All animals in the woods recognize the sounds and the body language of other animals they live with. Now what do I mean by body language, you ask? When a deer stamps one foot, it is not keeping rhythm to a beat, but communicating through body language and sending a clear message. The message is caution, uncertainty or challenge. The deer is saying, "I know something is wrong, I have not figured out what; move so I will know for sure." Body language is another form of communication. We will get into body language later, as it is an important part of the communication process that needs to be understood when you are communicating with the whitetail deer.

For me, learning about using deer calls came after I had used several unsuccessfully, thinking all I had to do was to blow a deer call like a trumpet, and whitetail deer would immediately stop whatever they were doing and run to me. Hell, it said on the back of the wrapper to blow several times, pause and wait a while, blow again, then be ready to shoot, because they can come from any direction at any time. However, it never worked for me that way in the beginning. So what went wrong? Heck, I can read instructions as good as anyone can, so where did I screw up? The answer is, just like with any product on the market that you can buy, there are good products that do what they say they can do, and there are the ones that could work but don't. You also need to know how to use the product correctly. If after you have used the product correctly or been shown how to use it correctly it still does not work, it is a good estimation that what you are using just does not work. At that point, you need to find another product that does the same thing and works.

Now you do not have to be a rocket scientist to come to this conclusion, but what you do need to know is that because you used a deer call and it did not produce the effects it was supposed to produce, you should not stop using deer calls. I did until I learned that the tones of some calls sound more realistic to whitetails than others. Some calls on the market will not attract a deer even if you sat in the middle of a wildlife preserve surrounded by whitetails. You can use them all day long and never get a deer to lift its head or look in your direction. However, some calls do work at the right time and under the right conditions. I found this out when I was a young hunter first starting out and after several years of hunting. My first experience having a deer call work happened unexpectedly.

I was headed toward a small hunting camp off Route 17 in the Catskill Mountains. One of the neighbors of my youth, Tony, nicknamed "The Moose," because of his long years of hunting, had invited me to hunt with him at his hunting camp for the weekend. I had gotten off the highway leading to the town of Bloomberg, New York. I was traveling on a winding road in the middle of nowhere, wondering if there was a camp at the end of the road or if I took a wrong turn. It was the sort of road you would not want to break down on for fear you would not see a soul for hours, and then you might wonder whom you might meet. There was a heavy fog followed by steady rain, which made driving to the hunting camp in upstate New York a challenge in itself.

Following the directions given to me, I reached the camp, drove through an open gate with stone crafted pillars formed by an artisan of long ago, and saw other hunters inside the open door of the camp. Trucks were being unloaded, and I recognized a few familiar faces while seeing the general confusion when hunters first get to camp and put away their gear. Suitcases, duffle bags, rifles, and boxes covered the ground around the vehicles, and I wondered whether I should park my truck and look for Moose or wait until others were unpacked and inside the cabin. I did not have to wait long, as Tony saw I had arrived, came outside the building to greet me with a few other club members, and showed me where to park.

It was a nice little camp, with a wood-burning stove for heat and a outhouse privy about thirty feet from the door, with most of the modern conveniences and a touch of rural, rustic charm, a charm that you would enjoy during a warm summer day, but not when the temperatures reached below 10 degrees, as it was in the middle of the night.

The camp was spacious on the inside, with bedrooms for the higher-ranking members of the club and sleeping bags on the floor for those who did not rank high on the list or young members of the club. My bunk would be a bed, as I was an invited guest who was made to feel comfortable and positioned close to the warm, wood-burning stove, which I enjoyed. You would never go hungry being a member of this club as Tony, who was of Italian heritage, did most of the cooking. Lasagna, sausage and peppers, chicken cutlet parmesan and fresh Italian bread filled the air of the camp, and you easily could gain five pounds in the week you were hunting, even if you ate only two meals a day. Moose saw to it that there was always a fresh pot of coffee brewing on the stove, pastry in the kitchen, and something always cooking on the stove or in the oven. I wondered at times if Tony ever hunted with all he did in camp, but he always managed to come home with a nice whitetail deer every year.

Opening morning was a scene resembling a hunting camp at rush hour. There were people getting dressed, others looking for their gear, lunches quickly put together and stored in brown paper bags, and breakfast consumed at a fast and steady pace by hungry hunters not wanting to waste any time.

I noticed and found it surprising that every hunter was carrying some sort of deer call. The calls were either attached to the hunter's coats or on a rope around their neck, others were packed in backpacks or hanging out of coat pockets. I turned to Moose and asked why everyone was carrying a deer call. I had never had any luck with using them myself, and seeing everyone walking with one looked a bit odd to me.

Moose replied, "The bucks are in rut now, and you may not get one to come by your stand if you're without one." He said he had an extra call and asked me if I wanted to borrow it. It was a buck grunt call made by Primos. Moose took the time to explain to me how to use it correctly. He told me to wait a while after I got to the stand, and then to use the call by holding it in one hand and with my other hand, form a loose fist around the end of the call that does not go into your mouth. Then blow into the call with two or three loud but not deafening grunts. Each time you blow into the call, open your loose fist as the call is made and wait. He said the reason for opening and closing your fist as you make each call is to reproduce the sound a buck makes as he opens and shuts his mouth when calling. Then stop, listen for movement, and look by turning your head and not your body, which would give away your presence. If you do not hear or see a deer after a while, try the call again and repeat the same process. I had never tried one of the Primos deer calls. I figured all deer calls were alike, and they just didn't work. I agreed and put it in my pocket, figuring I would not use it, but I did not want to be the only hunter in the woods without one, thinking at my young age that it was a tradition or superstition in the camp to carry one.

I got to my stand after everyone else was positioned, for I was the guest, taking last place in the pecking order of hunters to be driven to their stands. In this camp, visitors were positioned in stands known to produce opportunities to see whitetails as a sort of enticement to join the club, and the fact that I was the neighbor of Moose helped also.

I was in my stand for about two hours but didn't see a deer, and I wondered, if this was one of the good stands, what were the bad stands like? I reached into my pocket for a hand warmer, as it was a frosty six degrees that morning, and put my hands on the buck grunt call. I said what the heck, took it out of my pocket, and made several grunts as Tony instructed me to do. I waited about ten minutes and grunted again with three short grunts. Nothing happened, so I waited about fifteen more minutes and grunted again with two grunts, focusing the sound of my call in the direction of thick cover that was off to my left. It wasn't long, probably only a few minutes, when a nice eight-point buck ran from thick cover and out in the open. My .300 Savage was on my lap, and I slowly raised my rifle, putting the crosshairs of my scope on the deer's neck, delivering a sixty-yard shot that dropped the deer instantly.

Once the deer was down, I looked at the grunt call and said, "I'll be damned, it worked." This was the first time I ever had a deer respond to a call and I have used what I thought to be every deer call on the market, by every known manufacturer.

I got up from my stand and approached the deer, which had a thick neck from being in rut. I saw it was an older deer with a well-proportioned rack and massive body. I filled out my buck tag, field dressed the deer and began the long task of dragging the buck back to camp. When I got back to camp and saw Tony inside in the kitchen, he turned and said I was the first hunter back and asked how I did. I asked him if he had gone out, and he said he stayed in for the morning but would go out later. I told him I got a nice eight-pointer, and he immediately came out to examine the deer. He claimed it was a nice deer and asked if I used his deer call. I said, "You know, I never thought these things worked, but I have to admit, this call brought this buck straight in and out of the thick cover."

Tony looked at me and said, "Let me tell you something, there are plenty of deer calls that all claim to bring bucks to you, but this one works."

The right deer call is as important as the right location.

I hunted with The Moose, and later his son-in-law, in the camp one other time, and I remember the good times in camp and learned a lot about hunting from listening to Tony. Tony passed away a few years ago, but he was one of the best hunters I ever met. I know if there is a hunting club in the afterlife, The Moose will be there cooking Italian food and teaching new hunters what they need to know about hunting and calling whitetail deer.

I still was not convinced about using deer calls, as I had tried other deer calls during the rut. After I thought about my hunt a few times, I figured that possibly this buck might have been running through the cover, and it could have been a coincidence and not the call. Not wanting to rule out that by using a deer call I would call in deer, I bought several deer calls before I went on my next hunting trip and began practicing. I did notice that different calls had variations in pitch and tone, even though they were all buck grunt calls. I figured that maybe some deer sound different from others. Heck, all people do not sound the same, why should deer? So I figured I would try it and use other calls. I did not realize how wrong I was until I tried using another call on my next hunt.

I hunted with an outfitter in Colorado the year after I hunted with Tony in the Catskill Mountains. When I packed for the hunt, I packed three different buck calls, one of which was the Primos Buck Grunt that I had success with in Tony's camp, which I had purchased before the hunt. I arrived at camp and learned from my guide that it was a good time to hunt, since the bucks were in pre-rut and already chasing the does. I settled into the lodge, and the guide asked me if I wanted to sight in my rifle. Knowing it was a good idea to check to see if the rifle was still on, I went to the range and saw that my rifle was not bothered by the long drive and was still on the mark at 100 yards. I always like to sight in at 100 yards, as I know what my rifle can do at other distances and my shooting capabilities.

The hunt started the next morning, and as I sat in my stand for the morning hunt, I was entertained by seeing several small immature bucks chasing does in what could only be described as a staged show being put on for my benefit. I left the stand at noon when the guide approached, and I told him about the activity I had seen. He asked if I had seen any larger mature bucks, and I said no, but I saw a few nice smaller two-year-old bucks that were six and seven points. He asked if I had any luck calling in a larger buck. I said I tried calling. Reaching for my grunt call, I saw it was a buck grunt call, made from a manufacturer whose advertisement stated it would have bucks running in. The guide looked at the call and said, "That should have worked," but it had not called in a large buck. Thinking the stand I was in didn't have a larger buck in the immediate area, I shrugged it off and was thankful I saw the bucks I did see. The guide told me that there was a good ten-pointer that he had seen from the stand several weeks earlier when he was scouting, and again two weeks ago, and that I was hunting in a prime location to see a nice whitetail buck. I told my guide I would hunt the same stand after lunch until dark, and if there was a nice buck in the area, I would call him in.

I got to my stand around 2 p.m. and started working with the call after I was settled in. I waited between callings and managed to see a small eight-pointer, but that was not what I was looking for; besides which, he came in before I started calling. I returned to the lodge that night and thought tomorrow would be a better day, since there was snow forecasted for that night, and that alone would get the deer moving better.

I got to my stand the next day with a four-inch blanket of newly fallen snow on the ground, and I sat there thinking someone would walk out of the woods singing, "Walking In A Winter Wonderland" at any minute. The trees were heavily covered in snow with the pine boughs low to the ground from the weight of the snow, with whitetail tracks covering the ground in every direction. I tried using my buck grunt call several times, but the morning ended without me seeing a buck and only a few does. I got back to my room in the lodge and looked for my other deer calls. I found one of the buck calls I packed was cracked. I thought for a moment and realized I bought this new call recently to replace one like it that had cracked the year before. Now the new buck call was cracked. It was made by a company up north, and I was thinking about writing them a letter, telling them that their calls needed to be made of studier material, since they cracked with normal use. I never did get to write them a letter, and I never replaced their buck call either. I had tried it several times, and each time produced the same results, with me not seeing a buck and the call not having the results the manufacturer claimed the call would produce. I had the Primos Buck Grunt Call with me and a deer call named The Can. I remember looking at it when I bought it and thinking, this will never work, but I figured I would buy it and try it and see. I had never used The Can before, but I figured what the heck. The Can was designed to imitate the Estrus bleat of a doe, (the breeding sound made by a doe), and I decided I would try it. I returned to my stand after lunch and figured I would try it after the woods calmed down a bit from my activity of moving to my stand. I was in the stand about forty-five minutes and started using this new call. It wasn't thirty seconds when a large nine-point buck ran out of the snow-covered pines. Shocked, I looked at the buck for few minutes, but before I got the opportunity to position my rifle for the shot, he disappeared. I tried calling with The Can several other times that afternoon. I could see signs of deer movement through the pines from snow falling off the pine branches and heard sounds of deer crashing through underbrush. I never got a good opportunity for a good shot, but this deer call did work.

That night upon returning to camp, I told my guide what happened, and he stopped the truck and looked at me. He was familiar with The Can call and asked me if I also used a grunt call when the nine-pointer first came out or right after using The Can call. I said no, because I didn't want to spook the buck that was out of the cover. He asked how far the buck was from me, and I said about seventy yards. The guide told me that the buck came out to see what was out there, and since he didn't see or hear any deer, he went back to where there were does, in the pines. He also said that was the time I should have used the grunt call, so the buck would come out further to investigate, thinking there was a rival buck too close for comfort. We parked on the side of the road for about an hour with the guide explaining to me the proper ways to use deer calls and when to back off from calling. I had thought I knew when and how to use deer calls and showed him what I had with me that afternoon. He looked at the two calls and said they were about the two best calls a hunter could have. I told him about the other calls I had with me, and when we got back to the lodge, I showed them to him. He smiled and said for me to come with him. We went down to a store in the main floor of the lodge where hunters could buy what they forgot to pack, and there was a section with about ten different deer calls. The two other calls I had with me on this hunt were in the selection, which was behind the counter, but not any of the Primos deer calls. I asked the guide why the lodge didn't stock Primos calls, and he told me that the lodge got their deer calls for free from a vendor who stopped in once a year, and the owner gives him a free hunt. In return, the vendor supplied the lodge with these inexpensive deer calls and some hunting equipment. The lodge made money on hunters who forget to bring their calls and other hunting gear and buy the ones the lodge gets free and sells at a high price.

He told me the Primos calls were the best you could own, and that he used their grunt call himself while hunting. We sat down and ate dinner together while my guide told me of different hunts, large bucks that were seen and some taken by hunters who knew when and how to call, usually bringing their own deer calls. Dinner turned out to be an evening of talking at the table long into the night, and I decided I would try using both of the Primos brand deer calls the next morning.

I got into my stand by 6 a.m., and it was just about turning first light. I reached into my pocket, taking out The Can, used it a few times and then the grunt call. I blew into the buck grunt call loud enough to be heard by anything in the pines, which was about seventy-five yards. An area of the pines exploded a few moments later, as a ten-point buck with high tines bolted out of cover with eyes wide open and ears rotating to locate the source of the call. I hesitated and then used the grunt call again, but softly, and the buck started moving forward. He was about sixty yards away and stood behind several trees when I raised my rifle. After a few minutes, the buck stepped out from the trees and began to walk parallel to me. I whistled and the buck stopped long enough for me to drop him with a shot to the buck's spine.

I climbed out from my stand and examined the buck as the guide was driving to me. He was not far from my stand when he heard the single shot, and he knew I had taken a whitetail. It was the buck he had spotted, and he congratulated me on taking a buck in the 180-class range. We loaded the buck into his truck and began the drive back to camp. I told him how I called the buck in, and he told me that he sees many hunters and all different styles of hunting in this business. He said the hunters who get large and trophy-size deer, know when and where to hunt and how to use deer calls to bring deer in close to them. He also stated that if you want to call in a trophy, you have to learn to speak a deer's language. I laughed and looked at the guide and said, "Speak a deer's language?"

He looked at me and said, "All deer can speak and respond to what they hear from other deer. What do you think you were doing when you used the calls to get this deer? You called out to the buck and said I am here and ready to breed. Then you used the grunt call to answer the doe, and this big fellow said, 'Hey, wait a minute, she's mine and came charging in to see who was after his girlfriend.' You know, you hunters use these calls, and you don't know what the calls are saying."

I looked at the guide and said, "You're right."

I talked to the guide for the remainder of my hunt. There are a number of deer calls on the market, all claiming to bring a buck to you, but like everything else, there are the good and there are the bad. Some calls actually scare deer away I have found. I learned this by using one such call on a hunt for whitetails in Nebraska. I was hunting again with a friend of mine name Cheech, and we were hunting property outside of Sioux County by Harrison that had good whitetail hunting. I was on my stand the third day of the hunt and had a deer call which was made by a manufacturer other than Primos. I was in my stand for about an hour and saw several deer in a field about 150 yards away. I started blowing this grunt call. It was during the rut, and I was trying to entice a large twelve-point buck closer to my stand from the field. I had spotted the buck, and it was a nice thick-racked deer in the 170-class range. The buck started to move and was coming to my direction, browsing as he was moving. At about 100 yards, I blew on the grunt call as I normally do to get the deer's attention, and the buck turned in the opposite direction and bounded off. Surprised by the actions of the deer and knowing I was not winded by the deer, I figured it was the call that actually spooked the buck. It was not until the same situation happened two other times during this particular hunt that I realized the buck grunt call I was using would actually spook more deer than it attracted. I have tried many different calls by all the different manufacturers in the years I have hunted.

After my Nebraska hunt I decided I was going to follow the advice of my Colorado guide and learn how to use all the deer calls I could find and master the deer's language. I figured that if I could call whitetails to me, and knew what each tone meant, I would be the one to determine the outcome of each of my hunts.

I decided to call a friend I had made who was the caretaker and manager of a state park close to where I was living. There was no hunting in the state park, but

Not all deer calls are the same.

it was loaded with whitetail deer. I told the manager that I wanted to do research and would like permission to come to the park wearing camouflage and use several different whitetail deer calls to see the deer's reactions and responses. He was not too keen on the idea, but agreed as long as it was during daylight hours and the rangers for the park were on duty.

Having permission to do my research, I decided to buy every buck and doe call on the market and try them all. I spent several months in the state park, getting to the park at different times and on different days of the week. I also wanted my research to entail different seasons and different times during the year to get accurate responses. I recorded my findings during the pre-rut, rut, and post-rut periods, which also entailed the early hunting season for archery, for empirical evidence as to what whitetail deer calls worked the best.

I have found in my research that some calls actually have a tendency to put deer on their guard, some scared deer away, others worked some of the time, and one worked almost all of the time. I did find, and I want you to know, that you have to be in an area that holds deer in order to use a deer call effectively. I mean that if you have selected an area, set up a stand, and there are no deer moving through that area during the day while you are there, no whitetail deer call on the market will help, because you will be talking to no one.

This is the main reason why hunters have no luck with deer calls. It is not that the call doesn't work. It could be the call you are using, if you are using one of the calls I found that did not work, but it is probably the area. It is like fishing and having the best bass boat on the market, the most modern equipment ever made, a tackle box full of lures of all kinds, bait well full of fresh bait, but you are fishing in the middle of a field. You can fish all day and you won't see or catch a thing. You might get a ticket for loitering, but that's it. What I am trying to say is that you first and above all have to be in an area where there are deer. This is important, and the actual first step for calling a whitetail deer. The second step is your understanding how to use the deer call and what the deer call is saying to deer.

The Grunt Calls

Both bucks and does make grunt calls. The pitch and the tone produced determines what you are saying while you are speaking the language of a deer. Some hunters do what I call "Over Grunting," thinking that because they cannot see a deer that no deer are in their area, and they think they can attract a deer to them by doing this, and a deer will possibly hear one of their grunts at some point. This is a total misconception, as doing this will scare deer away that you cannot see. Over grunting is as bad as waving a flag at a deer while you are in your stand. You are simply telling deer, "Here I am." It is important to remember, each time you use a grunt call, always use the call as if there is a deer within calling range, and you are another deer communicating directly to them.

Does usually bleat when they vocalize, but they do grunt at times. I have heard does grunt when they want to scare another deer away, and when they are communicating to correct their young offspring. The doe grunt is usually a high-pitched tone. If the doe wants to scare another deer away, her grunt is followed by the doe using her front legs to stamp at another deer. You do not want to imitate the high-pitched tone grunt of a doe, as many times you will be attempting to scare a deer away with this tone. The grunt tones you will be interested in are low-to-medium pitched tones, each with their separate and distinct sound.

The Attention Grunt

This is a soft, short call made by a deer to announce their presence to other deer. This is a call used to get a deer's attention. You use this call when you see a deer, it is not close to you, and you want a deer to stop what it is doing and move closer to you. You want the deer to look for the deer that made this vocalization. If done correctly, the deer will look in your direction and move towards you, looking for you, thinking you are another deer. Once the deer begins to move towards you, call again, but stop if the deer stops moving. If the deer stops moving, look at the deer to determine if the deer is alerted or just figuring that he can hear you and thinks he should be able to see the deer who is calling him. Refer back to the signs deer make in Chapter 13 to help you understand the body language of a deer. Once the deer is closer enough for a shot, stop calling and prepare to shoot.

The Aggressive Grunt

This is a loud and sharp-toned grunt. It is a challenge call, and you are attempting to challenge the dominant buck in the area to come out and fight. It can also be used with antler rattling to signify two bucks fighting one another, which will trigger a dominant buck to rush out and investigate who the fighting rivals are and to assert his position. This is a very effective call. When you use this call, be prepared to see a buck come in quickly. You make this call by blowing hard and using short, pronounced bursts of air into the grunt call. Once you use the call, be prepared and ready to react quickly.

The Mating or Tending Grunt

This is a call designed to trigger a buck into thinking another buck is in his area and looking for his does. It will make a breeding buck come out and see what buck is there, so he can show him that this is his territory. It is a short, medium-sounding call that sounds like it is coming from a deer's gut, which bucks make to let breeding does know, this buck is ready to mate.

Those are the main vocalizations that bucks make when communicating, but bucks do make other grunts also. I observed a nice eight-point buck one afternoon grunting at a fawn who was trying to get the buck's attention. The buck grunted at the fawn with a sharp tone, which sounded like more of a bark than a grunt. The buck was showing and expressing his annoyance to the fawn. I have heard this grunt several other times, each time when a buck was annoyed and another deer was in the area. I call this tone an annoyance grunt that a deer makes. It is an attention getter, as I have seen other deer's response to this grunt tone, and it does get a deer's attention. I have been unable to reproduce this barking grunt at this time. Other tones sound like wheezes and roars and are used to get other deer's attention, but sound louder than the attention grunt. Some hunters are under the impression that only a doe or fawn will bleat. This is not true. Bucks bleat and will generally bleat to other bucks or does to come closer. You will hear bucks bleat usually in the summer and pre-rut. To familiarize yourself with the different grunt calls and to be proficient, you have to practice. The are no shortcuts, and there is no quick mastering to calling. The more you call and use the different grunt calls, the more comfortable you will feel when using the call. Just as you have to practice at the range with your firearm or bow, calling requires practice also. Calling will work, but you have to practice using a call, see the reaction of the deer, and know what each call will and will not do. I will say, that it will not take you long to learn how to call, and having a good call will make all the difference in your success.

Just as there are calls that bucks make to communicate, does communicate by bleating. A doe bleating will trigger a buck to respond before, during and after the rut. Knowing how to use a doe bleat call is important and a good tool to have in your arsenal of equipment.

The Doe Bleat Call

Using a doe bleat call is great for early season bow hunting, because you can call in both a buck and a doe. When using a doe bleat call, you hold the call the same as a grunt call. One of your hands is used to hold the call to your mouth and then place your other hand around the end where the sound exist the call with a loose fist. You blow into the call and open your fist as you make each call, to replicate the opening and closing of the deer's mouth, as the call is made. Bleats are generally soft calls. You are not trying to blow a trumpet, or attract a deer from another ridge top.

Distress Bleats

Distress bleats are made by young deer. Fawns bleat to signify they are in trouble. If you use a fawn bleat call or bawl call, you will generally have does rushing towards you in response to the call. You can also trigger a buck to walk in to investigate what is going on, and do not be surprised if you call in a coyote with the same call. I have used fawn bleat calls during bow season and have seen coyotes respond to the call, thinking there was an injured fawn and an easy meal for them. The distress bleat is loud and continuous. You blow into this call loudly with definite intent, as a fawn would do if injured or caught. With this call, the fawn is screaming for help. I blow into fawn bleat calls for about 20 seconds, and then I pause for about the same length of time and repeat the call with a frantic tone. If you ever heard a fawn or rabbit caught by a predator, you would never forget the sound. If you want to hear the sound of a fawn or rabbit caught by a predator, most sporting good stores have electronic calls you can listen to, and you can buy tapes or CD's with the call of an injured fawn. You'll know you have mastered the call the first time a predator rushes in or does fly to your location.

I like to practice with my deer calls during the off-season. In May or June, depending on your area, and after the fawns are born, you can sit in a tree stand or ground blind and try the fawn call. I was amazed at the number of does that responded when I used this call. I have actually had does come within ten feet of me while I was sitting in a ground blind.

On one hunt in Lew Beach, New York, I was laying down on the ground when using a fawn bleat call. There was a large oak tree, which had fallen on the top of a ridge several years ago, with a hollow area on the ground under the tree that allowed a hunter to lie under the tree completely camouflaged with plenty of room to move around. The fallen tree was about four feet in diameter and was in a perfect location, as it was at the edge of a ridge, and you could overlook a slope and bottom that had a small brook running through and leading to a swamp. I was down under the tree, using the fawn bleat call and looking down the ridge. After the third time I blew the call, two large does came running and stopped right next to the blow down I was under. One of the doe's legs was about twelve inches from my shoulder. I was hunting for a buck and thought I would see one coming out of the swamp to investigate the calls I was making. I didn't want to take a doe, but I wanted to see the reaction of the doe if I touched her foot. I reached out, smacked her leg, and said, "Get out of here." The doe jumped up (I think she did a 180 in mid air) and flew down the ridge and into the swamp. Both of those does came rushing out to aid the fawn. Now I don't recommend you try to grab a hold of a deer's leg as I did. For one, their hoofs are sharp, and you could get seriously hurt. I did enjoy seeing the doe's reaction to both the fawn bleat call and to my touching her leg.

Throughout the many years I have been hunting, I have seen number of hunters using rattling antlers. Giving a fair estimation from what I have observed and even seen on TV, 98% are using the method of calling in deer by rattling completely wrong. Though hunters have called in several worthy whitetail deer by rattling, I do believe more whitetails are taken by coincidence when rattling than by the actual act of calling. The majority of hunters performing rattling do not shoot record size whitetails, and out of the hunters who do shoot a buck from rattling, only a very small percentage take deer in the 180 or better class range. The vast majority of hunters are not able to call in a buck, especially in areas where the ratio of buck to doe is greatly out of balance. Now you may be asking, what does he mean that 98% of hunters are rattling completely wrong? I will tell you why and how you can greatly improve your ability to rattle in a large buck, which will also improve your chances at taking a mature whitetail buck of trophy size.

You already know now that all animals can communicate. Did you know that during a fight, all animals communicate as well? Have you ever seen two dogs fighting that did not communicate by growling and barking? Have you ever seen squirrels in the woods fighting? Were they barking and chattering at one another, or were they quiet? If you have seen animals fight, you know they are not quiet when they are fighting. Neither are whitetail deer. However, most of the time when hunters try to attract a buck by imitating two deer fighting, all he does is rattling, or raking brush to imitate antlers connecting and brush flying without vocal communication. Now if you are an immature deer, and hear the sound of two deer fighting, you investigate, right? You would if you were an immature deer because you do not know any better. That is why when a hunter rattles antlers, the first deer to show up are the immature bucks. They are the two to three-year-old deer in the seven or eight-point ranges that would not know any better. They have alerted the mature deer, but most of the time the mature bucks stay in cover. Some hunters can see them, but usually if they are taken it is with a firearm and not at a close range. Yes, mature bucks can be shot by rattling alone, but the chances are limited and only in the most ideal conditions in areas where the buck ratio is much higher, but not in your average hunting areas.

Large, mature, trophy-class whitetail bucks did not get to that age and size by accident. Their senses are acute from knowing how to separate between something that is real and something that does not sound right. They come within a distance that they can hear and then determine while they are holding in place and listening if the sound they hear is real. If it sounds authentic, the mature deer will come in and show his presence. Mature trophy class whitetail bucks are not new to fighting as a young buck, and that is why you see mostly immature bucks when rattling, if you do see a buck at all. Most of the time when you see or hear bucks fighting you are at a distance that you only hear the clashing of antlers and brush. If you were closer, you would hear the vocal communication that takes place. I have witnessed more than four dozen bucks fighting and at a close enough distance that I have heard their communication, their grunting during the fight. The sound is a combination of air passing from the deer's mouth and at the same time low, and heavy grunting combined. Force being exerted by the air sounds combined with the grunting is what a mature, trophy-class deer hears as well as the crashing of antlers and brush. If he is standing and listening, that is the total of the authentic sounds he is waiting and listening for. If the fight does not sound real and authentic, he moves off. Most hunters do not know this or have not witnessed two deer fighting at a close range to them. The main reason is that if they were that close to deer, they would be spotted by the deer, and the deer would not stay around to fight. This is also what I observed at the state park when I did my research on the different whitetail deer calls. For calling to work, it has to sound real in every aspect. Whether you are using a grunt call alone or combining calls, it must imitate an authentic sound or act.

There are several deer calls on the market today. Some work and some do not. I will not mention every manufacturer of deer calls on the market, as I am not advertising, nor I am saying you need to buy them all. I will say that through my research, I have found one manufacturer of whitetail calls that has consistently proven to perform the best by actual pitch and tone sound, and that is the whitetail calls made by Primos.

Every deer hunter should know that the best whitetail deer calls on the market are made by this manufacturer. I travel around the country hunting, and I have done so for many years. If I found a better deer call on the market, I would use it, but there are none better. I have enclosed what I feel all whitetail deer hunters should have if they are looking to be successful in the field or want to bring home a trophy whitetail buck. Now I am not saying you need to buy every one I list at one time. What I am saying is that every one I have listed does work. I do recommend that a new or experienced hunter have several in his hunting bag or pack to equal several situations and periods you will hunt.

I guarantee, if you use whitetail deer calls correctly, and at the proper time, you will not be disappointed. There are not too many guarantees that people can give you in the sport of whitetail deer hunting. Though there are many claims to fame, I have found few that actually meet the mark. Researching by using all the different whitetail deer calls currently on the market, I have proven repeatedly, with my success and the success of those whose knowledge and abilities I trust, that the calls designed and manufactured by Primos are without a doubt the best out there. Here are a few of them I feel you should have as standard whitetail hunting equipment in your search for the master of the woods, the whitetail deer. Remember, to pick up the ones you will need for you first or next hunting trip, and add to them over time.

Buck Calls

For the best deer calls visit www.primos.com

Trophy Grunter

This buck call has a great tone and is a good call to have as it reproduces the actual sound and pitch grunt.

Grunt Call

This call is good to use in both early season and post rut hunts. I have found this call to be very effective to call in both buck & doe.

Still Grunter

The Still Grunter is an accurate sounding Grunt call that was smaller than traditional calls. With perfect tone and pitch, you won't be disappointed

Big Buck Grunt

The inhale-only feature makes this call 100% freeze proof, which allows you to hunt trophy bucks in extremely cold weather.

Little BIG Roar

The Little BIG Roar reproduces aggressive buck grunts that you will most commonly hear during peak times of the rut. Now you can reproduce the aggressive grunts that bucks make when their testosterone levels are through the roof.

Challenge Wheeze

The Challenge Wheeze is a sound bucks make when they want to challenge another buck to fight or want to run smaller bucks out of their area. This call is often referred to by many hunts as a snort-wheeze, can be very effective to call in dominant bucks. It is most effective in the rut and pre-rut when bucks testosterone levels are

Buck Roar

The Buck Roar is the most effective deer call since "THE CAN®". The "Roar" is a deep, resonating sound that is made by aggressive bucks during the rut. Bucks make this "Roaring" sound when their testosterone levels are through the roof. Whether the rut is in full swing or just beginning, bucks will make the "Roar" when they are trying to get an Estrus doe to stop or warn other bucks to get away from a 'hot' doe. This call comes with an instructional video.

Hands-Free Buck & Doe

Time and time again you need a call that would allow you to call while keeping your hands on your gun or bow. Here it is. The Hands-Free Buck & Doe is the perfect choice for those close encounters.

Doe Calls

For the best deer calls visit www.primos.com

Deer Bleat & Bawl

The Deer Bleat & Bawl™ is the call that has received so much attention over the last 15 years. Hunters just cannot believe how the bawl brings does charging in during the early season. This call also reproduces a short bleat and Estrus Bleat, perfect for all-season

Hardwood Fawn Bleat

The Hardwood Fawn Bleat is the "Original" call introduced in 1986, which started the craze of calling does. Made from select hardwood, it reproduces the bleat and bawls of young deer or fawns which appeals to the maternal instincts of all does during the early bow season.

Estrus Bleats

Estrus Bleats tell bucks that a doe is ready to breed. Whitetail deer respond quickly and dramatically to the "quivering" doe Estrus Bleat produced by "THE Original CAN". This is, by far, the best call known to call in bucks during the pre-rut, rut, and post-rut. This is a fast acting call.

THE Lil' CAN

"THE Lil' CAN" is perfect for early season calling. Smaller than The Original Can, it fits nicely into you pocket and has great tone representation. I recommend both this call and The Original Can to every hunter. It is a fantastic early season call that brings in deer to your area. Be prepared to have deer respond quickly when using this call.

THE GREAT BIG CAN

This call is used in conjunction with a grunt call. Its sound means a hot doe is with a buck, which only increases the urgency of another buck to get in on the action. "THE GREAT BIG CAN" has been tuned to be louder and longer for long-range calling. It's perfect for windy days and hunting wide-open fields.

The Long CAN

The Long CAN" produces longer, more intense Estrus Bleats, which lets bucks know there is a doe that's ready to be bred. During the pre-rut and rut this is the sound bucks are listening for. Be sure you are set up in an area where bucks have to come in and search for the doe when you call.

The e-CAN

With the push of a button, you can have a perfect Estrus Bleat every time. This call is designed to have the exact sound and volume as the "Original CAN®". Keep "The e-CAN" accessible when hunting, so you can draw deer in or stop them for a shot.

e-DEER

All the advantages an electronic call can offer are yours with the e-DEER. Place the e-DEER speaker set where you need the deer to go and set-up where you are concealed. The e-DEER remote works from as far as 60 yards away. Other electronic calls are shallow in comparison to the realistic sounds of the e-DEER. This call includes wireless remote and tree strap. The e-DEER produces the sound of Estrus Bleats, grunts, snort-wheezes, and rattling horns.

Chapter Eighteen

Hunting Clothing

Throughout my years in both teaching new hunters and in hunting in the field, I have found that during new hunter training, much emphasis is placed on firearm and bow selections, different stands to use, and locations to hunt, but little is mentioned concerning what a hunter should own for hunting apparel. We have seen the camouflage craze and seen different companies all saying a hunter will be invisible in the woods if he uses their product. There are clothing manufacturers that claim a hunter will be scent-free if they wear a particular type of outfit, and we hear about both odor-and scent-lock clothing.

You can buy lightweight, medium weight, and heavyweight clothing. You can wear one-piece zip-up camouflage suits, camouflage bibs, camouflage overalls, and camouflage over-wear, camouflage bug netting over your clothes—you can even buy camouflage underwear. Let us not forget lightweight, extra light, mediumweight and heavyweight red plaid outfits. Then there are the blaze orange coats, the blaze orange pants, the blaze orange jumpsuits, and the blaze orange bibs. How about the down-filled shirts, the down-filled pants, the heavy cotton pants in gray, brown, green and black that you can wear? Hold on, I am just getting started. There is long underwear that will keep you warm when the temperature gets down to the teens. Then there is what is referred to as the artic wear, the polypropylene, the 100% cotton, the cotton-filled, fleece-lined and stretched cotton underwear. You have facemasks, open hoods, closed hoods, detachable hoods, spandex wraps, thinsulates, Microskin flex masks, Nordic gear, Yukon beanies, Alaskan-style, bomber-style, balaclavas and even a thermologic hat battery to give you a heated hat or hood.

You can find scent-free soap, scent-free washing machine detergent, scent-free antiperspirant, scent-free wipes, and even scent-free chewing gum to take with you in the woods. So where does a new hunter begin?

If you had three walk-in closets dedicated for hunting apparel, one would be for warm weather hunting clothing, the second for when the temperatures begin to get brisk, and the third to be dedicated to cold weather wear, you would be covered. In the real world, that just does not happen. Well, not right off it won't, but as time goes on, one does tend to acquire more and more. After a while, if you are like me, you will have one walk-in closet and two other closets just for your hunting apparel. Weight of clothing has always been an issue of concern. If you were to hold a insulated parka for cold weather hunting and your bib of choice to keep you warm, you will know how much these two items weigh while you are wearing just them alone. You do not want to dress and look like Ralphie's brother in the "Christmas Story" to stay warm in the woods. Micro-fiber insulation clothing weighs less, as do vapor films used to create the water repellant property in

Layout all your clothing you will be taking.

clothing. If you are hunting in the frigid climates, these could be your best option and weigh considerably less while offering you more freedom of movement while still maintaining a level of comfort.

If you live up north and hunt with a firearm where the temperature is 20 degrees when you go hunting, you might not want to stock up on lightweight hunting clothing. However, if you live up north and bow hunt, chances are you won't need thermal and down-filled outfits, either. If you both bow and firearm hunt, you will have at least two different weight outfits as a rule. Be selective and know what you want and what you will need to stay warm and comfortable under changing conditions.

As new hunter or a beginner just starting out, you will probably know if you plan to hunt with a firearm or bow, so your selection will be easy in the beginning.

Let's talk about your firearm hunters right now. The region you hunt and the temperature you will be hunting in will determine what you will need. Years ago, bright red and red plaid was the most popular color of hunting clothing. This has changed, and many states are changing laws that make a hunter wear the color blaze orange for their hats and coats or a blaze orange hat and vest when they are hunting with a firearm in the field. It has been found to be the most visible of colors for a hunter to wear in the woods and is considered the safest. In the beginning, some of the old-time hunters were against the change, as they thought the whitetail deer would be able to spot them in these new outfits while they were hunting.

The fact of the matter is that all whitetail deer are colorblind. If a deer didn't spot you when you wore red because you didn't move when you were on your stand, the deer won't spot you when you wear blaze orange when you are on your stand and don't move. Deer respond to movement, sound and scent, not color. Remember, this when you are selecting your clothes, as the color is designed to protect you and others while hunting. Another thing to remember when picking out your hunting outfits is to buy clothing that is loose fitting and not tight. You want some freedom of movement without restriction. I have the rule when buying coats, shirts and pants, to buy one size larger than what I need. This will allow you to layer your clothing beneath. As the weather conditions change, you can adjust by removing or adding what you need to maintain your personal comfort level. Save the tight-fitting clothes until after the hunt for you to change into. One thing to think about that is not size or weight related is how easy a piece of clothing such as a bib or jumpsuit comes off in the field. This can be especially important for women and youths when "urges of nature are calling," if you know what I mean.

Another consideration that you will find important is to pick outfits that have many pockets. The more pockets the better; trust me, you will find the need for them. On pants, look for padded knees, cargo-style pockets, and wide loops for sturdy leather belts and rivets for suspenders. Talking about suspenders, you may think in the beginning that you never wore them and a belt will be adequate. When you are hunting and your pants have extra ammunition in your pockets, spare magazine clips, compass, whistle, rangefinder, alcohol wipes, field dressing gloves and whatever else you put in your pants pockets, they may have a tendency to drop around your ankles at times while walking or climbing a ladder to get into your stand. This might not bother you if you are a mooner, but it could prove to be an annoyance otherwise. When wearing suspenders, you can still wear a belt loosely to carry your hunting knife, mag lite holder and drag rope, but suspenders might be a good idea to keep those pants in place where they belong.

With coats, I tend to look for coats that have linings that can be removed and coats that are reversible, especially in the mediumweight coats. If you are hunting an area that has cold weather conditions, look for coats with zipper hoods that can be easily removed when not in use. Remember, you are not just going to wear these outfits when walking through the woods. You may be climbing into a ladder tree stand, using a climbing tree stand, and you will be shooting a firearm while wearing them. Make sure you can move easily in the outfit you choose.

Look for outfits that are water resistant. Few are waterproof, but many can be found that are water resistant. This way if it starts to drizzle while you are in the field, you will not get soaked during the trip out of the woods. One thing that many hunters usually overlook is how a coat or jacket will get rid of moisture from within. As a hunter, you will get active at times and sweat, and if this moisture has nowhere to go, the day can become miserable. Be sure to read labels and to pick the garments that will suit you the best.

Bow hunters will be hunting when rifle hunters are usually not in the woods and camouflage hunting clothing is allowed for the bow hunter. The bow hunter will have to decide on the pattern of clothing they prefer, and are not limited to the blaze orange color clothing. Now you may be asking, why does it matter if you are wearing camouflage if deer are colorblind? The answer is that when whitetail deer look through the woods and you are motionless, you won't be detected. If you are wearing a camouflage outfit and are walking or in an open stand, the camouflage pattern will blend in more naturally than a solid object. For this hunter, I do recommend full camouflage from head to toe. Wearing a facemask is important for a bow hunter, as you want to be totally concealed when in the open. When a person

Camouflage clothing is important for the bow hunter.

is wearing blaze orange and hunting with a firearm, he can get a shot off at 100 yards or better. The bow hunter has to be within a much closer range to a whitetail, and the chance of detection at this close range is much greater. The camouflage pattern in his hunting outfit gives the bow hunter a greater edge for concealment. But if you are hunting in a stand that has the bottom half of you covered, what matters is what a deer can see, which is from your waist up, but remember you may have to stand for a shot so full camouflage is a definite plus. Bow hunters have a large variety of clothing to choose from, besides the various patterns in different outfits made by many manufacturers. You can select from hardwood patterns to leafy brush patterns, from snow-white patterns with branches to gray- and green-bark patterns. You can match your outfit to the location you plan to hunt in all different styles of outerwear.

Rain gear is too often overlooked or simply forgotten about when hunters are looking for hunting outfit. I can't count the number of hunters I see sitting in their cars, trucks and campers when it starts to rain. All you have to do is drive by an area where hunters park their vehicles and see the number of hunters sitting in them when it is raining. Before, during and after a light rain is prime time to be hunting, but you see hunters in their vehicles because they either forgot or do not own raingear. You don't want to buy just a poncho. Ponchos are good to have as a last resort, but not as your only type of hunting rain gear. Look for a rain outfit that has either a jacket with a hat attached, or a jacket with a removable top portion for a hat. This way the back of your neck does not get wet when it rains, and you can remain comfortable when you are in the field. You also need rain pants that go over your pants. Remember to buy a good rain outfit. You do not want to buy a rain outfit that you will wear once and find that it rips apart, because it is too thin. You also want the size of the outfit to be loose and not restricting when you are wearing it over your hunting outfit. If you wear a medium hunting outfit, you want a large-size rain outfit because it has to go over what you are wearing and still provide you with flexibility.

Young hunters are totally amazing. I see them all the time, and many of them, I believe, dress to show how tough they are. By this I mean they will wear a hunting jacket, jeans and a pair of either sneaker boots or low-rise boots (if they wear boots) and what they wear is seldom waterproof. I remember being in one camp where several of the married men brought their young sons hunting during rifle season. Some wore padded hunting shirts, jeans and low-rise boots. One had on two shirts, a denim jacket, and a pair of sneaker boots that were not waterproof. Now mind you, the temperature outside where we were hunting was about 35 to 40 degrees. Not too unbearable, mind you, but enough to put frost on the pumpkin. I hunted in this club and had a stand that could fit four hunters comfortably. It was an enclosed stand about twenty-five feet off the ground, with sliding Plexiglas windows, a roof, carpeted wood floor, a propane heater to keep you toasty warm. I do love my creature comforts at times.

I got to my stand, and was there for about two hours when one of these lads walked by my stand, looking like a frozen popsicle, shivering and returning to the cabin. I waved him to my stand, got him to warm up a bit, and asked him why he went hunting dressed as he was. His comment was that it wasn't that bad out, and he was going back because he didn't see anything. He didn't see anything because he was too busy trying to keep warm before he decided to give it up. He did come back the following day wearing heavier clothes and waterproof boots. You know, you can always tell when some youngsters have been out hunting during hunting season a few days later. They come home and develop a sore throat or begin a cold from being outside for long periods improperly dressed, by getting wet or cold feet, and going from a warm cabin to cold weather conditions not prepared. Then again, I remember how it was when I was a youngster and knew everything myself.

I want to impress upon you that if you plan to take your son or daughter on a hunt, make sure he or she is dressed properly for the hunt. Nothing will turn them off quicker, than if this is their first hunt, than sitting and waiting to see something quietly while they are cold or have wet feet. My way of thinking is that you can always take a piece of clothing off if you get too warm, but if you don't have it with you and you get cold, you're miserable. Being cold or getting cold, wet feet have spoiled many a hunt for new hunters.

Footwear is a topic of concern, especially if you are prone to getting cold feet when you are sitting outside and trying to remain motionless on a stand. If you are hunting an area that is damp or has bogs, an area where you have to cross a creek or streambed, and are wearing anything less than waterproof boots, you are going to get wet, cold feet. Water-resistant is not the same as waterproof. Water-resistant means that water will run off the sides or off the top of the boot, not that water won't seep through them. You can take water-resistant boots and put several coats of waterproofing on them, and they are still only going to be water-resistant. Water-resistant boots are not the boots to be wearing when you are hunting a wet, damp area, and the waterproof paste for waterproofing is used on boots that are already labeled waterproof as a covering for the seams and as the boots begin to show signs of wear. Besides which, once the waterproof paste is applied to your boots, it has to stand for a few days to allow the paste to dry. In an

A plastic bag over your socks will keep you warm once you get to your stand.

earlier chapter, I told you how to beat the cold and keep you from getting cold feet on a stand. I will repeat this tip, as I feel it will help those of you to be able to sit longer on your stand with warm dry feet.

Bring two plastic bags with you to your stand that you can slip your stocking feet into. Once you get to your stand to sit, take your boots off. If your socks are dry, or if you have also brought dry socks with you, remove the sock if it is wet or damp from your foot and put the dry socks on first. Then put your dry sock and foot into one of the plastic bags, and then into your boot and lace it up. Putting your feet in dry socks and into the plastic bag and then into your boot will warm your feet, as the plastic bag will hold the heat in. Never walk to or from your stand wearing the plastic bag over your feet in your boots. You feet will perspire and get wet, and you will get cold feet from this. This is only for when you are sitting on your stand stationary and to keep your feet warm. Naturally, if you have a medical condition like a cut or bandage on your foot, I do not recommend this. If that is the case, I do not recommend you being on a stand in the first place, but I am not a physician or claim to be giving you any medical advice. I recommend two different boots to bring with you when hunting: Waterproof boots that are insulated to keep your feet dry and warm; and walking boots that will support your ankles when walking over rocks and uneven terrain.

If you have a long walk to get to your stand to hunt and are wearing long underwear, an insulated shirt, a coat and heavy boots, chances are you will be sweating by the time you get to your stand. What I usually do in this case is to carry my long underwear and a heavy shirt in a carry along or backpack to my stand. Once I get to my stand, I take off my boots, coat, and then my pants and quickly put on my long underwear, then redress and put my boots on. This way I am toasty warm on my stand and not sitting there perspired with damp undergarments. I don't recommend you get naked, but you can quickly redress in layers; it sure beats sitting there damp and wet to start-off your hunt. That is, if you are hunting an area where the climate is a bit cold, like the northern part of the country, which I hunted for many years. Now that I have my home in Missouri, I have not found it all that necessary to put on a show for the wildlife and redress in the woods. Besides, there was never any music when I undressed in the woods.

For people who hunt where the air is not blowing a warm, mild tropical breeze, such as states like South Dakota, Michigan and New York, you may want to invest in long underwear as a needed addition to your hunting clothing. I recommend that when looking for long underwear, go for the best you can find and afford. If you are going to be hunting in temperatures below freezing, and especially if you intend to stand hunt, buy the best. Look for long underwear that is rated for either artic or below zero temperatures, even if you only will be hunting when it is just below freezing. Wind chill temperatures, temperatures around the freezing range, and hunting in the early morning when the thermals are rising will make you wish you had bought the best long underwear on the market.

Remember to dress in layers, even when putting your socks on. I would put one pair of light socks on, then my long underwear bottoms, and then a pair of

Dress in layers.

thermal socks over the light socks. The long underwear will keep the lighter socks in place like a seal before you put on the thermal socks. If you are still hunting and moving, you don't want to bundle up as you will be moving, but if you will be on a stand, layer up.

Ear protection is good to have available, especially if you are wearing a hat that has earflaps. I know, I know, you are sitting there saying you don't want to look like an Elmer Fudd, right? Trust me, if you buy a hat with earflaps, you can leave the flaps tied up if you feel the need to make a fashion statement. However, you will be glad you have them if the wind picks up on a chilly November day, when Mother Nature wants to blow into your ear and say hi. Many hunters today don't want their ears covered, as they want to hear every sound in the woods without it being muffled. Some wear hearing enhancers that magnify sound; I use one myself. On days when it is a bone-chilling cold, you can hear a deer snap a twig at fifty yards, as sound will carry in temperatures that are bitter cold and dry, even with your ears covered by the flaps.

Gloves are important for every hunter to have. When selecting your gloves, try to stay away from tight-fitting gloves. I personally enjoy hunting with cotton mittens that have a slit in them and open up to allow a hunter to shoot with bare fingers. I like this because you have greater control and can squeeze the trigger better when shooting a firearm. For bow hunting, if you are using a release, a good pair of cotton camouflage gloves work well. Buying gloves will come as a personal preference, and the main idea is to buy two pairs, as one glove or a pair of gloves always finds a way of disappearing on you.

I am enclosing a Hunter's List of Clothing as a general list for a new or experienced hunter to have. You can refer to it or make one of your own as a checklist for when you are going on a hunt locally or away to an outfitter in addition to the equipment list in Chapter 16.

Hunting Clothing List

Firearm Hunting Clothing

- ❍ Heavy wt. blaze orange coat
- ❍ Medium wt. blaze organge coat
- ❍ Blaze orange jacket
- ❍ Regular outdoor coat
- ❍ Regular outdoor jacket
- ❍ Blaze orange hunting vest
- ❍ Insulated vest
- ❍ Hooded sweatshirt
- ❍ 2 regular sweatshirts
- ❍ Longsleeve sweater
- ❍ 1 shortsleeve sweater
- ❍ 1 hunting hat with ear flaps
- ❍ 1 soft hunting sock hat
- ❍ 1 cotton face mask hat
- ❍ 1 thermo face mask
- ❍ 1 pair of waterproof boots
- ❍ 1 pair of walking boots
- ❍ 1 pair of camp shoes
- ❍ 1 pair of regular shoes
- ❍ 1 pair of good slippers
- ❍ Spare boot & shoe laces
- ❍ 2 pairs of gloves
- ❍ Hunting shirts
- ❍ Regular shirts
- ❍ 2 pairs of hunting pants
- ❍ 2 pairs of regular pants
- ❍ 2 separate belts
- ❍ 3 pairs of long underwear
- ❍ 6 pairs of regular underwear
- ❍ 4 pairs of termal socks
- ❍ 6 pairs of regular socks
- ❍ 4 hunting hankerchiefs
- ❍ 6 regular hankerchiefs
- ❍ Rain gear
- ❍ Extra rain gear/poncho
- ❍ Silicone boot dressing
- ❍ Suitcases/duffle bags
- ❍ Toiletries
- ❍ Towels/wash cloths
- ❍ Camera/extra film
- ❍ Sleeping bag/blankets
- ❍ Pillow
- ❍ Cell phone/charger
- ❍ Wallet & extra money
- ❍ Emergency Kit
- ❍ Medications Needed

Archery Hunting Clothing

- ❍ Heavy wt. camouflage coat
- ❍ Medium wt. camouflage coat
- ❍ Camouflage jacket
- ❍ Camouflage netting overwear
- ❍ Camouflage bib
- ❍ Regular outdoor coat
- ❍ Regular outdoor jacket
- ❍ Camouflage hooded sweatshirt
- ❍ Regular camouflage sweatshirt
- ❍ 2 camouflage hunting shirts
- ❍ 4 regular shirts
- ❍ 2 camouflage hunting pants
- ❍ 2 pairs of regular pants
- ❍ 6 pairs of socks
- ❍ 3 pairs of long underwear
- ❍ 6 pairs of regular underwear
- ❍ 4 hunting hankerchiefs
- ❍ 6 regular hankerchiefs
- ❍ 1 cotton camouflage face mask
- ❍ 1 net camouflage hooded face mask
- ❍ 1 regular camouflage hunting hat
- ❍ 1 soft camouflage hunting hat
- ❍ 1 longsleeve sweater
- ❍ 1 shortsleeve sweater
- ❍ 1 camouflage arm guard
- ❍ 1 pair of waterproof boots
- ❍ 1 pair of camp shoes
- ❍ 1 pair of regular shoes
- ❍ Spare boot & shoe laces
- ❍ 1 pairs of camouflage gloves
- ❍ Rain gear
- ❍ Extra rain gear/poncho
- ❍ 2 separate belts
- ❍ Silicone boot dressing
- ❍ Suitcase/dufflebag
- ❍ Toiletries
- ❍ Towels/wash cloths
- ❍ Camera/extra film
- ❍ Sleeping bag/blankets
- ❍ Pillow
- ❍ Plastic bags – all sizes
- ❍ Butcher phone number
- ❍ Cell phone/charger
- ❍ Wallet & extra money
- ❍ Emergency Kit
- ❍ Medications Needed

Chapter Nineteen

Preparation Before the Hunt

As a new hunter or someone who has hunted for a few years, you are probably feeling a little overwhelmed between selecting what to bring with you, what to buy, last-minute shopping, and trying to figure out where everything is scattered where you live that you need to bring on a hunt. Let me tell you new hunters something that many of the experienced hunters already know: *Preparation Before the Hunt* can be a bit confusing, but even more so if you wait until the last minute to organize. If you think you are confused, take a look at sporting goods stores, the hunting department in any large department store, or the different places that sell firearms and archery equipment, and you will see what I mean.

I cannot tell you how many hunters wait until the last three days before a hunt to find out their firearm needs an adjustment or must be fixed. Their scope is clouding up or lost its seal and needs replacing. Archery hunters who are seeking repairs notice for the first time that the bowstring is frayed or that the nocking point on the string is off, possibly even a loose wheel. Venison seekers cannot find their hot seat because they accidentally left it in the woods the past season, or hunters needing to pick up ammunition to sight-in and hunt.

I remember one year that my wife, Mary, and I were going to hunt whitetails while staying at a lodge in the Adirondack Mountains with a friend and his young son. On our day of departure to begin, we got up at 6:00 a.m. to meet them at their house and then begin our drive with two vehicles to the mountains. We arrived at their house around 8:00 a.m. and learned that our trip was going to be delayed because my friend's son, while packing their car that morning, realized that his lever-action rifle was missing the screw that held the lever in place. Knowing my friend had several rifles, I told him to bring an extra rifle, and we could get it fixed at a gun shop in the area we were going to hunt. His son wanted to get his rifle fixed before we left, and we waited for the local gun shop to open at 10:00 a.m.

Preparation is an important key to success.

and did not get on the road until close to noon that day. I asked my friend's son if he had sighted-in, and he told me he did last year and that he did not fire a shot last year after he sighted-in, figuring his rifle was still sighted in for this year's hunt. I shook my head and told my friend that his son needed to sight in when we got to the hunting lodge. After we got to the lodge and my friend's son began to fire his rifle at a target, which was eighty yards away, he learned that his rifle was off by six inches on the elevation, hitting the target high, and was off side-to-side by close to three inches.

He said, "That's not all that bad."

Surprised by his comment, I looked at him and said, "You're right; if you were going to use that rifle as a club, it would work just fine, but if you're going to shoot with it, lets get it sighted-in." He was having problems, and I asked if I could see his firearm. I discovered the mounts for the scope were loose, so I tightened them with a set of Allen wrenches I had with my gear, and the boy managed to sight-in his rifle to an acceptable degree of accuracy.

Rifle ranges are usually packed with last-minute hunters all trying to sight-in their rifles, with some finding out for the first time that their rifle has a problem or needs to be repaired.

In the previous chapters, I have enclosed lists for what hunters should bring with them on a hunt. I have enclosed both Equipment Lists and Clothing Lists. Preparation before a hunt does not mean just packing and getting ready. It also entails knowing where you are going to hunt and getting the necessary maps of the area to make your driving easier. While you are acquiring maps, it is a good idea to pick up a local topographical map, or a "topo map," as they are called. If you already did not pick one up when you were scouting areas to hunt, now would be a good time to get one and bring along with you on your hunt.

Topographical maps are good because they show you elevations, streams and hollows where deer could hold up in. I strongly recommend having one with you on a hunt. It is not vital to bring the topo map into the field, but it can come in handy to check locations. If you hunt and have a backpack in the field, which is another idea I strongly recommend, you can slip a topo map into one of the zippered pockets so it is out of the way but available.

Sighting-in and shooting your rifle or bow should be done as a regular activity during the year to maintain accuracy and to correct any changes that occur. If you practice several times a month, your firearm or bow will be sighted-in already, as well as your being comfortable with what you are shooting. Accurate shot placement can be the difference between coming home with a whitetail deer or a Christmas tree on top of your vehicle. Now don't tell me you thought when you saw Christmas trees on top of hunter's vehicles returning from a hunt, your idea was that the hunter was just filled with the Christmas spirit while they were in the woods. It could happen, but it has been a long tradition that unsuccessful hunters return with Christmas trees. Have you ever seen both a deer and a Christmas tree on top of a hunter's vehicle together? It is usually one or the other. When you are going away hunting, which would you prefer to come home with?

Topographical maps show ridges, streams, and funnel areas.

If you are hunting out-of-state, you may need to think about airline reservations as well as a place to stay if you are not staying at a lodge or camp. Will someone pick you up, or will you need to rent a vehicle? All options must be thought out and well planned in advance.

Talking about vehicles, what about your vehicle? If you plan to drive your vehicle on a long hunting trip, when was the last time you had a tune-up, an oil change, a brake job, checked your vehicle's antifreeze, had your transmission checked or checked the 4-wheel drive fluid level? Part of being prepared for a hunt is also making sure you are able to get there and back without your vehicle breaking down. Having your vehicle break down when you are away from home is not pleasant and no way to start or end a hunt. Take the time and see to it that your vehicle is up for a long drive. If you were putting off getting new tires, this is a good time to replace them. You may be driving in a location when it begins to snow and wish you had better tires. If you are driving to the mountains where the temperature drops to below freezing, checking your antifreeze levels could prove to be important. Are your windshield wipers in need of replacement? Check them out, as this minor repair can be the difference in being able to see clearly should it happen to rain heavily or snow while you are driving. If the weather is going to be cold, you may consider bringing an ice scraper and lock deicer with you. If you bring a lock deicer, do not leave it in the glove compartment of your car or truck, where it will not do you any good should your vehicle's locks freeze up. Put it in your suitcase or duffle bag; that way it will be inside with you. Bring an extra set of keys for your vehicle; put one set in your pocket and another set in your suitcase so it will be in the cabin or lodge in case you lock one set in your vehicle accidentally.

Having your vehicle prepared to make a long drive is just as important as remembering to bring all your hunting gear with you. One thing that is often overlooked when checking vehicles is the spare tire. Does your vehicle have a spare tire? When was the last time you checked to make sure the spare tire was full of air? Do you have a lug wrench and a jack? You may need a star lug wrench for leverage in case the lug wrench that comes with most vehicles slips or the lugs are too tight. No one expects to get a flat, but people do, and being prepared is good. I usually pack a small tool kit that I bring along on every hunt. I make sure it includes duct tape in case a hose leaks, black electrical tape, an adjustable wrench, a socket set, pliers, a few screwdrivers, and a hammer. If you do not have a break-down, you may be able to help someone who has and is stranded on the side of the road.

Do you have an emergency road kit with flares? It may be a good idea if you picked one up. They are inexpensive, and having one could help if you have a breakdown. Some emergency road kits have air pumps with a long cord that can be plugged into a vehicle's cigarette lighter in the event you have a tire needing air. Having one could be the difference between being on the side of the road waiting or being able to drive for help. As well as an emergency road kit, you should also pack an emergency medical kit. They also are inexpensive, and you can usually buy a good one at a pharmacy or retail store for under $30. Make sure there are bandages of different sizes: wound dressing, ointment for cuts or bug bites, scissors, and adhesive bandages. A box of bandages alone is not considered a substitute for an emergency kit.

If you are going to a lodge or hunting camp, tell someone where you are going and when you plan to get there. It is also good to tell someone in the camp or lodge when you expect to arrive. This way if you do have a break-down, someone will call and either look for you or tell someone to look for you. It may not be a life-threatening delay, but it is better to be prepared in every way. It is just as important, if you are only going on a one-day hunt, to let someone know where you are. Do not say, "I am going hunting," and leave it at that. Tell someone so that person will be able to call either a ranger, conservation officer, or a police official, and tell him or her where to begin a search. Do not give a general area, as some areas cover a big distance and many roads. If you know the name of the road you will be parking your vehicle on and where you are going into the woods, let someone know the name of the road and in what direction your stand is located. This is not because you cannot take care of yourself, but because any number of accidents could happen, and it could save your life. You owe it to yourself and those who care about you to take all possible precautions. You could trip and have an injury while you are a mile in the woods walking or dragging a deer back to your vehicle. You could be walking out of the woods at dusk and your flashlight stops working. Accidents are not planned events and could happen to anyone at any time. The question is, did you prepare?

I have been on a few searches for hunters in my years of hunting, and it is not easy when all you have to go by is that the person is in the woods hunting or somewhere in the woods at a camp. One such search involved a few of the members of a hunting camp I belonged to in upstate New York, along with members of another nearby club, the area conservation department and the state police. I was asked to participate in the search because one of the members of my club and myself hunted the particular area the lost hunter was hunting. We knew the area well, and the weather was due to turn nasty, starting with freezing rain changing to snow as the temperature was going to drop well into the single digits during the night. The lost hunter had a cardiac problem and was told by his physician that he should not hunt this season. The hunter told his wife that he would not exert himself and would only hunt close to camp. Hearing this from a conservation officer who came looking for me at my hunting club, I decided to participate, bringing several of my club members who volunteered to search as well. We broke down into teams, each with either a conservation officer or a state police officer, and spent most of the evening with lanterns and two-way radios searching, but we were not able to find the lost hunter that evening. I learned the next day that the hunter had walked close to a mile away from his camp and climbed to a ledge on a ridge that overlooked a funnel area below. He was nowhere where he said he would hunt and was found the following day by state police with the aid of search-and-rescue dogs. I also learned that the hunter had a massive heart attack and was found sitting on the ledge with his rifle on his lap. His medication, which should have been with him, was back in the camp cabin in his suitcase.

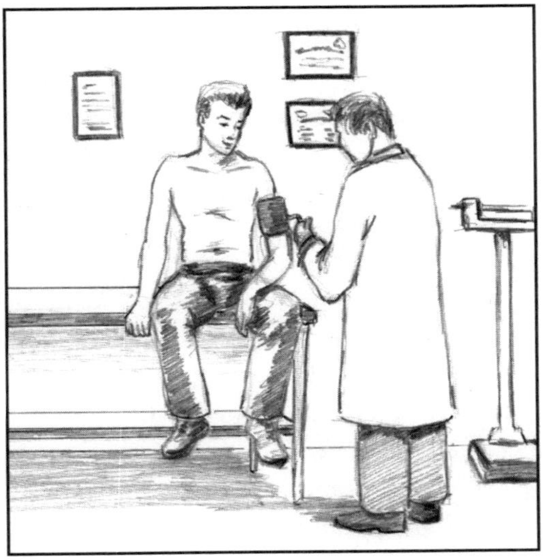

Remember to visit your doctor, for medication refills.

It is important that every hunter realize that there are times when you should not be in the woods. If you have a medical condition that warrants you to stay away for a day or the season, you should follow what your physician recommends. If you are on medication or need to have medication with you, make sure you have secured enough medication for your trip and have it accessible. Do not wait until the last minute to get extra medication if you need it. Some doctor's offices require 48 to 72 hours to supply pharmacies with refill orders, and then you may have to wait a day longer if the pharmacy is out of what you need.

Are you physically prepared for the hunt? Have you been going to work, and when you get home, eat dinner and then watch a bit of TV before going to bed? On weekends, do you do what is needed around the house but not get enough exercise? Hunting requires physical exertion. Whether you are walking in the woods over uneven terrain or up on a mountain or even a ridge, you need to prepare. If you are out of shape, start walking long before your hunt; go to a gym two nights a week or ride a bike on weekends. If you have a climbing tree stand or even a ladder stand, start practicing early enough to get into shape for the hunt.

As well as checking your vehicle and medications, you need to check to make sure that you are ready for the hunt. If it is a pack-in hunt on horseback and you never rode a horse, I would look into spending a few days on horseback at a riding stable. I know two of my close friends, Lenny and Steve, who thought they were in good shape until they went on a pack-in elk hunt where they rode a horse for eight hours to get to their camp. They both are in good shape, as Lenny is a retired gym teacher who exercises every day, and Steve is a retired NYPD detective. Both were in good shape physically but never rode a horse. Lenny did go once or twice horseback riding, but was not prepared for the long horse ride. Steve never wants to look at another horse again; at least, that is what he told me. They did rest every so often on the hunt, but an eight-hour horse ride to camp is still long for anyone who has never ridden a horse. I have been on a few, but I also own and ride horses. I have not ridden in several years, and if I were going to go on a hunt that involved riding horses, I would brush up myself.

If you have never ridden a horse before, you should try it, as it can be a lot of fun. You also will have a new found respect for the cowboys who spent most of their day in a saddle. When I was younger and in South Dakota, I would spend as many as six to seven hours riding in the Dakota badlands. I enjoyed riding then, and as I got older, my time in the saddle with horses changed from the seven-hour jaunts to a one-hour ride. Be aware that trail riding is a bit different from riding on horseback to an outpost hunting camp. During horseback rides to a hunting camp, you will be following a guide with packhorses and usually not on a well-worn trail. The difference could possibly mean riding between two trees that a horse can get through, but it is also nice to be able to pass between those trees with your knees still intact afterwards. Horse pack hunts can be fun with several surprises thrown in if you have never ridden before. Not to say you should not try one, but try to prepare for the horse ride well in advance. Outfitters have horses that are gentle, but their saddles are hard and do not come with shock absorbers in the seat.

It goes without saying that you need to sight-in your rifle, but it is a wise idea to take an extra rifle with you on a hunt away from home or a spare bow if you are going to be shooting archery. Anything can happen, and if you need a spare firearm or bow and are without one, you could have a problem. I generally bring an extra firearm or bow as a rule, and you should as well. Remember if you bring two rifles to bring enough ammunition for each. Since we are discussing ammunition, you should remember when you buy ammunition, if you are buying two or three boxes, buy the ammunition with the same lot numbers on the boxes of ammo. The lot numbers will be found on the inside flap that opens on one end. Look to see that the numbers match in each box.

Manufacturers make ammunition in runs, meaning that if they are making 180-grain ammunition in the 30-06 caliber, each bullet in the lot number will have the same grains of powder added as signified by the lot number. Having two different lot numbers can cause a small problem. If you sight-in using one lot number and hunt with another box with a different lot number, the amount of grain in the different lot number could vary your shot by as much as three inches at 100 yards. Be aware—if you sight in with ammunition from one manufacturer and use another manufacturer's ammunition with the same number grain to hunt, you could be off as well and by as much as eight inches. It is always important to

Buy matched ammunition serial numbers, when buying more than one box.

make sure you sight-in and hunt with the same manufacturer's ammunition and the same lot numbers. There are many different ammunitions, manufacturers, grain sizes, and calibers to choose. All are good, but some are better than others. It will be up to you to decide which ammunition is right by practicing with each. Make sure you feel comfortable with what you have chosen, and have consistent, accurate results by making periodic trips to the range. Make sure that the rifle or bow you bring with you for a spare has been sighted-in and practiced with prior to the hunt. If you need to use the spare, it is good to know it is on target and ready to use. Once you get to where you are going to hunt, it is a good idea to test the accuracy of your firearm or bow. You want to make sure what you are using to hunt with did not change settings by possible movement on the ride and is still accurate. Most outfitters or hunting camps will have a range where you can check your firearm or bow for this.

If you are going to your own hunting camp, most members of the camp will call one another before the start of the hunting season to discuss the food you will have in camp. You should select who is going to bring what, and make a list of what you will need. Remember, you will need food for breakfast, lunch, and dinner. Some members of the camp or club may choose to stay in one day or an afternoon, and it is a good idea to bring food enough for the days you or others will be in camp. Some camps hunt for a week, while others stay open the entire season. If you are a member of a club, someone could bring breakfast foods. Others bring lunchmeat and bread, and some can bring pans of food prepared a week before the hunt and frozen, if you have a large freezer in camp. You need to decide on drinks like soda or fruit drinks, coffee and tea and whether you will have snacks in camp. Usually this is decided at a club meeting prior to the season, and people decide what they need to pick up. All in camp pay an equal amount of money for this. If you are hunting by yourself or with another, you can make a list of what you need. Do not forget cups, spoons, forks, napkins or paper plates, toilet paper, as well as a good supply of garbage bags. Be sure that what you bring into camp returns with you when you leave camp, as far as extra food or trash. Mice and other critters have a way of getting into cabins that are unoccupied after a hunt.

Call your butcher well in advance to schedule processing of your deer.

Okay, you have your vehicle and transportation covered, you made out your list of equipment and clothing and have that in order, your rifles or bows are sighted-in, and you have that covered. You even made an emergency contact list and packed an emergency kit; what about the deer? Are you going to butcher the deer yourself in camp, or wait until you get the deer back home? Are you going to have someone else butcher and process it? It is recommended that you know, in advance, what you plan on doing if you are successful and shoot a whitetail deer.

If you have read this book and followed the steps I have written, you can plan on shooting a deer, as you have prepared for this hunt by not leaving the outcome to only chance. If you want to get the deer processed, make sure you know who will be doing it and have phone numbers and directions to get the deer to them. If you are using an outfitter, the outfitter may be able to help you. If you are hunting locally in your own state or a nearby state, it would be wise to have all information available before you make the hunt. Speak with the butcher you have chosen to advise him of your hunt and that you would like him to butcher your deer. Let him know your approximate return date so he will expect you. Later in this book, I have included chapters on both field dressing and processing your deer yourself. It is important for every hunter, even if he does not plan on processing a deer himself, to know how it is done. Believe it or not, processing a deer yourself is easy, and you may enjoy making some select cuts yourself, saving a processing fee. Processing fees can range between $75.00 and $150.00, depending on how you want to process your deer and the cuts you select. Some butchers can make breakfast sausage, summer sausage, and even polish sausage out of venison. Naturally, processing like this is in the higher range charged by butchers for their service. You can even make deer jerky out of venison, which is fast and easy to make. If you enjoy the taste of jerky, you will appreciate venison jerky, especially if you have made it yourself.

Preparation before the hunt is as important as the hunt itself. If a hunter has prepared and is organized with lists of all that is necessary to bring with them on their particular hunt, it will make the hunt and the time before the hunt enjoyable. You will find that lists come in handy as you can prepare for your hunt well in advance. You can pick up what you need at your leisure if you do not already have it, check it off the list, and put the item where you have stored what you intend to take with you. Designate one area of your home where you will store these items to make it easier when you do pack. This way you are not tearing the house apart to find things. Relax, take your time, and the *Preparation Before the Hunt* will come a lot easier.

The proof of a successful hunt.

Chapter Twenty

Safety at Home and in the Field

The issue of safety has long been debated between state officials, firearm and archery manufacturers, local enforcement agencies, and hunters. As hunting grew from the necessity to sustain life to a modern-day sport, so has the concern for education in the way of mandated courses, which became a requirement in many states. The first state to act by introducing hunter education classes was New York in 1949. New York pioneered hunter safety and had mandatory classes as a requirement for new hunters seeking a hunting license.

For more than 25 years, I was a teacher of hunter education classes in New York. As well as teaching, I was involved in training men, women and youths by conducting seminars that instructed both young and experienced hunters about the sport of hunting and the art of taking a whitetail deer. To me, safety at home and in the field is the utmost of importance and cannot be overemphasized in any hunting journal or publication.

The hunter education classes teach new and young hunters firearm and archery safety, but programs have been expanded to include topics concerning responsibility and ethics. I believe that hunter education classes are not enough and that *Safety at Home and in the Field* is the responsibility of every firearm or bow owner, parent and person who takes their firearm both inside their home and into the field.

Years ago, in the time of flintlocks, muzzleloaders and black powder pistols, firearms were complicated. You would need the combination of three elements in order to have a firearm discharge. The process was to pour powder down a gun barrel, place a wad of paper over the end of the barrel, insert a ball over the wad and use a ramrod to push the ball and wad down to form a tight seat, then, by adding a primer, the hammer would strike and create a spark, which ignited the powder. Advances in ignition systems brought about firearms that became more modern. Today, with high-speed bullets, quick loaders, and automatic firearms, all the guesswork has been removed. Unsupervised or unknowledgeable handling causing accidental discharges became the fear, which prompted the rise for more safety awareness. Now you might think that safety awareness when handling a firearm is elementary, but statistics prove this not to be the case. Do you know what is the single, most-owned firearm that causes the most injuries and fatalities in this country today? It is the unloaded gun. The reason why I say this is that when people are interviewed after accidental discharges of a firearm, the answer given in over 95% of the interviews is, "I didn't know it was loaded."

Coming from New York a few years ago and being a teacher of hunter education and a hunting instructor, it was standard to have a rifle in a locked gun case while in my vehicle with the ammunition in a separate area away from the firearm. At game checks, officials would check to make sure I was following all precautions in this manner. Having this drilled into my head from the time of my youth hunting, I rarely loaded my rifle until I got to my stand in the woods. Most of the time in the beginning, I was walking in the dark following other hunters, and there was no actual need to have a loaded gun. It was illegal in New York to be in the woods before sunrise with a loaded firearm. Hunting started usually at sunrise, not 5:30 a.m. when you were walking to your stand.

On one hunting trip, I was standing with my wife, Mary, getting ready to go into the woods. I had just locked my vehicle when we were approached by a game warden who was driving and stopped. The conservation officer checked our licenses, and after seeing they were in order, asked to see our firearms to see if they were loaded. If they were, there would have been fines issued, one for hunting before sunrise and another for having a loaded gun in a vehicle.

Now if you live in a state like Missouri, you might think this is a bit strict, but be mindful that different states have different laws and hunting regulations. Just as many states have changed their regulations concerning what a hunter should wear, some states go a bit further with safety and institute regulations concerning firearms in vehicles and the carrying of firearms to and from the field. I was trained to be safety conscious at all times and try to pass that on to everyone I teach or share a hunt with while I am in the field.

I was hunting many years ago when I was much younger with a good friend of mine named Gene. I was staying at his house in Livingston Manor, New York, and we planned to go hunting the next morning in a spot he was familiar with. Gene had been telling me about two bucks that he had seen several times during the season, and he had a good spot picked where we could both sit where the deer crossed during the early morning hours.

We got up the following day after the alarm clock rang, and I saw it was 4:00 a.m. Mind you, I have never been a morning person, even during deer season. I always felt it was more sportsmanlike to allow a deer to sleep in before you shot him, but Gene never felt the same and was shaking me when I turned off the alarm and fell back to sleep. I got up and said, "Do you know what time it is?"

Gene looked at me and said, "It's five minutes past 4:00 a.m., and why aren't you dressed?" I reminded him that it doesn't get light for another two hours, but Gene insisted I get dressed because we had about a forty-five minute ride to get where we were going to hunt. I got dressed, grabbed a quick cup of coffee, and before 4:30, we were in my truck heading for a spot in Lew Beach.

Traveling down the road, we saw whitetails crossing the gravel road, and Gene looked at me, saying, "The deer are moving, so you had better get moving." The road was pretty winding, and there was snow on the ground, so I was using some caution, but I guess my driving was a bit too slow for Gene. Local people have a way of getting to their stand without fear of trees jumping out in front of them and saying hello to you. It must be a local thing, and you needed to be a ridge runner to understand.

We got to where Gene said to park and got our hot seats. I shouldered my rifle, and we were on our way into the woods. Gene had already gotten his buck, so he was acting as a guide for me to shoot my buck. Gene led the way, and I was familiar with both the area and the trail we were on. State land was to the right of us, and a hunting camp owned the land to the left of the road. We got to a rock shelf that overlooked a nice area below, and Gene said that was the spot. It was still dark, and I couldn't see five feet in front of me, so I agreed. I quietly asked Gene about the general area where he saw the deer and where they would be traveling. He told me that the deer usually came from the right, and if they followed the same pattern, we would see them right after sunup. I looked at him and asked if he sat up there often. I was surprised that he knew where the deer would be coming from at sunup and how many times he probably hunted in this spot. It turned out that this was one of Gene's favorite hunting spots, and he had taken several nice bucks from this area by sitting on the spot where we were now sitting. It was about seven degrees; I was sitting on a hot seat on a rock, which was not what I would call comfortable. I was also thinking that hunting would be a lot easier if they sold venison in the supermarket, so I could go in at 10:00 in the morning and buy a venison roast, cutlets, ground meat, or a package of tenderloins. However, no, this was fun, sitting on a rock in the dark, freezing my butt off and getting a wedgie at the same time. I thought how some people vacation and go to Hawaii or the Caribbean, but I sit in the snow and get to enjoy this. How foolish am I to think I would enjoy being warm, comfortable, or just being back in bed?

Well, the sun was starting to come up, and the squirrels were beginning to stir and move about. I focused on the area to both the left and the right when I saw brown movement to the right and picked up my .270 Remington. Gene said to wait, as it was a small four-pointer that was coming out of the heavy cover in the woods first. He said a nice heavy-rack seven-pointer should be following him. I waited, and about two minutes later, I saw two deer coming out of the woods. One was another small buck, and the second was the seven-pointer. I put the cross hairs of my scope on the buck's neck and waited for the whitetail to stop. The moment he stopped, I slowly squeezed the trigger and heard "click." Surprised, I threw the bolt open to find my rifle was unloaded as the deer, hearing the sound of the bolt of my rifle opening, trotted off.

Gene looked at me, smiled, and said calmly, but louder than he normally spoke, "Don't you think that rifle would work a lot better if there were bullets in it?" I was so accustomed to walking in the woods while it was dark with an unloaded firearm that I never loaded it when we got to where I was going to hunt. Well, I never got a buck that day, and I took a lot of ribbing over my unloaded rifle, as I was reminded of it by several of Gene's friends in the days that followed when I was with Gene and his friends hunting. Always being told to load my rifle, as we set off into the woods. After that incident, I always remembered to load my rifle when I began my hunts and when I got in the woods in my stand. I also remember to this day the look on Gene's face when he realized my rifle was empty and can still hear the words he told me that day.

Safety in the field is a continuous process of being mindful that you have a loaded firearm that can kill. Whether it is a rifle, shotgun, muzzleloader, compound bow, or crossbow, you can have an accident at any time. A common rifle used for hunting is the 30-06 with a cartridge of 180 wt. grain bullet. This bullet, when fired, leaves the muzzle at 2700 feet per second, has the energy in foot-pounds of 1368 at 400 yards, and continues traveling if not stopped. When shooting at a whitetail deer, it is good for a hunter to know if there is a suitable backstop, should your shot miss its target.

Always be aware of your back-stop.

A hunter should not take some shots, as the picture shows, if the hunter does not know what is on the other side of the hill. It is impossible for me to describe every situation you will encounter in the field. What is important to remember is that you, as a hunter, have the responsibility to be safe and use good judgment when shooting. The best rule to follow is if you are not sure, do not take the shot. Once the bullet is fired, it cannot be recalled.

If you are hunting with other hunters, be mindful of their direction. Know where they will be hunting and the possibility that they could be turned around and approach you from another direction. You may be hunting on state land, and there could be other hunters in the woods of whom you are not aware. Always clearly recognize the deer you are shooting before you shoot, and shoot accurately to deliver a quick, clean kill.

When walking in the woods, make sure your firearm is on safety. If traveling to your stand in the dark, have your firearms unloaded, and load them after you get to where you intend to hunt. This will avoid accidental discharges if you lose your footing and fall.

Before climbing into your tree stand, have a rope attached to your stand and attach the other end of the rope to your firearm. I generally put a small balloon over the end of the barrel and attach the rope to the rifle sling and around the

Safety in the field is important.

butt stock. Once I am in my stand, I then lift my rifle with the barrel facing down and unloaded. The balloon keeps any unnoticed dirt or snow from getting into the barrel. I also leave the balloon on the end of the barrel while I am hunting. I do this to prevent any rain or snow from entering the barrel should the weather change. The balloon will not deflect your shot and will keep your rifle barrel dry. I also recommend you use this technique if you are still hunting, especially if it is during a light rain or snow.

If you are crossing a fence with another hunter and there is no opening or gate, hold the firearm of the other hunter after it is unloaded, and let him or her cross the fence first. Then pass the unloaded firearms over to the other hunter one at a time, then cross the fence yourself. If you are crossing a fence by yourself and there is no opening or gate, first unload your firearm. Then place the firearm on the other side of the fence, laying it flat down on the ground if possible, then cross the fence.

Never cross a snow bridge if possible. A snow bridge is a stream that appears to be frozen and crossable. Many hunters have fallen through snow bridges, and I learned this as a young hunter in South Dakota while hunting with a friend and hunting companion named Bob. We were hunting for whitetails in the Black Hills when the outside temperature was 10 degrees below zero. Having just entered the woods and about 150 yards from my truck, Bob saw a stream that appeared to be frozen that we had to cross. I looked at the stream and said I was going to go down river a bit to find a narrow area, because I didn't like how it looked. Bob went out about five feet and tapped on the ice with the butt of his rifle and stamped one foot, saying it was okay. As I turned to look down the stream, Bob had taken a few more steps, and the ice let go. He fell to his shoulders before I got to him and managed to pull him out of the stream. He said he had dropped his rifle in the stream. I looked at him and said to forget it, I needed to get him back to the truck. By the time I got Bob back to the truck, his pants were already iced. I got the truck heater going, helped him off with his boots and pants, and covered him with a blanket I kept in the truck for safety purposes until he stopped shivering. That was my first experience with snow bridges, and I have never crossed one since. Bob was lucky. Had he been alone, the outcome might have been different.

Safety in the home is equally as important as safety in the field. Many hunters store their firearms in wood and glass gun cases in their den that can be easily opened by a child, even when they are locked. The best precaution would be to have a gun safe to store your firearms to protect them from being handled when you are not present or from being stolen in a break-in. I do realize that a gun safe can be costly. There are other things you can do to prevent a firearm from being accidentally loaded and discharged.

Even if you have a firearm in a gun cabinet, I believe all firearms should have either a bolt or action cable lock or a trigger lock. By having one of these locks, a firearm cannot be accidentally fired. The locks are inexpensive and generally cost less than $10.00 each. When a firearm is purchased, the owner should buy a lock at the same time. I have found that several good and reputable gun dealers will throw a gun-locking mechanism in at no additional cost if you ask them at the time of purchase. How many accidents by children picking up a firearm could have been avoided if there was a lock on the trigger or the action?

Safety in the home can also take place if ammunition is stored in a separate place than the firearm itself. If the firearm is stored in a locked gun cabinet, the drawers underneath are not where ammunition should be stored. The compartments underneath are for extra rifle clips, slings, rifle cleaning kits, ammunition belt holders, deer calls, and scents, but not ammunition. All ammunition should be stored in either an ammo box or metal boxes that have sturdy locks attached to them to prevent opening except with a key. I found that a separate storage room on a top shelf that cannot be reached by children to be a good place. Whatever place you choose, make sure it in a separate room that is cool and dry, away from all firearms, in a locked case, and above the reach of any children in the house.

Store your firearms with a trigger lock in a locked gun cabinet, ammunition should be store in a separate location.

If firearms are on display, use an approved lock for safety.

Pistols are a fascination among young children who see cowboys on TV shooting while riding horses. If you own a pistol, it should be stored separate from other firearms unless you have a gun safe, where it can be stored safely. If you do not have a metal locking case for your firearm, you can store it safely by first making sure it has a trigger lock attached to it.

I have found that a good place to store a pistol safely is inside a closet, straight up inside and above the door. There is usually a 2-foot area inside most closets straight up as you walk in. You can install large hooks inside in that area where they are up high and not seen. If you put trigger locks on your pistols, this is a good place to keep them if you do not have a locking pistol case. If you put it up

Pistols should be stored high and preferably out of sight.

high this way and inside the master bedroom closet, the pistol will also be close to you at night.

We have discussed firearm safety up until now, but archery safety is equally important in the home as it is in the field. Broadheads are sharp and have razor edges designed to pierce flesh and cut through bones to deliver a fatal shot. Compound bows are always under tension, and accidents can happen if they are drawn back without an arrow and released. Compound bows are designed to transfer energy and have that energy released by the flight of an arrow to its target. If a bow is drawn back and released without an arrow, pressure is transferred directly to the limbs rather than the arrow, and the limbs can either shatter or fly apart, causing the person releasing the string or anyone nearby to be seriously injured. A 45-pound compound at half-draw can send an arrow at 180 feet per second and easily go through half-inch plywood at thirty feet with a target tip. This is good to remember when you are storing your bow at the end of the season or between shooting at the archery range. Modern compound bows today are designed to have an arrow leave the bow at speeds of 300 feet per second and can penetrate a piece of half-inch plywood at a distance of 35 yards. Many hunters store their compound bows with arrows in a hard bow case, but it also recommended that you store your bow in a locking case and out of the reach of curious children. Broadheads should be stored separately as you would ammunition. For personal safety, check your bowstrings and cables periodically. Touching a cable or string with a razor sharp broadhead could cut it instantly, but most times, it will cut only a few strands, causing an unsafe condition if it is not seen. When unnoticed, it could break under the pressure of the bow at full draw, causing injury to the shooter or anyone nearby. It is recommended that you use bow wax regularly or at least after every practice session before you lock your bow away for the day. If you store your bow, arrows and mechanical release in the same hard bow case as most bow hunters do, make sure the case is locked and in a safe place for storage.

The crossbow is becoming the bow of choice, and many hunters are getting into both target shooting and hunting with a crossbow. Some states allow hunting with a crossbow; some states allow crossbow hunting for handicap hunters, while other states are still looking into whether they will allow crossbow hunting in their state in the future. Hunting with a crossbow can be and is safe, but one has to be aware of a few things about crossbows. With a crossbow, you

Safety in the field is important.

are holding the string of the bow back to full draw and in a locked position when it is cocked. To release the string from that cocked position, it is extremely hard and can be dangerous if done by hand. Most manufacturers of crossbows recommend that the release be done with an arrow (called a bolt) being fired. Now if you shoot a crossbow bolt into the ground and hit a rock just beneath the ground, you will shatter the bolt. I generally bring a target designed to have crossbow bolts shot into it, just to shoot a bolt into at the end of a day of hunting if I have not shot at a deer. This is about the best way of doing it. Mechanical cranks that draw the crossbow string back are not recommend to be used to release the crossbow strings when they are at full draw positions.

The crossbow I have is a 175 lb. crossbow, which can deliver a bolt accurately at 75 to 80 yards. I have not shot a deer past 60 yards to date with a crossbow, as I feel comfortable shooting at 55 yards or less. If you place your shot accurately with a crossbow, a whitetail should drop within thirty yards from where the deer was shot. Safety with a crossbow is as important, as with any bow. The hunter with a crossbow should be mindful that the crossbow limbs are always under considerable pressure and should be checked regularly. Crossbow cables need to be waxed, as does the arrow rest. Cables should be checked, as it is very easy to accidentally touch the fixed cable or bow string with a broadhead while the crossbow is at full draw. It is also important to remember never to carry or lift a crossbow at full draw up to your stand. Always cock the crossbow once you are up in your stand and in place, raising it from the shoulder plate up to your stand by a rope with the crossbow facing down.

It is extremely important to be mindful where your fingers are while holding the crossbow in position before you shoot. If you are holding the crossbow to your shoulder and supporting it in the palm of one hand, make sure your fingers are not resting on the top area where the bolt sits. If they are, and you shoot, the force of the crossbow string coming across the bolt rest can sever your fingers. This is a very important safety step to know when firing any crossbow. Some crossbow manufacturers, having this safety step in mind, have constructed their crossbows with a separate grip under the bolt rest. Even if your crossbow is equipped with

When using a crossbow be mindful of finger location.

this bottom grip, always be mindful of the force your crossbow exerts and where your fingers are when holding the crossbow.

Safety at Home and in the Field is important, and the life you save by practicing safe handling of firearms and bows could be that of a fellow hunter or your own. You owe it to yourself, your fellow hunters, and your family to observe safety at all times.

Chapter Twenty-One

Shooting a Deer with a Firearm and Bow

In the time I have spent teaching new, young and veteran hunters how to successfully hunt for the whitetail deer, I was amazed at the amount of people who thought the middle of a deer's body was the place to target their shot. Though it is possible to kill a deer by shooting it in the middle of its body, there is a good chance that by doing so, you may spend the afternoon, evening, and most of the next day trying to find the deer. You may find your deer, but in actuality, the chances of finding your deer with that shot are remote. By aiming at the middle of a deer's body, there is a good chance that you will totally miss the vital organs, which are located behind the front shoulder to just shy of the middle of a deer's body.

With the internal anatomy of a deer standing broadside, it is possible and very likely to shoot through a whitetail, never hitting a vital organ to drop the deer. Shooting at the middle of a deer's body will result in either shooting trough a deer's diaphragm and possibly only nicking a deer's liver, if you hit it at all. A shot such as this could have the whitetail traveling for miles and dropping in a location far from where the deer was shot.

On my property, two years in a row, I have had a whitetail buck die next to one of my food plots after it was poorly shot during the firearm season. The first deer was a good size seven-pointer that my wife and I found at the edge of our biologic food plot that was shot directly through the middle of the buck's body with either a .223 or a .243 rifle. The entry hole was rather small and barely noticeable. I called the local conservation officer, thinking the deer died from a disease after I did not readily see a bullet hole. The conservation agent pointed out the entry hole, showing the entry hole in the diaphragm, and we estimated that the buck traveled several miles before it died. The second buck was a small-rack eight-pointer that appeared to be shot with a muzzleloader and was shot low in the middle of the deer's body, partially gut shot. I found that buck about fifty yards away from where I found the other buck, and it had traveled a good distance before it died.

On both of these deer, it was apparent that the shots were aimed at the middle of the deer's body, and both deer traveled a distance before they died and became food for coyotes. The property that borders mine on one side is a large piece of property owned by a young couple that my wife and I know very well, and they do not allow hunting on their property. When they are away, I keep an eye on their property for them.

One of my other borders, which borders this couple's land also, is a very large parcel of land that is closed to all hunting. Knowing this, the conservation agent and myself determined both the bucks traveled a good distance to die.

I hunted upstate New York in the Catskill Mountains for a number of years and had a hunting friend named Gary who lives in a small town at the base of the Catskill Mountains. Gary was your typical hunter who worked hard six days a week, and when hunting season came, he would spend a week to two weeks at the hunting camp. Gary is a great person, but he cannot hit the broad side of a barn. He hunts with a semi-automatic 30-06 and does so because in his mind, if he fires four shots, one will probably hit the deer.

He collects quality firearms, and I have hunted with Gary many years. His biggest drawback is the fact that he never goes to a rifle range, except to sight in, once a year for an hour. If he is within four inches, he thinks his rifle is sighted in.

He is the person I see coming back from the range with a small bandage just above his right eyebrow because his scope sits too far back and hits his eyebrow every year, but he doesn't correct it by moving it forward and bore sighted at a gun shop. So when I go to the range with him, I listen to him cuss after he cuts his forehead. In fact, I bought a .35 Remington from him because of this and still have it today in my gun safe. For five years in a row, he would cut his forehead until he got tired of it and sold me the gun. I moved the scope forward, and it works fine for me. I just do not use it and rely on my .308 Browning or my .300 Savage, but I keep it in my collection.

I cannot tell you how many times I offered to take Gary to the range with me, but he was always too busy, doing something that needed to be done. I did see him shoot a doe one year, and he did hit the doe twice before she dropped. Nevertheless, I have to admit, Gary was in my wooden ground blind with me hunting, and the doe offered him a broadside shot at less than fifteen yards. At that distance, he could have thrown his rifle and hit the deer.

Gary always aimed for the middle of the deer, despite all my efforts to get him to change, and began hunting with his semi-automatics. He has been aiming this way all his life, and despite the fact that he loses more deer than he finds, he will not change. I am surprised because Gary has lived upstate most of his life, and I have found country people (ridge runners) are quite good shots.

I had a good friend named Paul who lives not too far away from Gary, and Paul could shoot a fly off a tack at 80 yards with iron sights. Paul was one of the first people to help improve my hunting skills and would always aim at a deer's neck if at all possible, which is what I do myself. In all the years I have been hunting and using a firearm, my favorite shot is the neck shot. Deer seldom take a step after you have shot them in the neck. That is not to say you do not have to aim for

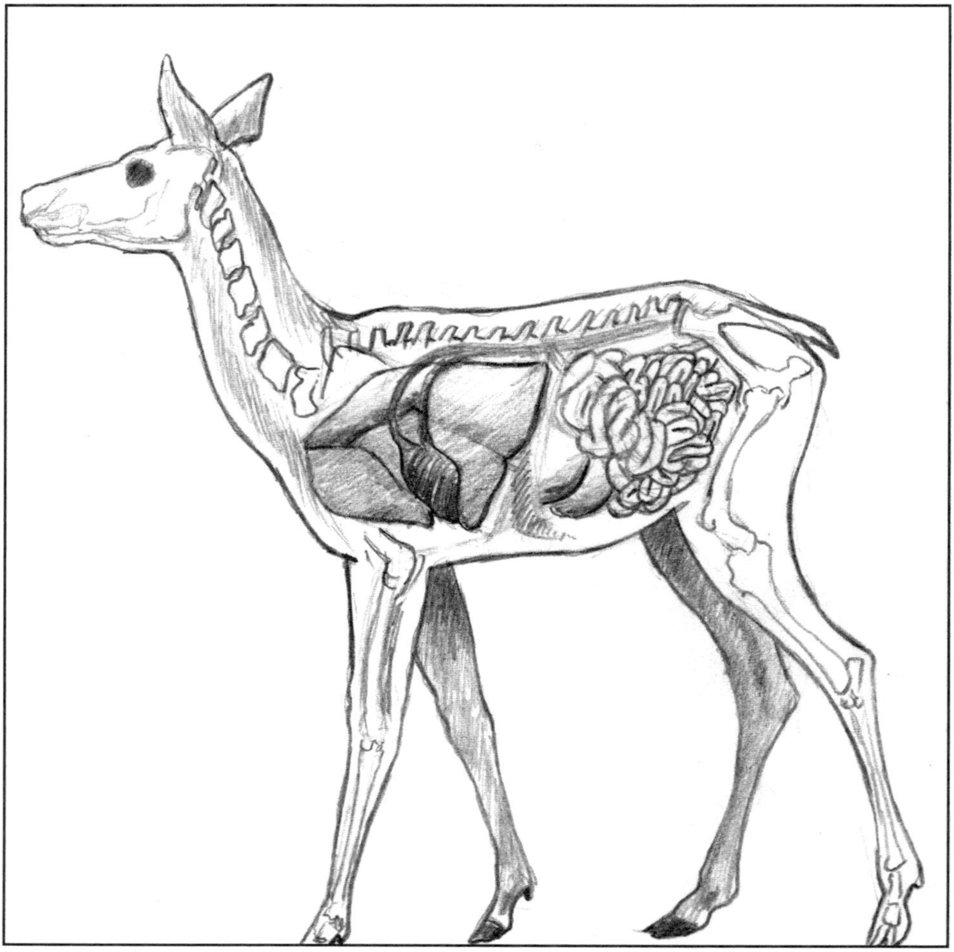

Anatomy of a deer.

a particular spot, but on neck shots, you can break a deer's neck bone or major artery, and that will drop a deer instantly. I find it to be the quickest and cleanest shot besides the spine shot when using a firearm.

In the two views show above and on the next page, you can see both the skeletal and organ structure of a whitetail deer. Though it is possible to hit an organ like the upper diaphragm, this would not necessarily be a fatal shot. If the whitetail does die from this shot, it will be a long, slow process, and chances are you would not retrieve your deer.

In the next drawing, you are looking at a deer as if you were above the deer in a tree stand. See where the heart and lungs are located? If aiming at a deer in this position, you should be aware of both the deer's skeletal structure and the position of the vital organs for an overhead shot.

Be aware that the internal anatomy of other big game animals, such as the moose, pronghorn, goat, sheep, and elk are very similar, but for our purposes, we will concentrate on the whitetail deer.

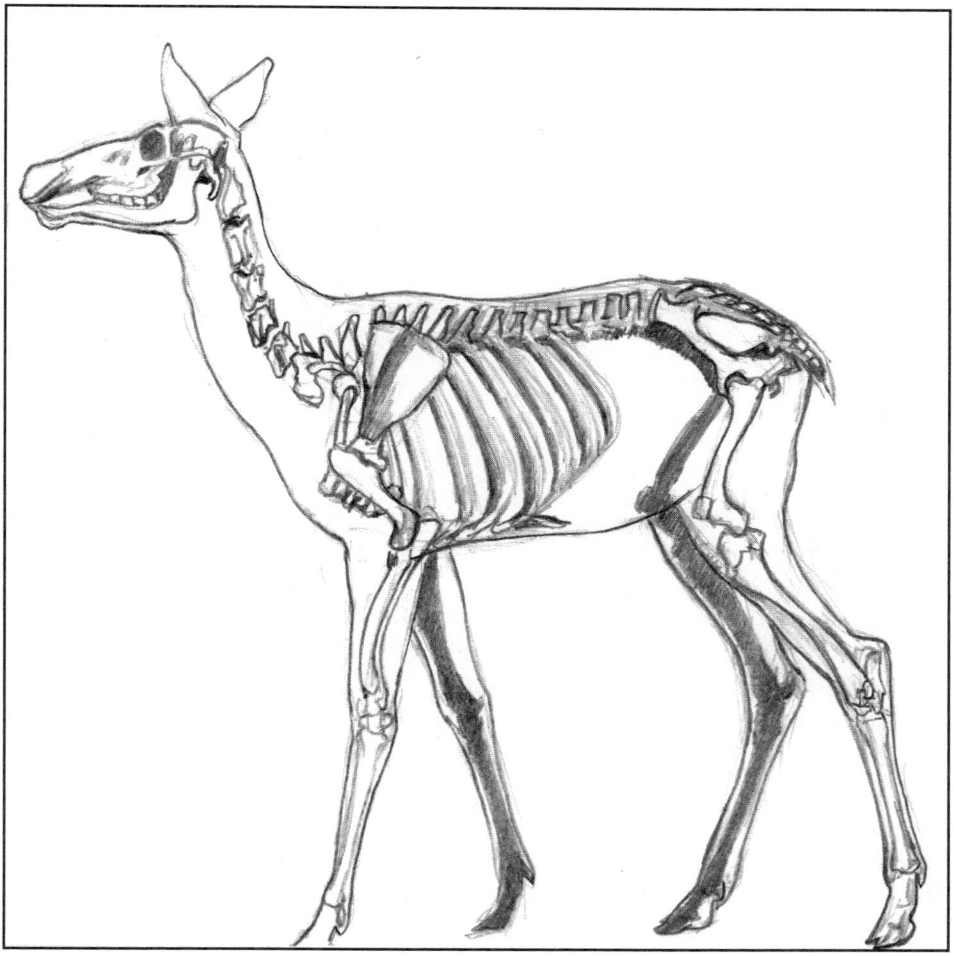

Skeletal view of a deer.

Bullets harvest deer by delivering massive shock, together with tissue and organ destruction. Bullets fired have considerable pounds of energy behind them, which can tear apart and break through bones, tissue, and the organs themselves. Whitetails die from shock, damage, and a substantial loss of blood.

Arrows fired from a bow have razor-sharp broadheads that are primarily designed to cut. Whitetails are harvested by cutting veins, arteries, and vital organs that result in the loss of blood. A well-placed shot through both lungs will cause the lungs to collapse and fail, thus resulting in death through suffocation. I personally recommend a heart shot or neck shot whenever possible as a quicker way to down a deer with a bow.

When using a bow capable of projecting an arrow above 45 pounds of pressure, a shooter who has the ability to fire an arrow deliberately and to the target effectively with every shot will cause a deer to drop much quicker with a neck or heart shot delivered from a bow. If you are able to use a high-poundage bow, a shot in these areas will drop a deer with an arrow as quickly as if you were using a rifle.

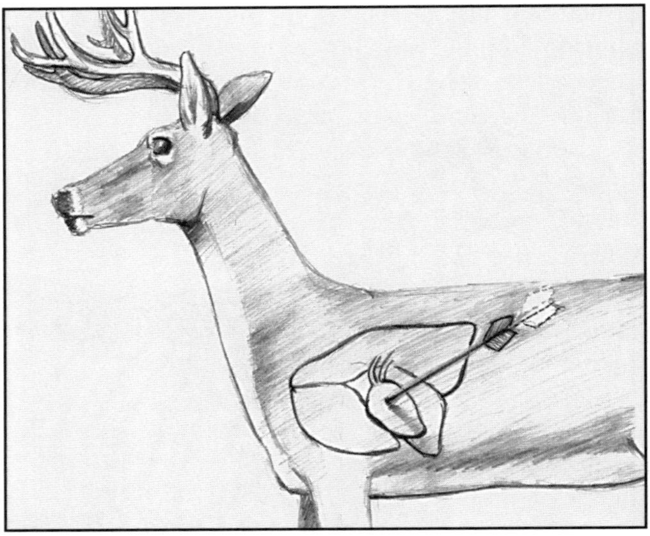

Perfect heart shot.

I have proved this repeatedly, as most of the deer I have taken with a bow have traveled less than forty yards when shot, if they did not drop instantly.

Too many hunters who shoot with a bow practice with a bulls-eye target, which I consider to be foolish. I have yet to see a deer in the woods with a target and bulls-eye strapped to them. If you take a target shooter who has the ability to place an arrow in the bulls-eye at thirty yards into the woods with you, chances are that he or she would find it difficult to shoot a whitetail deer. Yet when hunters practice at home or at the range, a majority will be shooting at round targets, thinking, "If I can get a tight group, I can kill a deer." That thinking is as wrong as saying, "If I have a gun that is sighted-in, I will always kill a whitetail."

Many times while hunting and in thick cover, you see parts of a deer but not the whole deer. The identification process is not easy for a beginner, and I will repeat a good way to see deer, as I did with my wife and also explained in an earlier chapter. Just remember that all things in the woods are vertical. To find a deer, look for the horizontals in the woods. Look for an ear twitching or the flicker of a tail; look for a horizontal patch of brown. Sometimes that is all you will see in the beginning. If you want to practice while someone else is driving, and you pass a section of woods that have deer, look through the woods for the horizontals, and you will focus on deer that are standing there. It took my wife, Mary, several times, but after a while, she was able to see deer in the woods easily while I was driving. After a while, you will be surprised at how many deer you will see by practicing this way.

I would like to point out that it is important for a new as well as a veteran hunter to avoid taking shots at moving deer. Whether you feel you are proficient with a firearm or bow, shots taken at deer moving should be avoided at all costs. Your chance of wounding or crippling a deer more than triples by taking these shots, besides the fact that these shots are unsafe.

Firearm and bow hunters have the responsibility to make quick, clean, and accurate kills and to recover all game that they shoot. Not some of the game or most of the game, but all of the game they shoot. If you do not feel this way, do not hunt, and take up another sport. Accurate shot placement is the key to both a quick, clean kill and the recovery of the game. It is important to know where whitetail's vital organs are located and not just have a general idea; their skeletal structure is just as important. They are the keys to place effective and accurate shots to drop the whitetail deer as quickly as possible. However, even the best of shots can be altered by the sudden movement of a deer or a branch that cannot be seen. If uncertain, do not take the shot.

While using a bow, the broadside shot offers the best penetration when aiming at a whitetail. It is the best of shots for a neck shot, a heart shot or the double lung shot that many recommend, because even the least amount of penetration will down the deer. You do need a minimum of 10 inches of penetration, and I usually recommend at least 14 inches to be sure. With the poundage available today, many bow hunters are able to shoot through a deer, which is recommended to deliver the maximum amount of damage.

When using a bow, many states require a minimum poundage weight to hunt with, which is about forty-five pounds. When I was teaching young or new hunters to shoot, I always recommended a fifty-pound bow. Youngsters may find this difficult to draw back, but I have seen a large number of hunters with forty-five pound bows not recover deer that were shot in the lungs. It may not seem like a big difference from forty-five to fifty-pound bows, but the difference is significant. To place an arrow at thirty yards into and through the heart of a deer, a fifty-pound bow is needed. At thirty yards, you will also drop a deer with a neck shot using a fifty-pound bow much easier.

Now many of you reading this may wonder how you judge yardages when you are in the field. As a new bow hunter, I found this difficult myself and often set up targets at different yardages to practice. To effectively practice before hunting, it is important not to shoot at only twenty-five or thirty-yard target distances. Practice is always the key, but another key is to practice at different yardages.

In the beginning, start your practices at twenty yards, then go to just above thirty yards; I usually practice at thirty-five yards. I also practice at forty yards but will only shoot at that distance with my seventy-pound compound bow. If I am using a crossbow, I practice at fifty-five to sixty yards as well. Once you have placed accurate shots at one distance, increase your distance by ten yards and practice again. Set up targets at different yard ranges and learn to judge distances.

Today you can buy a digital range finder, which takes all the guesswork out of determining yardages. However, back when I was a youngster, we did not have range finders, and you may not have yours with you all the time. It is a good practice to shoot without a range finder in the beginning. Once you can determine yardages accurately, then you can check yourself with a range finder if you have the time and if the deer is gracious enough to stand there and wait for you to figure out which pin to use when aiming at him or her. I have found the deer I have shot not to be that gracious and in a hurry most of the time. But then again, many were New York deer that were always in a hurry for one reason or another. In my new home state of Missouri, I'll be darned, if they aren't in a hurry here as well—go figure....

You will be glad you learned how to judge distances when you are in the field bow hunting, as eight or ten yards can make a big difference. Another

Elevated shot placement is important.

consideration is if you practice from the ground at a straight distance to your target and then sit twenty-five feet up in a tree stand, though your point of aim is the same, your arrow will hit the target differently. It is important to practice from an elevated position if you intend to hunt from an elevated tree stand.

More deer are missed or shot poorly by bow hunters who hunt from an elevated tree stand and practice by shooting at targets while they are on the ground. To get a clearer picture of this, get a twelve-foot ladder, a helper, and a piece of string to mark the distance from the base of the ladder to an object twenty yards away on the string and mark the string. Then stand on the top of the ladder, carefully, and have your helper walk to the target with the string and you will see how long the string comes to the target. Now realize this: while you are sitting in a tree stand that is twenty or thirty feet high: will change your impact by as much at twelve inches within twenty-five yards. The same is true when you are hunting the side of a steep ridge and aiming at a deer positioned thirty yards away and down, or when you are at the base of a hill shooting up. Not all shots at deer will be on the ground on even terrain, and it is important to know where you will be hunting and practice accordingly.

Ground level shot placement is important.

On quartering away shots, you have to determine shot placement in a three dimensional view. You have to be able to pick your shot placement and determine where the heavy bones are positioned inside a deer to avoid them, and the forward angle into the vital area if you are in an elevated stand, as most bow hunters are. The angle is very important and will determine the arrow path. The lesser the angle, the better your opportunity will be. The backbone and shoulder blades shield much of the vital organs, and you have to aim further back than you would if you were on the ground and on the same shooting plane as the deer is on. On the ground, the quartering away shot needs to be well behind the shoulder and lower to shoot through the heart of a deer, which sits low below the lungs.

Note the angle of the arrow in the shot from the elevated tree stand for a heart shot as opposed to the same shot from ground level. A quartering away shot is a good shot for a bow. Quartering towards you is not a recommended shot for a bow hunter, as it is extremely hard to make an accurate shot to hit the vital area of a whitetail and should be avoided until the deer presents a better position for you to shoot.

Chapter Twenty-Two

Tracking a Deer After the Shot

After the shot, tracking begins.

You have waited all year for this. It is your time of year, and what you have waited for through the spring and long summer months is finally here, the beginning of the whitetail deer hunting season.

You are in the woods and have picked this spot after you have done a number of scouting trips before the season, determining this to be the perfect spot to place your stand. There are many signs showing whitetail deer activity, which indicates this as a good crossing point between the feeding and bedding areas. You have decided to use a portable tree stand and have gotten up early to get ready and get into your stand a half hour before sunrise to allow the woods to quiet down.

You made the long walk through the woods with your Maglite® and walked as quietly as possible so you would not draw attention to your presence. You were sure to tie two ropes to your climbing stand, one to attach your unloaded firearm and another to a small pack to be able to pull both of them up to you when you are at the desired height.

You have locked the tree stand to the tree and checked your safety harness again to make sure you are in a safe position and are pulling up your firearm or bow. You are set and await a trophy whitetail to step out of the cover at first light.

You remember all that went into this day, the planning and preparation, and you are going over in your mind what you have included in your pack that you may need today. You made a checklist long before the season, and as you picked up what you needed, you checked it off the list and were sure to put it in a location where all your hunting equipment and supplies were easy to get to when you packed for the hunt.

The squirrels are beginning to stir, and a turkey has just left its roost and flown to the ground to begin his day of foraging with others in his flock that are now leaving their roost and calling to one another. You count about twelve in this group, all good size, and you estimate they average between twenty to twenty-five pounds each. You watch them wander off, as you are not here to shoot a turkey, but the most elusive of all big game animals, the whitetail deer.

What was that? You see movement in the brush and the back of a whitetail moving in heavy cover. You cannot see the head yet, but the body is large, and in a few moments, you will know for sure. Your heart is pumping hard. You wonder if your breath, which is beginning to form a small cloud of warm air coming out of your mouth, will be seen from the ground if the deer looks up. You freeze in place, slow your breathing, trying not to hyperventilate as you see horns of a mature whitetail buck.

You slowly raise your rifle from your lap as the buck makes his way to the end of the cover. He is standing about seventy yards away from your stand. You put the butt of your rifle stock to your shoulder, click the safety off slowly, put your finger on the trigger and begin to squeeze. A squirrel begins to chatter, and the deer takes an unpredicted step forward as your shot is fired.

You hit the deer, but it is farther back than you wanted, and the woods exploded as the deer took flight through the woods toward cover and out of sight.

Your heart is racing a mile a minute; you're breathing heavy, and you are experiencing one heck of an adrenalin rush. That is all part of the feeling you get when you shoot a deer. I get that feeling every time I take a deer myself. If I didn't, I would have stopped hunting a long time ago. Its part of the feeling you will have with seeing sights and hearing sounds that you alone, as a hunter, will experience. Others will only see it on TV and miss most of the feelings, sights and sounds only you will enjoy. You are part of the cycle and a part of nature in its purest form.

Like most, you will not be able to express all that you experience, for how do you describe the smell of the woods? You're sitting next to an apple grove where just a few feet away an alfalfa field was just hayed, and the aroma fills your lungs combined with the scent of apples in a grove and flowers below. How would you describe a turkey leaving its roost, or seeing a barrel owl flying through the woods in search of food? You will see a show of nature with every hunt or every passing of time on your stand.

Watch the deer after the shot to determine the location.

Now you have a task facing you. You have just shot a mature buck, and as luck has it, your shot was off the mark and further back than you anticipated. The first thing you should have done was to mark in your mind the last place you saw the deer standing and focus on that spot; pick either a rock, a tree, a brush pile, or something that will help you walk to the exact spot you last saw the deer, *after* you check the spot where the deer stood when you hit him.

You have the spot fixed in your mind where you last saw the deer before he went into the woods. You know the spot the deer was standing when you shot him, so now what do you do? Well, the very first thing to do is unload your firearm, then put the safety on and lower your rifle down the tree. In case you've forgotten, you are twenty feet up in a tree. Don't laugh; some people forget this after they have shot a deer, and eventually you will hear stories about hunters who have walked out of their tree stands after they shot a deer. It does happen. However, so it doesn't happen to you, start to climb down from your tree stand, and be sure to adjust your safety harness as you descend, keeping it attached to the tree until you have both feet on the ground.

You're on the ground now, and you have put your stand together. You don't want to carry it with you when you are tracking the deer, so you leave it by the tree you climbed. You have the tree marked with red or orange surveyor's tape so you can find it again easily. If you are hunting on state land, be sure it is locked to the tree. If you are hunting on your own property or on another's property, and no one will be hunting there, you may not need to lock your stand to the tree. Nevertheless, I have heard of many hunters who have lost their stands accidentally after they did not have them securely locked to trees. Enough said.

If you shot your deer in one spot, and the last time you saw the deer was in a spot further away, go to the spot where you actually hit the deer. Once you are there, look for hair and blood.

Look at the hair: Is the hair color white? If you have shot your deer further back from the heart and the hair is white, it is a good indication you might have gut shot the deer. You can determine this by picking up some of the hair and blood and seeing if it has a foul smell. If it does, and the blood is a dark red color, it is a good indication that your deer is gut shot.

Let me take this time to tell you a little about the blood you will see. If you shoot a deer and the deer runs off, you go to the spot you hit the deer and look for both hair and blood. If you find dark hair and pinkish blood with bubbles in it, it is a sign of a deer hit in the lung area, and chances are your deer will not be far if you are using a rifle, shotgun slug or muzzle loader. Whitetails shot in the lungs generally will not go far, especially if both lungs are penetrated. I have seen them travel 200 yards when hit in the lungs, but generally, with a good solid lung shot with a firearm, the deer will travel less than 100 yards. If there is a ridge nearby, deer will head up the ridge as an escape from what they perceive as danger and generally be found at the base of the ridge or half-way up the ridge with its white belly showing that it is down. If you are hunting near a swamp or a pond, many deer will head for water. If the shot is poor, and did not go through the deer but just grazed him, the deer may lay in the mud. I have seen deer with broken legs lay in the mud and roll their side in it. Whitetail deer, if shot poorly, don't just lie around and die. Some will if not disturbed, but the majority will not. Why not, you ask? Because your average hunter is impatient. We will discuss more about that.

If you reach the spot of impact and you see white hair and no blood, one of two things has happened. You either shot at the deer and hit the deer low and just grazed the hair off it, or you hit the deer low and it is bleeding internally. In that case you *wait* for a minimum of forty-five minutes to one hour from the time you hit the deer to begin your search. Mark the point where you hit the deer and then again at the last spot you saw the deer before it disappeared. It will take a while before the deer feels weak and wants to lie down.

If you get to the spot you hit the deer and see rich, red blood and a lot of it, mark the spot and go to the last spot you saw the deer before it disappeared and mark that also, then *WAIT* about thirty minutes before you start looking. You need to wait to allow the deer to lie down. With rich, red blood and a lot of it, you made a good hit and the blood is pumping out. In about thirty minutes, the deer will seek a spot to lie down.

Most hunters are *impatient*. No, not you, I am talking about everyone else who hunts whitetail deer, but not you. You are the exception that we all want to become —congratulations. Let me know if you are interested in buying a bridge, as I have a good deal for you and would like to speak to you later on. So hold that thought.

Now for the rest of us who are impatient, we need to curb our enthusiasm just a bit. I know you want to run through the woods and find your buck, but if you do that, you will be added to the list of hunters who do not recover their deer.

Whitetail deer will take their last breath trying to get away from you or any movement or noise they perceive to be danger when they are wounded. Your absolute best way to recover your deer is to let the deer lie down and bleed. Your deer will lie down, but only if you stay put and don't begin the tracking process for one hour as a rule. Now that person who I was talking to who isn't impatient, you should wait an hour also. By giving any deer that ran off one hour, it is almost a guarantee that the deer will lay down. Once the deer lies down, blood will be pumping out, and the deer will get weak. The longer the deer lays down, the weaker the deer will get. That is a guarantee. However, if you go running through the woods now, two things will happen. First, you will be pushing the deer to either run or use every bit of strength it has to move further away. Second, your deer will be pumping adrenalin throughout its body, and should you recover the deer, be prepared for a strong-tasting deer when you cut it up to prepare it for dinner.

Have you ever tasted venison that tasted gamey? Many hunters who race down their deer after the shot is fired cause their deer to have a stronger taste. If you allow your deer to lie down and die, you can avoid this strong-tasting venison. This I have proven many times to hunters. Deer that have been pushed and run until they expire taste like meat that was unprepared or cooked rather poorly. Of course another reason is that many people who are otherwise good cooks do not know how to properly prepare venison. Later in this book, I will give you recipes that will have venison melting in your mouth. Getting back to the hunt....

You have shot the deer a bit further back than you wanted, and low, indicating possibly a gut shot deer; what do you do. You wait a minimum of one hour to play it safe. Now look for blood. You may not see blood on the ground, as it could be hitting brush or saplings, but you walk slowly, but *not on the tracks of the deer or blood path. Not stepping on the blood*, you stay to the side. If you have a young hunter, keep him or her off the tracks or blood trail.

With every splatter of blood, mark it waist high with orange surveyor's tape so you can see it from a distance. You did remember to put orange or red surveyor's tape in your pack, didn't you? This is another reason to have it. Not just to mark the trail to your stand, but to track the deer you shot if it did not drop instantly. Oh, you do have it? Good, you had me worried; let's continue.

You have found blood, and the trail is good. What do you do if the blood trail stops? When that happens you look back at all the orange tape tied to trees and bushes and see the direction the deer is heading, and then look about ten to twenty feet ahead for more blood. If you have not seen an area with a large pool of blood, indicating the deer has laid down, slow down. You can either go back to camp to get help, which will give the deer time to lay down if it did not already, or just take a twenty-minute break and slow down a bit. I recommend you go for help to have more eyes looking for blood. If the temperature is below 30 degrees, the meat will not spoil if you wait until the next day to track or resume tracking. Naturally, it is best if you find the deer this day, but if darkness occurs, stop the

Mark with orange tape where you find blood.

tracking. In one night, your deer will be okay from predators, as they like a foul smell to locate their food. Your deer will be safe until morning; resume tracking at first light with help.

If you had to wait until the next day, relax. There is an excellent chance your deer is down; the meat is still good if the temperature was below 30 degrees during the night. You are on your way to recover your deer.

Make sure you bring your fellow hunters or friends to the spot you last saw blood, and have them see the tape and the direction the deer was traveling. Have the others stay off the deer's tracks, and also them to call out when they see blood. Be sure to continue to mark blood sightings. If the deer has traveled and the blood trail stops, have all make wide circles to try to find blood or the downed deer. Chances are your deer will not be lying too far ahead from when you left the trail the night before.

Bow hunting tracking is a bit different. When you hit a deer with a bow and the deer does not drop instantly or within eyesight, mark in your mind where you

Get help to track your deer whenever possible.

hit the deer with the arrow and again where you last saw the deer before it disappeared. Stay in your stand or on the ground where you shot the deer and wait for at least one to two hours before you begin the tracking process. Deer hit with an arrow do not die from shock or rapid blood loss. They do have some shock, especially if they are hit with a high poundage bow or crossbow arrow or bolt, but it is not the same as with a firearm. You need to allow the deer to lie down, and it is extremely important not to push a deer hit by an arrow. Whitetails shot with an arrow can travel far if pushed. Be patient. Relax, have a cup of coffee from the Thermos you don't want me to see you have in your pack. I will turn my head and not see you drinking your coffee or tea, or the soda can you snuck in your coat pocket that I heard sloshing around. You are forgiven. Don't let it happen again, but for now, you are forgiven. You could have at least brought one for me also, but we won't get into that now. Now is the time to relax and decide where you are going to hang the buck. Will it be in your den or proudly displayed in your living room? Naturally, it will be with your wife or husband's permission, because let's face it, if you are the king or queen of your castle, then I am the tooth faerie. That being said, you are thinking about where it will be displayed with prominence as you wait. You are relaxing and taking a sip of refreshment as you look for your orange surveyor's tape, your field dressing knife, or wondering if you have to dress your deer out, or is someone going to do it for you?

Just so you know, I almost have my wife, Mary, to the point that she can do the whole process herself. She allows me to finish it so I can keep in shape and don't forget how. Ahhh, the gracious wife who is always thinking on our behalf.

Err… getting back to the deer. You want to be sure to wait between one to two hours with a bow shot to allow the deer to lay down and feel at ease that they are not being followed or pushed.

You begin your search the same way as if you used a firearm to shoot the deer. You go to the point of impact and look for your arrow, if you shot through the deer. If you find your arrow, and it passed through the deer, look at the color of the blood to see if there is any hair. If it is white hair, smell the arrow to see if it has a foul smell indicating a gut shot or determine the position your arrow went into the deer.

If you shot poorly and do not see any sign of the deer lying down after 60 yards once the deer is out of sight, end the tracking. Wait another two hours and begin tracking again. If it is late in the afternoon, end the search and give the deer the night to lie down. If the temperature will be below 30 degrees and the deer lies down and bleeds, the meat will be okay.

I hunted whitetail deer on Long Island, New York, and remember one hunt in particular where I was bow hunting. I was in the woods and got an unusual shot at a nice 10-pointer about three miles from my house in the woods. I remember this hunt because I had bronchitis; it was the opening of rifle season, and my doctor advised me not to go hunting. It was the first time in thirty-five years that I missed opening day of rifle season. I was calling my friends in the hunting camp I belonged to every six hours to get an update. I was resting but my phone bill was adding up.

On the third day, my fever broke, and I told my wife to drive me to a spot by the woods where I was going to go bow hunting on Long Island. I was following doctor's orders and not hunting upstate. I had my cell phone to call my wife if I felt bad in the woods. Besides, I told Mary I would be home in four hours regardless.

I got into the woods, sat on a blow-down and was about to put a hearing device in my ear to enhance the sounds of the woods and dropped the battery. I got on my hands and knees to look for the battery and saw three does running through the woods; they stopped about twenty yards away. Now you have to picture me on all fours, my bow across a blow-down to my left and the deer standing to my right. I slowly picked up a handful of leaves with the battery included and slowly put them in my pocket as I reached for my bow when the last doe looked over her shoulder. I froze and turned my head slowly to see a nice mature 10-pointer walking to me on my left side. I got to my bow, and as I was standing up, I fired at the buck, aiming directly at his heart. As I released the arrow, the buck turned in mid-air, and I shot the deer directly in the butt. I could not believe my shot, and to this day, I think I heard the buck say, "Ooooooo!"

The arrow went directly up that buck's butt and about four inches was sticking out of it when we found him. Well, I went back to my house on foot because my cell phone battery was too low to call. My wife asked how I was. I told her what happened, and she could not believe it was a 10-pointer and that I was only in the woods less than fifteen minutes before I got the shot at the buck. Well, I took my wife to where I shot the buck, and damn if that buck didn't go more than 600 yards before he dropped, even though I gave him a good two hours to lie down. After my wife and I found the deer, I field dressed it, and we were dragging him out of the woods when my friend, a conservation officer, was driving by on the road; I flagged him down. When he stopped, I showed him the deer, and he asked where I shot him. I told him to look inside, and he saw clear cut marks on the inside of the deer's ribs, showing the path of the arrow. I told him not to tell any of my friends where I worked, since he knew them all, as I did not want them to know where I hit the deer.

Well, the conservation officer, my friend, helped load the deer and hang it from a tree in my backyard, then immediately left my house and went to where I worked and told everyone the story.

My first day back to work from a two-week vacation, I had to take a driver's safety course with others from my job. My wife joined me for the class, and when we went in, everyone there had a bull's eye taped to the back of their pants, thanks to my friend. It took me until I retired to live that down, but I did.

The following year I shot a nice eight-point buck with my seventy-pound compound bow directly through both lungs at thirty-eight yards. I was in the woods about a mile from my house when the buck stopped by my ground blind and I made the shot. The deer ran about fifty yards, and I saw him lie down. I walked back to the house, waited two hours, and again started my tracking. It was near dark and the buck was not where I saw him lie down, so I marked the spot and went back home to pick up the hunt the next morning with my wife. The next morning was Saturday, and Mary and I set out to get to the spot marked where I last saw the deer and found blood. We followed blood, and I got to a small field and saw the deer. As I approached the deer with my bow in hand, the deer jumped up from a pool of blood and ran to the next woodlot.

I told Mary we needed to wait to let the deer lay down again, and we waited an hour. Now mind you, this deer was shot the afternoon before and laid down the whole night but was still not dead with a double lung shot.

We waited the hour, then I took the lead and followed the blood track to high grass. Mary walked behind me, and about thirty yards in the high grass, the deer stood up, and we both could see the lung shot from the day before. The deer was about another thirty yards away, and I put another arrow right next to where I shot him the day before. The deer ran sixty yards before it laid down. We let him lay down for close to forty-five minutes again, and then the deer died.

This is the first and only deer that I had this happen to. It took a lot for this deer to die, with two separate shots directly though both lungs with a seventy-pound bow.

When I field dressed this deer, there was not a drop of blood inside the deer, and how it lived as long as it did without being pushed is still a mystery to me. This deer never should have gotten up from where it laid when it first laid down, as the entire area where the deer laid down was covered in blood.

Whitetail deer have an amazing ability to surprise you, even after they are shot. When bow hunting, if I do not see the deer lie down, I now wait a minimum of two hours. Since that day, I avoid a lung shot and go for a neck or heart shot with the bow and with a firearm.

When going to track a deer or any big game animal, you have to be patient and wait. No matter how hard it is, you have to wait it out before you begin tracking.

Tracking in the snow is a piece of cake as opposed to following tracks in the rain or wet conditions. Different manufacturers carry a spray that will enhance the blood color on the ground and turn it blue to be seen easier. All you need is a bank account to buy all the bottles you need, for I have found them to go empty after the first fifty yards. They work quite well, but make sure you have about four or five spray bottles. Other manufacturers have tracking lights that enhance the color of the blood, which are supposed to work quite well. For the last few years, I have not found the need to use it, because with a neck shot, the deer always drops instantly. You will hear me say this a lot, but unless you are accurate in your shot placement, do not try a neck shot. I make it a habit to shoot every few weeks, and I feel that is necessary to ensure accurate shot placement.

For me to give you the key for effective tracking, the first rule is *WAIT* as long as possible: one to two hours if using a firearm, and two to three hours if you have shot a deer with a bow. No one will take your deer; relax and do the wait. Then mark the blood trail with orange or red surveyor's tape waist high everywhere you find blood to have a clear trail to where the deer is heading in case you lose the blood trail or it stops. If the deer does not lie down after sixty to seventy yards, stop and let the deer lie down, as you may be pushing him. Take your time, be patient, and you will find the deer. Whenever possible, get help, the more eyes looking the better. Do not give up; you owe it to yourself and to the deer to find it.

Chapter Twenty-Three

The Easy Way to Field Dress a Deer

Now that your deer is down, field dressing begins.

All the preparation has paid off, and you are in the woods standing next to a deer you have just shot and killed. You have approached the deer and determined by touching his eye with the end of your rifle barrel or bow that the deer is dead; what do you do now? The first thing you need to do is fill out your tag and attach it to your deer, which is the rule in most states. If you are hunting with a doe tag or bonus tag, fill out the tag and attach it to the carcass as required by law in the state you are hunting. I usually bring a few plastic ties to attach the tag, and sometimes I carry some plastic strips if I am going to attach the tag to the antlers. I wrap the tag in plastic to keep it in place with the aid of plastic ties.

I have found it much easier to take off my jacket or coat and lay it down on a dry spot and place my rifle or bow on my coat. I then take out a some alcohol wipes, which I carry in my backpack, and also some paper towels, and put them on my coat as well to be ready for the clean-up later on. I next take out one pair of long field dressing gloves and put the package on my coat as well, so all field dressing equipment is in one spot. If I am going to save the heart or liver, I bring large freezer bags and put them on my coat as well. I then reach for my buck knife, which I always use for field dressing. When I was younger, I used single-edge razors, but I prefer a buck knife with a three-to-four inch razor-sharp blade. I recommend that you lay out all your equipment that you will use first so you are not scrambling later on to avoid a mess or a problem. As with all hunting steps, preparation well in advance is an important key to remember. I usually put in my backpack or fanny-pack all that I need to field dress a deer. I have enclosed a list for you to copy or use, and I recommend that you look at mine and make one for yourself. This way when you are packing for the hunt, you have all that is necessary with you in one place for when the time comes to field dress your deer.

The length of rope will be for dragging your deer to camp or to your vehicle. I have included it in your field dressing kit, because I cannot begin to tell you how many hunters forget to bring it into the woods. If you have a length of rope in your field dressing kit, you will have it with you.

Field dressing a deer does not have to be a gory task as new hunters think. You have done the hard part already. You have shot a whitetail, and if it did not drop immediately, you have tracked it. Field dressing a deer, after you have done several, should take about fifteen or twenty minutes and is rather easy. It usually is the thought process of field dressing a deer that makes a new hunter nervous. Relax, and you will do just fine. I am going to walk you through every step of the process.

Note: If you shot your deer with an arrow and you did not recover your arrow with your broadhead, be sure to check your deer before you put your fingers in the deer to field dress it. Broadheads are razor sharp, and you can get a good cut from an imbedded broadhead or a broken razor piece if it is still in the deer. Check to make sure there is a clear entry and exit hole and there are no pieces of your broadhead embedded in the carcass. You should check your deer even if you shot it with a rifle, shotgun, or muzzle-loader. Bow hunting season often precedes rifle season. All deer should be checked to see if the whitetail has a bruise that could indicate a non-fatal broadhead entry.

Step 1:

Move the deer so that if possible, the belly of the deer is facing downhill or on a slight angle down slope. Okay, do that now. That wasn't hard, now was it?

You are doing this so that when you cut into the deer, the blood will come out and go down. There will not usually be much blood.

Position the deer in an open area so you are not fighting and working around trees or brush. It is also a good idea to find a dry spot to work so you are not kneeling in mud. If there is snow on the ground, that is okay. Try finding an area *nearby* that is open, as you do not want to have to drag your deer any distance. Field dressing is done in the field and not back at camp. It is much easier to move a field dressed deer as opposed to one that is not, as you will be dragging an extra twenty to thirty pounds if your deer is not field dressed. Some hunters do wait, but it is recommended that you field dress in the field.

Step 2:

While the deer is lying with its belly downhill, take out your field dressing gloves and put them on now. Field dressing gloves are long, oversized, and will allow you to put your hands into the finger portion and all the way up your arm to your shoulders. Now pick up your razor sharp knife—open it if it is a folding knife—and go to the deer. Standing to the side, insert your knife just below the breastbone and make a small incision about two inches. Stick the knife into the deer just enough to allow any gas to escape. If it took you several hours or from the day before to find your deer, chances are there will be some gas buildup. This is okay, but stand to the side so as not to breathe the escaping gas, as it may have an odor to it. If you have found your deer and it is still warm, the gas will be minimal, so relax.

Step 3:

Go to the back end of the deer and cut around the anus of the deer as shown in example 3a. Hold the deer's tail out of the way and cut around the outside of the vent as shown to loosen the vent tube. Then take about six inches of twine and tie the vent tube closed with a knot using the twine as shown in the example 3b. This is a simple process, and you are doing this to prevent any matter from escaping from the vent to the meat as you pull it through from the inside.

Step 4:

You are now going to go around to where you made the first cut and extend the incision on the belly of the deer to the pelvic bone. It is easier if you get on one knee and have the wind to your back so there will be no odor in your face. There should be very little odor, but it is a good idea to keep the wind hitting your back. Start by scoring the skin, then place two fingers between the inside skin and the outer skin (hide), raising it as you cut, not cutting too deeply, as you do not want to puncture any organs. After you have scored the skin, lift the skin with your fingers on one hand, holding it up, and insert the knife deeper. As you puncture the cavity, you will see the organs. Keep lifting the skin so you cut through to your first incision without cutting the organs down the full length of the belly. Once you have made this cut, lay the deer back down, and the organs will come out. You should now have the deer cut from the breastbone (bottom of the ribcage) to the pelvic bone. Some hunters cut higher, but it is not necessary, as the cut from the breastbone to the pelvic bone is all that is required for field dressing.

Note: You do not want to cut or remove the genitals of a buck. Leave them in place, as most states want the sex of the deer to be intact when going through game checks.

Step 5:

Now it is necessary to cut around the inside diaphragm to separate the organs from the inside cavity of the deer. This is a simple task, and there should not be much blood inside the cavity at this point if you have the deer's belly facing downhill. Separate the organs from the inside cavity. Then reach inside the neck and make a cut to separate the windpipe, then go to the anal vent and cut away any attachments to be able to remove the anal vent. There will be a small urine sack inside the deer's lower cavity. **Do Not** puncture it with your knife when you are cutting away any attachment to the anal tube vent, as it could spoil the meat if punctured. Be aware of this.

Step 6:

Now all organs are unattached and should simply roll out of the deer and be separated from the deer carcass. At this point, if you want to save the heart and the liver, you can put the heart in one bag and the liver in another. Even if you do not save the liver, you should inspect it. If you see any white pus areas, it could be the sign of a sick deer. If you notice them and are not sure, put the liver in a large plastic bag that you have in your field dressing kit and have it looked at, either at a game check station or by a veteran hunter who is familiar with field dressing and knows what to look for.

Step 7:

Now that the organs and intestines are separated from the deer, move the deer on its belly to allow any blood in the cavity to drain out completely.

Congratulations, you have now field dressed your deer in seven easy steps. While the blood is draining out, remove your field dressing gloves and put them in a plastic bag to take them out of the woods to dispose of. You can take a few alcohol wipes, clean your field dressing knife, and put the soiled wipes into the bag with your field dressing gloves to be disposed of later after you leave the woods. Wipe down your hands if you have gotten any blood on them, and use a paper towel to dry them off, putting any paper towels you used into the plastic bag.

All that is left now is to move the deer back on to its side and away from the field dressing area. If you shot a buck, you can raise the deer's front legs and put them on the antlers, attach a rope around the neck of the deer and then to your shoulder harness to drag the deer out of the woods.

Field Dress Step 1

Field Dress Step 2

Field Dress Step 3a

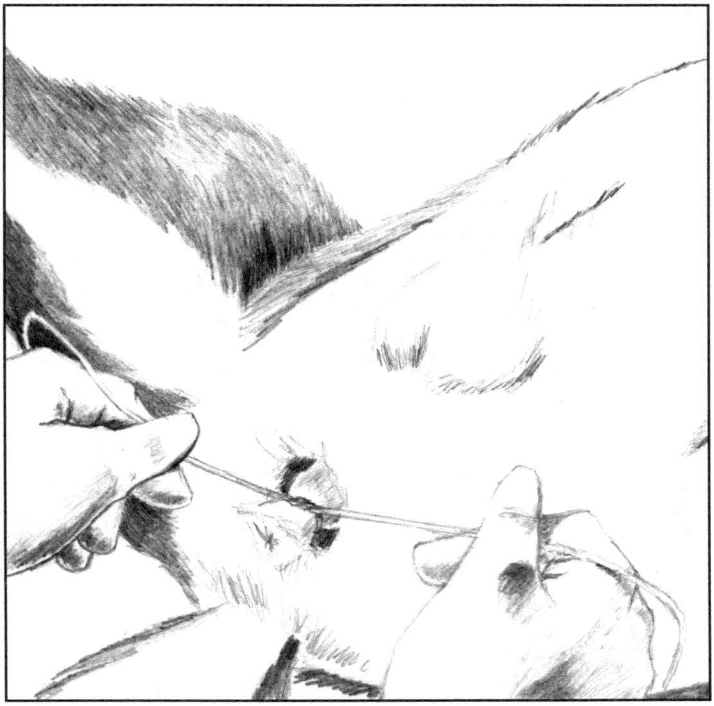

Field Dress Step 3b

Field Dress Step 4

Field Dress Step 5a

Field Dress Step 5b

Field Dress Step 6

Field Dress Step 7

Hang your deer to clean the cavity makes the job easier.

Remember that this is an animal, which can weigh from 90 to 195 pounds. You will be dragging the deer back either to your hunting camp or to your vehicle. Be sure to take regular breaks in between the dragging process. I recommend you walk fifty feet, and then put the deer down, and rest or catch your breath. This is not a marathon or a test of your strength or ability. You already proved your ability by harvesting this deer. This is the return process of getting the deer out of the woods safely.

If you have a buck and plan on having it mounted, you want to have the antlers and neck above the ground as not to damage either. Walk slowly; avoid rocks that you can stumble on or tree roots and blow downs. If you have to cross a stream, raise the carcass and avoid dragging your deer through water. Try to avoid leaves and dirt from getting inside the deer's cavity. Some hunters wrap their deer in an orange tarp, which is a good color for safety, which will also protect the deer's cavity.

When you get back to camp or to your home, lift the deer up by tying a rope around the deer's neck, and hoist him up as shown. Then rinse off the inside cavity of the deer with a pan of water or a hose, whichever is available, and wipe the inside cavity dry. Some hunters remove the flanks to give them a larger opening to work. *Do Not Do This* as this is the brisket area of the deer, and you are wasting meat. Also, do not cut away the flanks on either side of the incision you made for field dressing, which is a waste of meat as well. If your deer will hang for more than a day, put a stick inside the deer to make the opening larger to air out the inside cavity, then remove it later for transport.

After you have cleaned the inside cavity and it is airing, you are ready to transport your deer to either a butcher or home for you to process the deer yourself.

A pan of water and clean cloth will be sufficient.

Years ago, the majority of hunters would tie a deer to the top of their vehicles and drive back home to display their success in their quest and to show off their deer. This should be avoided, as many people, including children, when you pass on the road and in towns or rest stops can be offended by the sight of a dead deer with its tongue hanging out. If you need to tie your deer on top of your vehicle, please cover it with a tarp to avoid offending anyone. If the temperature is below 40 degrees, it will not spoil any meat if you cover the deer for a two or three hour ride home. If you have the room inside your vehicle or if you have a cargo carrier on the bumper, you can put the deer there and cover it, and that will work fine. There are some who do not believe in hunting, and young children could get scared at the sight. Common sense is the best way to look at this, and I hope you will use good judgment.

Hunting is a sport not to be thought of as offensive, but everyone has an opinion. It may be the end of November or December when you are returning with your deer, and many people can be out holiday shopping and not familiar with the sport you love. Think about it. You will not spoil your deer meat, by having the deer inside your vehicle or covered with a tarp.

On the return trip, decide how to process your deer. Will you have roasts, steaks, stew meat, chop meat or sausage? Never tie a deer on the hood of a vehicle for transport, because engine heat will harm the meat. A deer carcass can be hung for a few days if it is first cooled and the ambient temperature stays below 35 degrees, but I generally do not like to hang a deer long, as I like to process my deer quickly.

Chapter Twenty-Four

Skinning Your Deer

You have brought your deer back to camp or back home and decided that you want to either have the hide tanned or wish to process your deer yourself, and you need to remove the hide. You may have decided to have a trophy mounted and want to bring the head and neck cape to the taxidermy shop and then process your deer. Skinning a whitetail deer by yourself is a simple task. It will require a sharp knife with a blade around six inches long, and a gambrel with hooks set 24 inches apart. If you do not have these hooks already set up on a wall in your garage or shed where you will skin your deer, you can stop at a local hardware store and purchase hooks, a meat saw or a hack saw.

If you are taking your deer to a professional butcher, usually the butcher will skin out your deer for you and include a price from $25 to $35 for doing so, which will take him an average of ten to fifteen minutes. If you are having a trophy mounted and tell the butcher this, the average price for a butcher to skin out the neck and salt the hide for you to bring to the taxidermist is around $25, and then they will add another $5 to skin the remainder of the deer.

Skinning your deer is easy. Follow my steps.

These fees can be avoided by skinning your deer yourself. In the beginning, if this is your first deer, you can figure it will possibly take you about forty-five minutes to do it correctly with taking your time and not rushing. If you have help, you can take about ten to fifteen minutes off that time. After you have skinned a few deer, you will develop your own style and begin in a certain way. I have found the average time it takes to skin a deer correctly once you have done a few is about fifteen minutes. I prefer to skin a deer I have harvested myself and process my own deer to get the cuts of venison I like.

Many new hunters and even some veteran hunters wait to take their deer back home before they decide to skin their deer, as they wish to take pictures. Some say that by hanging a deer for three days, it will age the meat, which they say is more desirable. Then they will take longer to skin their deer, as the carcass is frozen and more difficult to skin.

I always like to skin a deer while the carcass is still warm, as the process is much easier. Then I will process the deer myself, but on occasions, I have waited 24 hours to process the deer. To be honest, I have not found a difference in taste by waiting and letting a deer hang as opposed to processing right off. Some say they can taste the difference, but I firmly believe if you have shot a deer and your deer dropped immediately or did not run a long distance before it expired, that alone is the major factor that contributes to the taste of the venison.

You will hear some hunters comment that they like to shoot a young deer as opposed to an older deer because the young taste like veal. Let me clear that issue up right now. I firmly believe hunters say this because they only saw a young deer and that was the only shot they got and used the taste excuse to cover themselves.

Venison prepared properly tastes the same if you shot a young deer of six months or one that is five years old. Remember this, and let the young ones grow up and put weight on them. The tenderloin of a six-month-old doe or a five-year-old doe tastes the same.

An animal that is grain fed as opposed to grazing is what produces the different taste. If you take a young cow, put it in a pen, and give it corn and grain, it is going to affect the taste of the meat. Not the age, but what it is fed, determines this.

Young deer eat what the older deer eat. Unless you shoot a fawn on mother's milk that is usually a tiny immature deer, which should not be taken, then you may end up with about 12 to 15 pounds of meat, if you are lucky. These tiny young deer do taste different, BUT should not be harvested. It is a myth, a story that has been told through the years, and some people now actually believe to be true because they heard it enough. If you shoot a young deer poorly and that young deer runs a while before it expires, it will have a strong taste, just like the older ones who run. How quickly you drop your deer, the preparation, and using a good recipe are the keys to delicious and mouth-watering venison that will melt in your mouth. That, my friend, you can take to the bank. At the end of this book, I will include a few of my select recipes, which will change the way you will cook venison in the future. I have several fantastic recipes, which I have prepared for my closest friends throughout the years. I know you will enjoy them and adopt several as your new way to prepare venison dishes, which will make anyone who eats it enjoy the taste of venison. Recipe number two is my all time favorite dish.

In order to skin your deer easily, you will need to make a hanging board, called a gambrel, to hoist your deer. This is very easy to make if you do not have hooks already set up in an area to work on your deer. You will need two large stainless steel hooks that you can purchase from a good hardware store, which can be nothing more than stainless steel coat hooks with three holes for screws. Take a piece of 2 x 4 lumber 48 inches long, and put each hook 18 to 20 inches from either end and attach the hooks. In the middle of the 2 x 4, drill a hole to put a rope, if you do not wish to mount the gambrel to a wall. Once that is made, you will need a skinning knife and a handsaw. For now, let us get to skinning your deer as the first step in the process.

Step 1

You need to have the deer laying flat on a long table or on the floor on a plastic tarp if you do not mind bending down for this step. You are now going to cut the legs off the deer one inch below the knee joint. You can use a saw, but I have found a circular or reciprocating saw to work just fine. Just be careful if you are going to use an electrical saw. It would be a good idea to have someone hold the leg as you do it. If you are doing it alone, be mindful of the position of your hand holding the deer's leg in relationship to the moving blade. This skinning step is simple and will avoid the headache of trying to skin an area that is not necessary to skin. You will not lose any meat by doing this, and it is a time saver.

Step 2

It is now time to hang your deer. Some people hang their bucks by attaching a rope to the deer's antler or head and then to a rafter or hook they have attached to a beam in their garage or having a rope over a tree limb. *This is wrong,* and you are making more work for yourself by doing this. Hang the deer by its rear legs, whether it is a buck or a doe. Make a cut through the skin about four inches above the knee joint into an area between the tendon, which is called the hock, and leg bone on each rear leg. Put one hook in one hole you have made and the other hook into the other hole on the opposite leg. If you do not have secure hooks on a wall, put a rope through the hole you drilled and hoist the deer up to where you can work on each leg just below the hooks.

Hanging a deer by the antler or neck will be a problem for skinning as you want to skin towards the head at all times. Remember that whitetail deer shed their antlers late towards the end of December or early to mid-January. If the buck you are going to skin has a weak antler and you try to lift it with a rope tied around the antler, you could have a deer fall into your lap when you have a razor sharp knife in your hand for skinning. Avoid the urge and hang all deer by their rear legs for safety.

Step 3

Now it is time to start skinning. Pick up you skinning knife and one rear leg on the deer. Cut the inside of the skin from the area of the leg you removed to the inside of the deer's thighs. Pull the skin firmly as you cut in a downward direction at the same time as you are making small cuts.

Do not let your knife cut too deeply, as you do not want to cut any meat; just remove the hide from the meat. Continue to free the hide on one rear leg and thigh, and then go to the next rear leg and do the same. Be sure to watch the hand you are using for pulling and the end of the knife. The same is true if someone is helping you by pulling and you are cutting.

Step 4

Once you have freed the skin around both rear legs and thighs and the tail, pull the hide downward firmly and it will peel easily, especially if the hide is warm. If you waited and the hide is cold, it may take pulling a little harder, but it will peel down. Use your skinning knife to free any areas that might hang up. The skin should come down about three quarters at this point and to the front shoulders.

Step 5

Now that you are three quarters done, cut into the skin on the inside of the deer's breast area by the center of the breastbone. Work with of your skinning knife, and grab the skin firmly, pulling the skin off the breast area of the deer and down to one of the deer's shoulders, then to the front leg and off the leg to where you cut the leg off. Use your skinning knife to free any area that is holding up by pulling and cutting at the same time. If your skinning knife is getting dull at this point, take some time to hit it with a sharpening stone or sharpening stick. A razor-sharp knife works the best at all times when skinning. Try to keep your skinning knife sharp, even if you need to stop to sharpen or change knives.

Be sure not to cut below the shoulder level through the neck, if you are having a mount done. Now do the same for the other front shoulder and off the leg, and then pull the skin down the neck to the base of the neck by the jawbone of the deer. You now have your deer skinned, and the process is almost complete.

Step 6

Take your knife and make a cut around the deer's neck and through the meat to the neck bone. Put the knife down, pick up your meat saw or hacksaw, and cut through the neck bone. This is not a large bone, and a few cuts from a sharp meat saw will sever this bone, releasing the neck and head. You can use a reciprocating saw to cut through this bone as it will not leave many bone fragments on the skin side of the hide. Besides, if you are taking the hide to the taxidermist, he will wash and prepare the hide regardless. If you feel comfortable with an electrical saw, be my guest and use it.

Trophy Mounting Step

If you are going to have the deer head mounted, you will need about ½-inch of the hide to present to the taxidermist. I recommend you call your taxidermist to ask them what they prefer. Most will want the hide to the end of the shoulder. You can give the taxidermist the entire hide, but it is not necessary. If you want the hide tanned also, you can give the taxidermist the whole hide. I recommend if you would like a deer hide tanned, use the whole hide of a deer and not one that is being mounted, as it will look better if you tan an entire hide to the neck.

Some hunters like to salt the inside of the hide before they bring it to the taxidermist. This is not necessary, and some taxidermists prefer you didn't if you are going to bring them the head and hide as soon as you get back, as they will sprinkle a chemical on the bare skin when they get it. Simply roll the hide to the head so that the skin is on the inside like a blanket and tie it on either end.

Congratulations, you did it. You have now skinned your deer in a few easy steps.

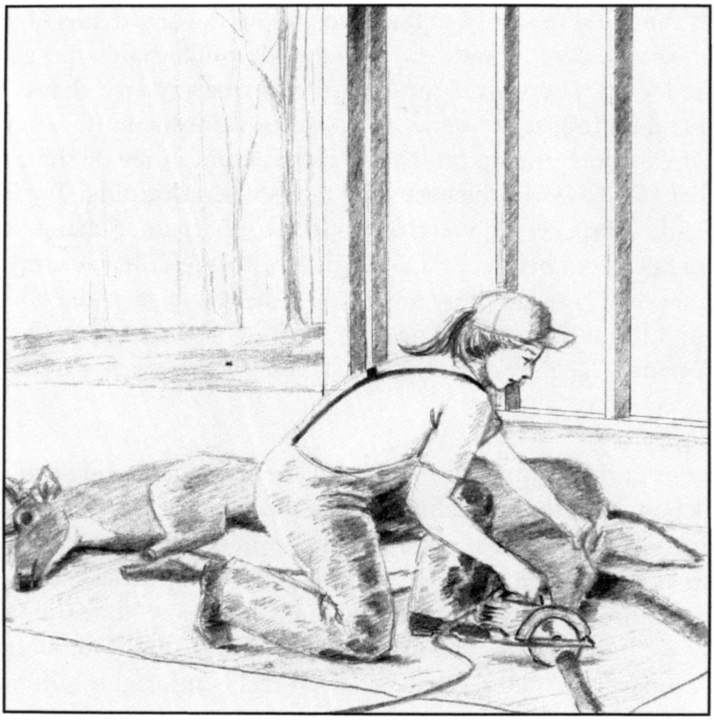

Skinning Step 1

Skinning Step 2

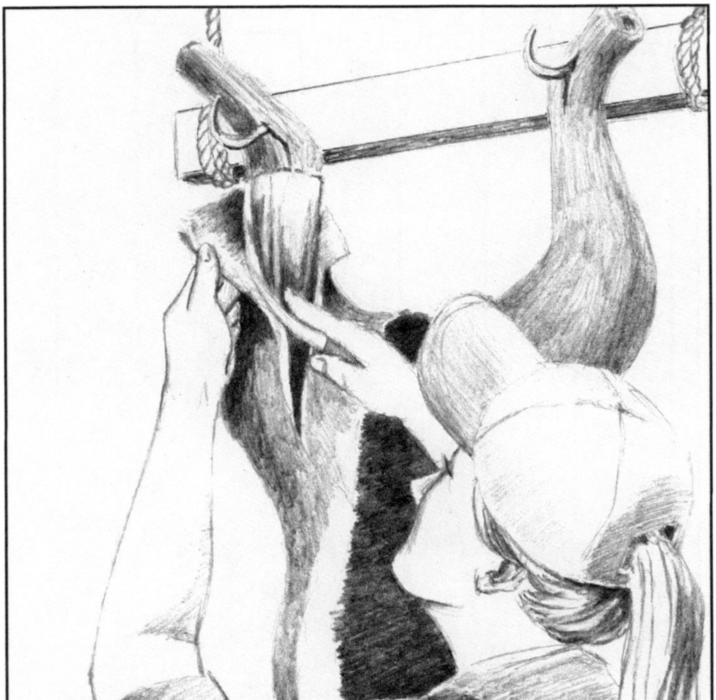

Skinning Step 3a

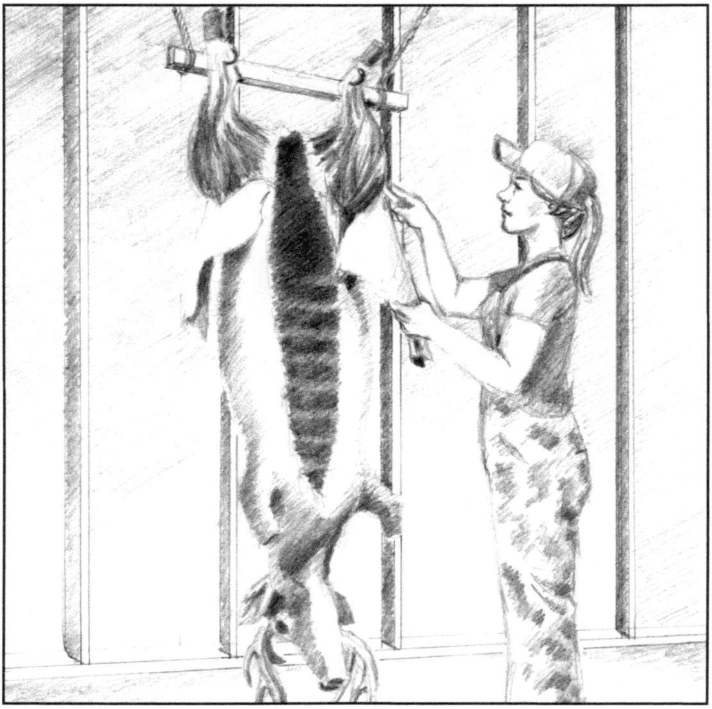

Skinning Step 3b

Skinning Step 4

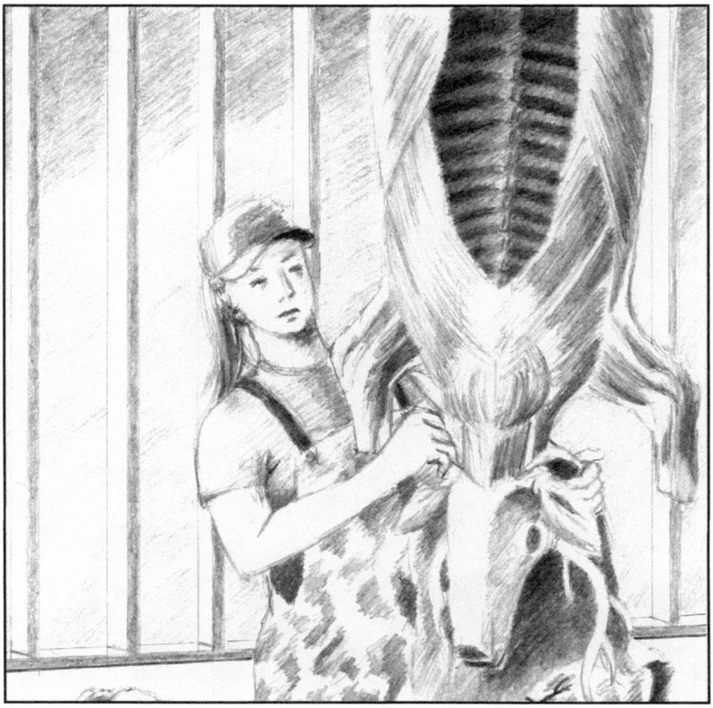

Skinning Step 5

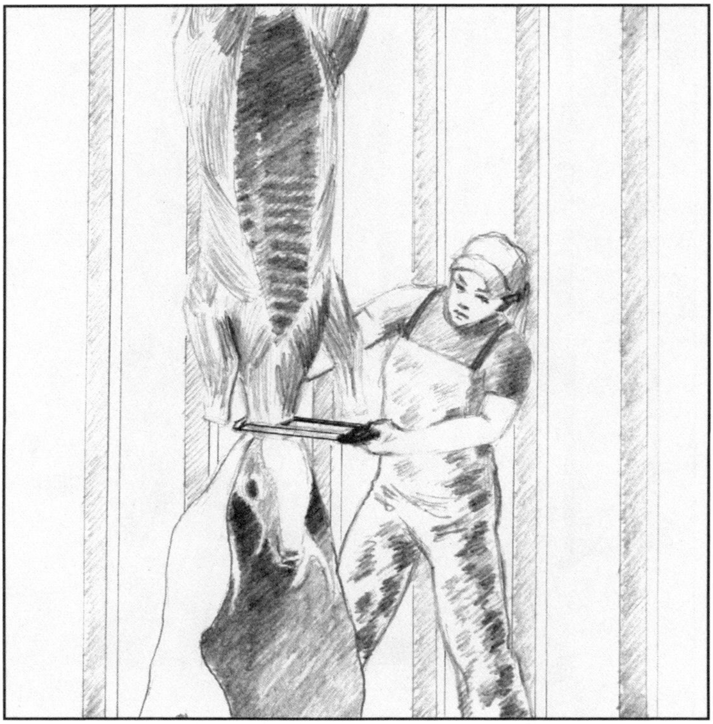

Skinning Step 6

Trophy Mounting Step

I did it!

Chapter Twenty-Five

Processing Your Deer Yourself

You have just skinned your deer, which you found to be easy, and would like to *Process Your Deer Yourself.* Good, you have made an excellent decision. With rising prices all around us, it is good to be self-sufficient, and it is not as hard as you might think. Venison contains more protein and considerably less fat than just about any domestic meats you can buy in stores. There is a large amount of people who enjoy the taste of venison and find it superior to the usual cuts of beef, chicken, or pork found in the supermarket. However, many hunters unknowingly spoil their venison and accidentally cause it to have a strong taste. Heat, moisture, and making a hurried cut while field dressing that allows the digestive juices in the stomach to flow on the meat will cause venison to have a gamey taste. A poor shot that allows your deer to run and pump adrenalin through your deer into the meat also harms the flavor.

More hunters than you think process their own deer, because they are looking for particular cuts of meat that they or their family enjoy, which some butchers will not do or will charge additional fees for. It is also a fact that if you bring your deer to a butcher who cuts up several deer during the hunting season, you may not get all the meat from your deer. No, I am not saying butchers keep your meat, but think about this—if you do not like ribs, and the butcher asks you if you want ribs and you say no, I just want roasts, steaks, cutlets, the tenderloins, some stew meat, and ground meat, the whole rib area won't be touched. Butchers make their money by butchering deer quickly, and since you did not want the ribs, that portion of the carcass will not be touched and will usually be discarded. You just wasted about ten to fifteen pounds of meat, as most butchers—not all, but most—will not bother to remove the meat from the ribs for stew meat or ground meat. Now, if you are butchering your own deer, all that meat will go for stew meat or ground meat, and you will not lose this meat. The same is true for the brisket area of a deer. Many butchers will cut that away, where if you butcher your deer yourself, you will not lose these two strips of meat that you can use, as the illustration shows, for soup meat, stew meat, ground meat or jerky. You will be surprised how much more meat you can have by processing a deer yourself. Just keep this in mind if you shoot only one deer during the season, as you will want as much meat as possible.

You do not have to be a butcher to process your own deer, and you might surprise yourself and enjoy making your own select cuts. I will guide you through the entire process, as I have processed my own deer for thirty-five years or more. I also bring some meat to a butcher I know to have polish sausage made from venison. If you like the taste of good polish sausage, find a butcher who will make it for you, and have polish sausage made from some of your venison. Trust me on this; it will be the absolute best polish sausage you ever tasted, bar none.

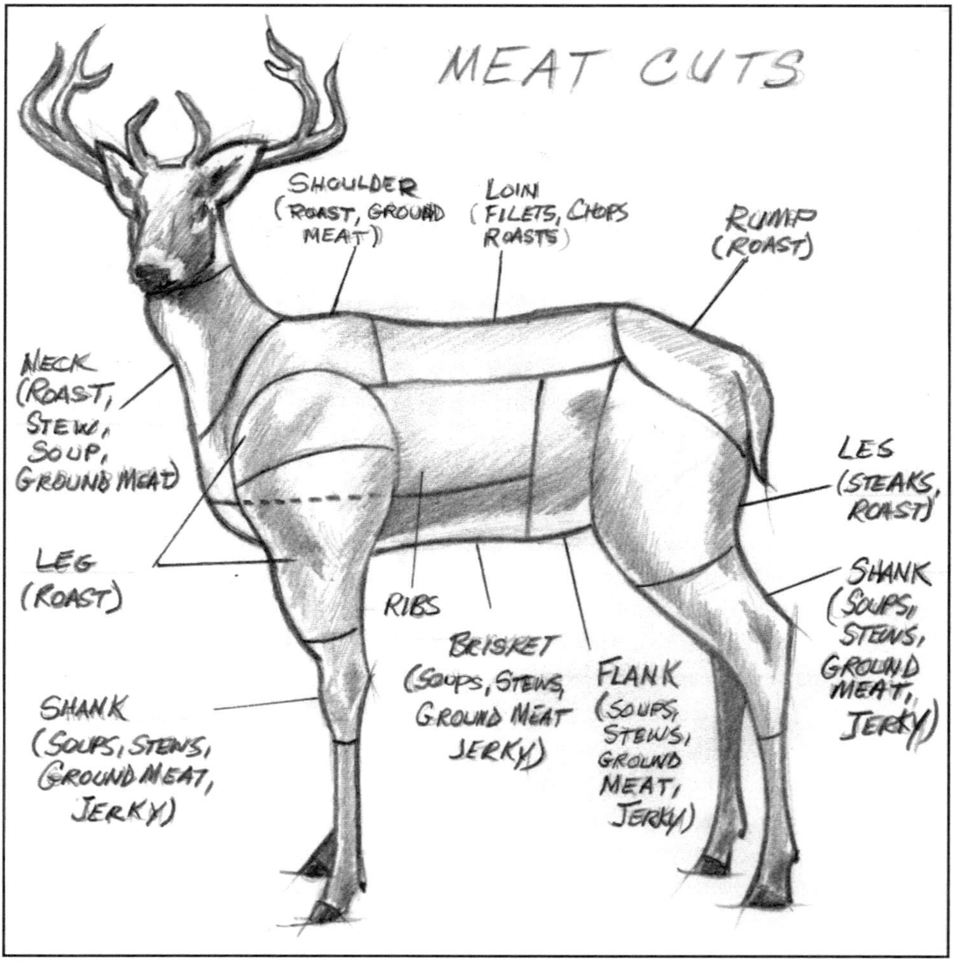

I have found butchers who take their time and trim all the meat off the bones, but they are few and far between. If you ask to have all the meat trimmed off the bones, the price for butchering will be a little higher. With this in mind, let us begin.

You will need what is called a boning knife, which has a thin blade about eight inches long. If you do not have one already and plan to purchase one, buy two of them and keep them razor sharp at all times. This way when one gets a bit dull, you can pick up the other to use. When the second one gets dull, stop and sharpen both knives, unless you have a sharpening strop and can keep them sharp by periodic stropping. You will also need a meat saw or hacksaw with extra blades. I find that blades do break, and it is good to have several new ones on hand and readily available. If you are going to buy a meat saw, buy two, one about fourteen inches long, which is standard, and a larger one. One will do, but there are times when the larger one comes in handy. When you are shopping, you might consider a vacuum sealer at this time. This way you can vacuum seal the meat you process, and it will last much longer while frozen. I suggest you have a good plastic wrap and use it to cover the meat if you do not have a vacuum sealer at this time.

Another thing you might want to consider is to go to your local supermarket butcher section and ask if you can pick up some plastic meat trays. You can lay the meat you cut on them and then wrap the meat in the tray with the plastic wrap. I have done this, and it works well with ground meat. If you do not wish to use trays, and even if you do, always double wrap your meat to prevent freezer burns. I also use or buy plastic trays, like the plastic storage trays you see in retail stores to store clothing. The trays should be about two feet long by twelve inches wide. You can also find them in a restaurant supply store or in the plastic kitchen section of a store. These will be to store your meat after you cut it off your deer.

The last item you need will be a meat grinder. You can buy a hand grinder or a good electric grinder that can make sausage also for just about $150. Trust me, you will use it repeatedly, and it is a good investment. I use mine many times during the year, together with my vacuum sealer.

Okay, before you begin, have all your tools laid out on a small table next to your deer. Put the plastic containers nearby, as you will use them soon. Some hunters like to cut the deer down the length of the backbone and have two separate halves to work on. I find this to be too much work, and I try to use the meat saw as little as possible. Many butchers are accustomed to butchering cows and other large animals and do this as a force of habit. I like to work easy, and avoiding this step of splitting a deer in two is highly recommended. Besides, you want as little bone fragments on the meat as possible, even though you will rinse off the meat later.

Note: Check again for safety purposes. If you shot your deer with an arrow and you did not recover your arrow with your broadhead, be sure to check your deer before you put your fingers in the deer to butcher it. Broadheads are razor sharp, and you can get a good cut from an imbedded broadhead or a broken razor piece if it is still in the deer. Check to make sure there is a clear entry and exit hole; there should be no pieces of your broadhead embedded in the carcass, inside or outside or imbedded in a bone.

Step 1

Your deer is hanging on the gambrel, and the first cut will be the inside tenderloins. I like to make this my first cut as the tenderloins are tender and much can be done with them. The tenderloins lie on each side of the backbone, and there are two of them. They are about 1-½ inches in diameter and about ten to twelve inches long, depending on the size of the deer you shot. They lie inside the body cavity on either side of the spine. Try to find each end before you cut, as you want to take the whole tenderloin. Put your knife into the cavity of the deer along the side of the spine and run it down the spine, pulling the tenderloins loose as you cut and remove the one side. If you leave them in the deer, they will dry out and spoil, and you will lose some of the tenderest meat on the deer. You will see the meat clearly, now cut the opposite side and remove the second tenderloin the same way as you did the other one. Do not make narrow cuts, as you want to take the entire tenderloin in one piece. If you did not take the entire tenderloin with one cut, relax and trim off the meat that remains and put it in a tray with the tenderloins. Whether or not you wish to age your deer, remove the tenderloins as soon as possible. I try to remove them in camp or as soon as I get my deer back home. Remember to do this cut first and as soon as possible. Once you have the tenderloins removed, you can leave them whole to cut later as steaks or you can fillet them, as they are excellent either way. If you see any silver skin on them or fat, remove it now or later, but it is best to remove as much fat as you can.

Step 2

The next cut I like to do is to remove the loins, or as they are frequently called, the back straps, which is what I consider the next tastiest meat on a deer. The loins are located on the outside of the deer on either side of the backbone of the deer. There are two of them, just like there are two tenderloins. They are covered with silver skin. Do not try to remove the silver skin before you remove the back straps, as you will lose too much meat in the process. Put your boning knife into the meat next to the backbone and cut in a downward motion along the backbone on one side of the back strap from the hips to the neck. Feel the thickness of the back strap and put your knife in, cutting from side to side to make sure your cut is close to the bone. Now put your fingers in where you cut; hold onto the back strap as you cut the other side along the ribcage, pulling the back strap out as you cut to remove it in one piece. If you see there is still part of the back strap still attached, remove the remaining meat with your knife and put it with the back strap in a tray. Try to get the entire back strap out on the other side of the backbone, as you will be making steaks out of this piece of meat.

Step 3

Now that the tenderloins and back straps are removed from the deer, you can start quartering your deer. This means that you will be removing the two front shoulder sections, the ribcage, and then the two rear hip sections. Let us start with the front shoulder sections, working one at a time. Lift one of the front legs and look into the armpit area. The front shoulders of a deer are similar to a cat in that they are not attached to the rest of the skeletal system, and removing them is quite easy. Begin your cut close to the shoulder blade and you will see how easy the front shoulder is to remove. There are no bones to cut, just meat connected by muscle. Lift the shoulder as you cut to expose the shoulder blade and cut around it, and the shoulder is free. Place the complete front shoulder into a plastic tub, then go to the next shoulder and repeat the process. You have now both front shoulders inside the plastic tub. The front shoulders you can make leg roasts (pot roasts), strip steaks, soup meat, stew meat, ground meat, and jerky. Now see how easy that was. Who said processing your own deer is hard?

Step 4

This step is simple, as all you will do is cut the ribcage off the deer that still has the neck attached. You will put this in a separate plastic tub, as you will be taking all the meat off the ribs and neck for stew meat or ground meat. If you like ribs or a standing rib roast, you can carve it later. Now pick up your meat saw and make a cut just below the rear thighs to sever the backbone. This is one of three cuts that you will use the meat saw for. I like to use a large meat saw for this cut, and it works a lot easier if you have some help to hold the ribcage. If you are doing this alone, just hold the ribcage with one hand and cut the backbone with the meat saw with your other hand. Once the ribcage is severed, place this into a plastic tub.

Step 5

You are almost done quartering your deer. All that is left is separating the two hip sections and then cutting the legs about two inches above the hock (rear knee joint), as depicted by the sketch. I generally cut right down the spine so there is a minimum of damage or waste to the meat on either side. The other line on the sketch on the legs shows where you should cut to separate the rest of the hind leg. Usually you will not waste any meat with this cut, but if you wish to pick at it, you could get some off the piece on the gambrel. Once you have cut through and two separate pieces remain on the gambrel, you can do that last cut with the meat saw. Place both hindquarters into the plastic tub and throw away the part that remains on the gambrel hooks.

Congratulations, you have now quartered your deer into manageable pieces to work with and to do your final cuts. Now this wasn't too hard, was it?

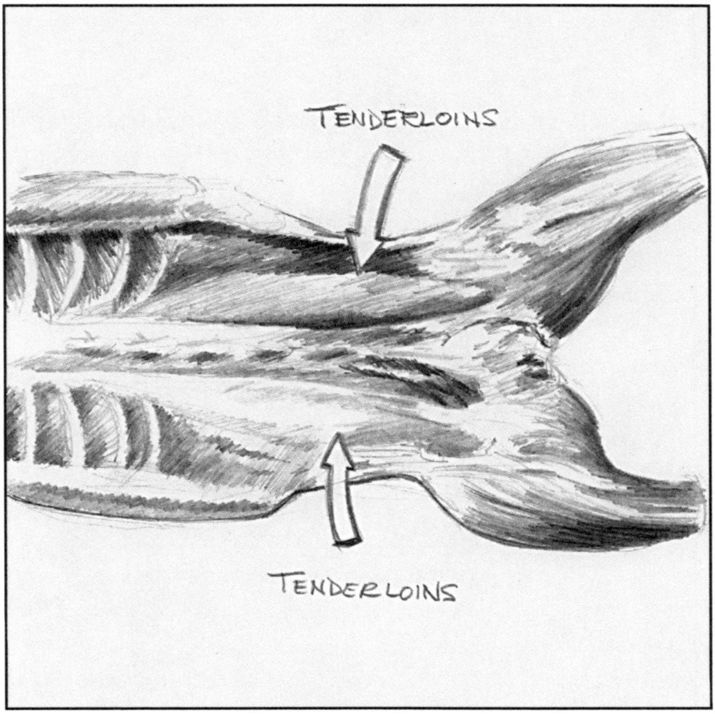

Processing Step 1

Processing Step 2

Processing Step 3

Processing Step 4

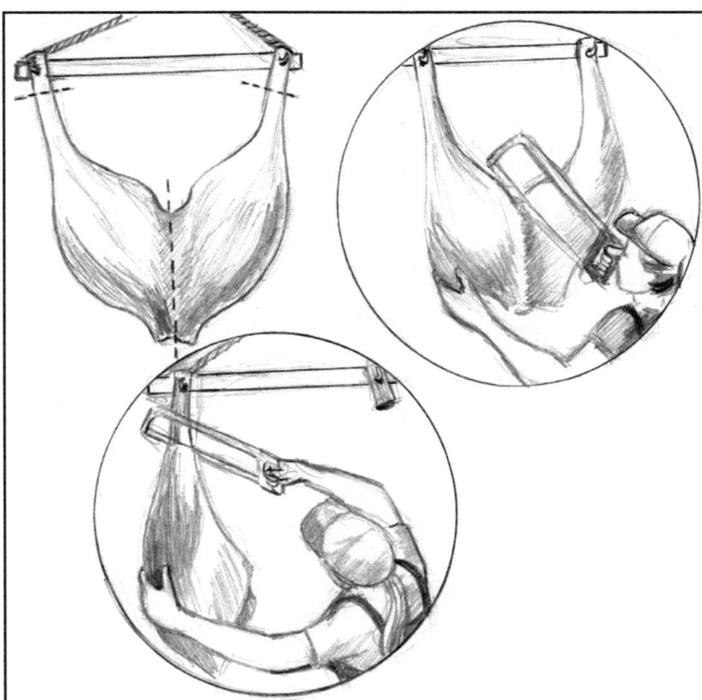

Processing Step 5

At this point, I would take and remove the leg part still on the gambrel and discard it. I would also take some time and do a clean up of your tools as well. Be sure to clean the meat saw and remove any bone or meat from the blade; rinse it under hot water and store your meat saw away, as you are done with it for now. You will be using a sharp boning knife to de-bone the meat, unless you prefer a bone in your steaks. I do not, and you may not either, so put away your meat saw after it is clean and dry.

Cutting the meat off the bone, or boning as it is called, is a simple task as well. It can be done in the field or in your garage, basement, or kitchen. All that is needed is a tabletop and a place to put your meat after it is cut and separated. You can sit at a table and take your time to get the select cuts you prefer. You can also spend time to trim off the fat and silver skin from the meat.

I generally put a few sheets of newspaper on a table and then a large cutting board for the final cuts. You will also want three plastic tubs. One will be for the select cuts, the second for stew meat cuts, and the third for meat you will grind. I have an empty kitchen garbage bag for waste and bones. The three plastic tubs can be three plastic bowls about the two-quart size each. If you like more ground meat than stew meat, make one bowl larger to hold all the ground meat. Once you have a place set up and your bowls are ready, get a sharp boning knife and begin. I generally like to have two separate boning knifes for this, plus a sharpening stone or sharpening stick handy to keep the knifes razor sharp.

Note: Remember to be careful, as the meat is cool and fingers can get in the way of the razor sharp knife.

Boning Step 1

Take the tubs that have the tenderloins; we will start with that. Trim away any remaining fat or skin, and make your cuts as you desire. Many people butterfly the tenderloins to have a wider piece of meat, but I prefer to filet them lengthwise. You can also cut them in three-inch lengths for coating with batter for the frying pan, whichever you prefer.

I generally cut them lengthwise, and after they are cut to my liking, I rinse them off in cold water and set them to dry before packaging for the freezer. When you package, be sure you double wrap if you are not going to vacuum seal them in a vacuum freezer bag.

Boning Step 2

Remove the back straps (loins) from the tub and place one on the cutting board lengthwise. You will see the silver skin on the top of the meat. You need to fillet this off the meat to remove the strong taste that the silver skin has. Place your boning knife under the silver skin, then draw your knife along the length of the back strap as you pull up the silver skin to remove the skin and not any meat. The silver skin does not come off easily unless you have a sharp boning knife. The silver skin is slippery, and using a meat glove or a skinning glove with grips does help. If you do not have a glove, take your time. You can use a paper towel to help you hold it firmly. Remove it all, or as much as you possibly can. Once this is done, cut the back straps into six-inch chunks to butterfly or to make a wider piece of meat, a steak. You will generally get around four steaks per side if you took the entire back strap from the deer. With smaller deer, you will get three per side. Wash off the meat in cold water and set aside to dry off. Once the back straps dry a bit and are still damp, you can wrap the back straps for the freezer.

You have now completed taking care of the tenderloins and the back straps. They are cut, packaged, and ready for the freezer. We will now work on a front shoulder. Relax, you are doing fine.

Boning Step 3

Take the ribcage and lay it on the table, as you want to trim off any fat from the flank on both sides of the adjoining ribs and then the brisket. Once you have removed the fat and any tough tissue, you are ready to remove the flank and the brisket. Remove the flank and cut it into two pieces, and you should wind up with four pieces, two from each side. Put them on the side and then remove the brisket. Once the brisket is removed, put it on the side also. Rinse all under cold water and lay to the side to dry off excessive water and then package as desired. I would label each package to know the flank and brisket when frozen.

Boning Step 4

With the flanks and brisket both trimmed, removed, and stored, you want to work to remove all meat from the ribcage and the neck. This meat will go for either stew meat or chop meat, depending on the size and the amount of fat and silver skin on the meat. Meat that has less fat and in chunks the right size for stew meat will go into the plastic container you have for stew meat. Meat that has silver skin and some fat will go for ground meat. You can judge accordingly. As most people do not like venison ribs, I do not bother cutting a standing rib roast, but if you do want to try one, keep 4 to 6 ribs intact and cut through to make a standing rib roast, and then de-bone the rest of the meat. Take as much meat as you are willing to cut off the bones. I generally will pick both the neck and the ribcage clean, as all meat can be used. The neck area especially has good stew meat that you can cut into two-inch cubes. I generally will use all the meat off the ribcage for ground meat.

Once you have removed all the meat from both the neck and the ribcage, set the skeleton to the side, by placing it in a large garbage bag for disposal. I generally place the skeleton in the woods, as my house is set one miles off a gravel road and surrounded by woods. I use one area of my property for this, as the coyotes will not take long to find it. If you do not have a place in the woods, take the garbage bag and set it in a good garbage can with a strong lid to prevent any small critters from finding it during the night. After you are done with the entire job, you can put the kitchen garbage bag that contains the scraps in the garbage can, for disposal as well.

The amount of people in your family and the size of the freezer that you will be using will determine how many serving size packages you will be making. I generally will package meat to accommodate two people, as the bags will be good to store in the freezer and not take up too much room. However, I do have several large chest freezers that I use throughout the year for freezing game I butcher. You now have two front shoulders and two hind sections to work on.

Boning Step 5

Pick up one front shoulder and place it on the cutting board. For those who want bones in their steaks, you can make an average of four to six steaks by cutting through the meat. When you reach the bone, saw through the bone section, and then cut the meat on the backside of the bone. I find this to be too much work, as I do not own a butchers electrical boning saw; probably you do not either. I generally will de-bone the front shoulder by running my boning knife along the bone to cut it out after I have trimmed off all the fat and silver skin. I suggest you do this as well. Trim off as much as possible before you de-bone your front shoulder. Generally I will cut through the side of the meat, and remove the top section to expose the bone. Then I cut out the bone that is showing carefully with my boning knife so I then have a bottom piece of meat with the bone cut out. After removing the bone, trim off any muscle, silver skin and fat until you have two large sections of just meat. You can cut steaks, cutlets, and roasts out of the meat. I generally will take one roast out of the large front section, then some trimmed steaks, and lastly the thin cutlets. Be sure to separate all the different cuts of meat, rinse them under cold water. After the excess water drains off, package them immediately and label each package.

Follow the same procedure for the second front shoulder. In the end, you will have four shoulder roasts, eight steaks, and several packages of cutlets. Remember to label all packages before you freeze them. Some states require you to put your license tag number on all packages of venison. If your state requires this, I suggest you follow the rules of your state for packaging venison. Any trimmed off meat can go for stew meat or ground meat.

As a suggestion for ground meat, since venison is lean meat, and you are trimming away most of the fat, when you grind the meat, add pork sausage to the ground venison. I generally buy ground pork, which you can find in the meat section of most supermarkets. It will add to the taste, and you will be able to cook your ground venison easier by doing this. It will not give a pork flavor to your venison, and it will add a good taste to your ground meat. I generally use a one-to-four ratio when adding ground pork.

Boning Step 6

You have completed de-boning the front shoulders, and all that is left is to de-bone the two hind sections. Start by placing a hind section on your cutting board and remove the fat and silver skin. Once you have done this, just like when you de-boned the shoulder section, cut the top meat off the bone by cutting into the side of the hind section to remove the top piece of meat. Once the top piece of meat is cut away, exposing the bone, work to cut out the bone and discard the bone, so you have two large hind sections. Just as with the front shoulder, I like to cut one nice roast from each of the two pieces of meat. I then cut several **????** inch steaks and cutlets. All excess meat I use for either stew meat or ground meat. Place the bones in your kitchen garbage bag ready for disposal. Rinse off the meat with cool water and allow draining before packaging. Be sure to label all meat so you will know the contents once the meat is frozen.

Congratulations, you have just processed you own deer and found that the process was not as difficult as you anticipated. Boning your venison enhances the eating qualities of venison, especially in roasts and the hindquarters. Once completed for the first time, you will develop your own style of de-boning and butchering your deer yourself. It took some extra courage and a sense of adventure to try it for the first time. The second time will be easier, and each time after will be even easier.

Remember elk, antelope or other big game animals can be butchered in a similar way. Boning game yourself has several advantages over the conventional methods of cutting up deer with leaving bones in. You can separate the choice pieces of meat from the connective tissues, tendons, off-grained meat, and excessive fat. Dirt, hair and bloodshot muscle can be removed easily. Your meat is boneless, compact, smooth, and easy to wrap and you are deciding the portions to wrap and not a butcher. You have also saved money and have done something from the start to the finish.

You are now self-sufficient as the planner, the hunter, the processor, and then the consumer. You should be very proud of yourself, because you have done what other can only dream about, you have graduated from one who watches it on TV to one who can do it all. You are a hunter, a sportsman, and from now on you will have a different prospective about the sport, for you have gone full circle in the entire process, from field to feast on your dinner table.

All that is left is to clean your butchering area, for the next whitetail deer to process, as you know the method of *Processing Your Deer Yourself.*

Boning Step 1

Boning Step 2

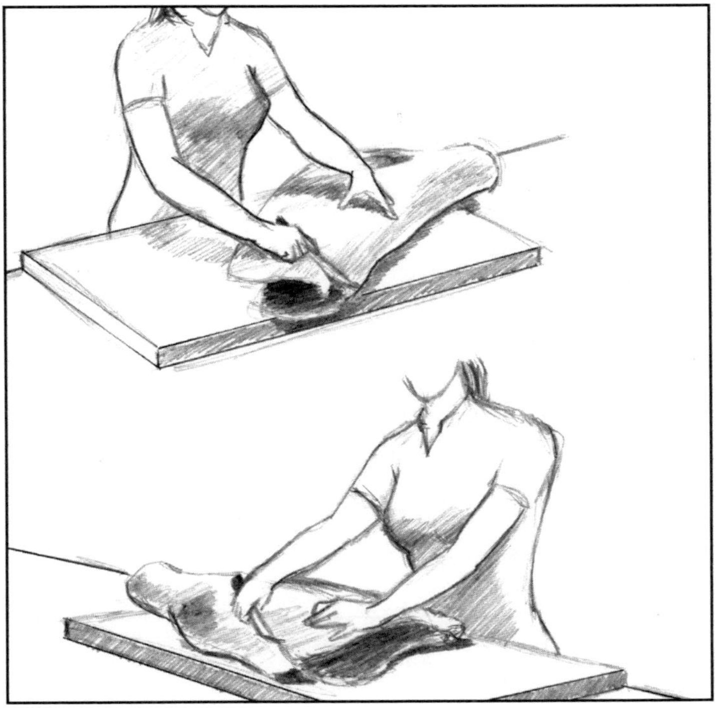

Boning Step 3

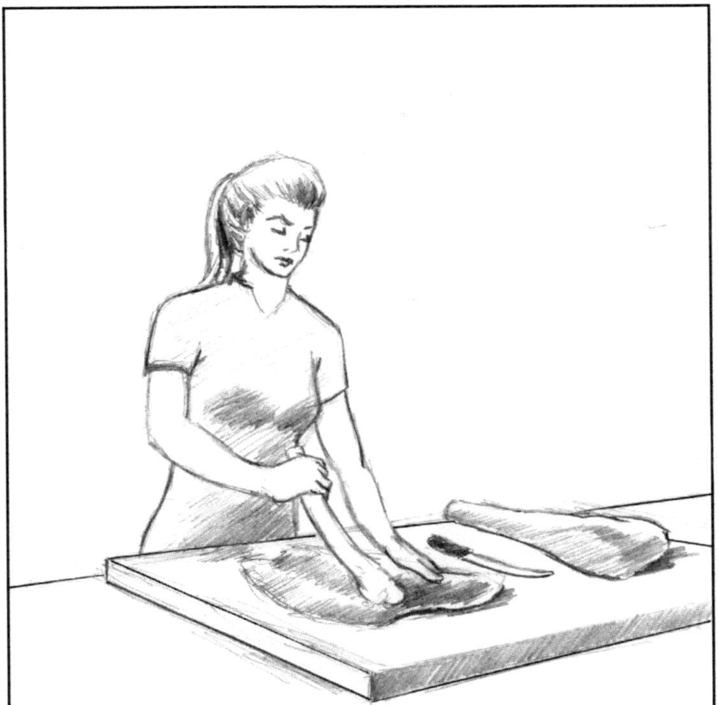

Boning Step 5

Boning Step 6

Memories of a hunt last a lifetime.

Chapter Twenty-Six

Survival Skills for the Woods

Preparation and survival skills will keep you from having problems in the woods, should you find yourself in an emergency. The best resources you have at your disposal are your mind, your determination to survive and your will to endure and come out of the emergency.

Some hunters, if they are hunting a new area, can easily be turned around and lose track of the direction they came into the woods and find themselves lost. If you keep your head and do not panic, usually you can get your bearings and come out of it okay. Never run through the woods or leave the area you first get turned around in, as you could wander further away from the target area people will be looking for you. If possible, follow your footprints and remain calm. You may come out of the woods a few miles from where you came in, and most of the time you will only be in for a longer walk than you anticipated.

You could experience an accident when climbing into your tree stand, falling out of your stand, or when descending. You may fall over a tree root or stumble on a trail, breaking a leg or arm. Any number of things could happen, but what is important is how you are prepared for an emergency and how you handle it.

If you do get lost and cannot find your way out of the woods, the first thing to do is to stop and admit you are lost. Do not panic, and remain calm. If you told others where you were going to hunt, they will be looking for you if you are in the woods later than what you told them you would be.

Remember, there is nothing in the woods to fear except your imagination. There are no man-eating dinosaurs, not that I know of. No fire-breathing dragons to carry you off that I have seen, and the headless horseman is only looking for people walking on roads. That lets you off the hook, because if you were on a road, you would not be lost. What you will need to do, if you have to spend a night in the woods, is to first find or build a basic shelter or windbreak. If you see no natural shelter in your immediate area, you will need to build a basic lean-to by first making a horizontal support between two trees that are close by to form a basic frame for a roof. Then cover the frame with evergreen branches to block any wind from coming into your shelter. You also want to have the opening of the lean-to away from the wind. If you use thick evergreen branches and pile them up, it will keep the wind off you as a good windbreak. You want to build your shelter by a stand of thick evergreens, so the trees themselves block some of the wind. Your shelter need only to be big enough to sustain you, not several people if you are the only one lost. Try to find dry ground that is flat and not on a hillside or too uneven of a terrain. You will also want to spread several evergreens on the floor of the lean-to to cushion you somewhat when you lay down.

After you have prepared your shelter, your next consideration should be a campfire. It is a good idea not to build a campfire too close to your shelter. You want the heat from the fire to radiate into your shelter, which will keep you warm without the worry of smoke in your shelter. This way when you sleep you will be between the fire and the shelter, giving you warmth. Have a large enough fire that will generate heat.

Make sure you clear the ground if it is dry, and you can encircle the fire pit area with rocks. Prior to building your fire, gather dry twigs to act as kindling, dry tree bark, or dry grass, and put it in the middle of where your fire will be. If there is snow on the ground, build a platform for your fire out of rocks or green tree logs, as they will not ignite. Once you have put the kindling in place, set larger sticks in a pyramid design over the kindling in the middle of the base. Light the fire, and as it grows, add larger wood. Keep a good supply of wood near you for the fire, as you do not want to be looking for wood in the dark; more is better.

Your campfire will be your signal fire. You can build other fires, but be sure not to light brush on fire that will spread. You want to signal for help, not start a forest fire with you in the middle of it.

Keeping warm for survival can make the difference.

Your next consideration is water. Even in cool weather, you will need water, an average of three quarts of water a day. Under usual conditions, a person can only last about four days without water. Chances are you will be found before then, but be prepared in any case and gather water or find a source of water. You will find that pure drinking water may not be readily available. Some mountain streams are contaminated with parasites, even though they look pure. The best way to purify water is by boiling it. You can make your problems worse by drinking water you think is pure that is not. Some of the water in mountain streams has parasites that can cause serious intestinal sicknesses that would double you over in pain within a day. Remember this before you take a drink out of a mountain stream.

Chances are you will not need food, as a person can go for up to two weeks without any food. You are in the woods, and there is game to eat for survival. It may not be what you are accustomed to eating, but there is food for you to eat. In order to keep a clear head, and if you are in the woods more than a day, you will need to eat. However, for now, concentrate on the issue at hand. You will do okay, and as I said before, people will be looking for you if you told someone you were

Making a fire.

going hunting and when you expected to return. Keep focused, remain calm, and you will be found.

A survival kit in a backpack is needed with useful things to help you, should you have to spend a night in the woods.

Hypothermia can occur if you are in the woods for a period of time and is usually induced by cold, wet conditions such as snow and freezing rain, or falling into cold water when conditions are cold, which could put you at risk. Hyperthermia occurs when a person's body loses heat faster than it can produce it. Hyperthermia can be prevented by layering your clothing by dressing properly and by drying quickly should you get wet. The symptoms of hyperthermia are uncontrolled shivering, slow or slurred speech, irrational behavior, such as feeling too warm in freezing conditions, and memory loss. High-calorie foods such as chocolate, candy, and raisins can help your body produce heat, but what is needed is warmth and shelter. Alcohol should never be consumed by or given to a victim of hyperthermia. Re-warm the victim of hyperthermia, remove wet clothing, and replace it with warm, dry clothing. The idea is to raise the person's body temperature without putting the person into shock.

Heat exhaustion is the opposite of hyperthermia and is when a person's body temperature increases during hot, dry conditions with the lack of sufficient water. The symptoms of heat exhaustion include nausea, headache, pale skin and muscle cramps. A good preventative for heat exhaustion is drinking plenty of water, taking frequent breaks if you are carrying or hauling equipment on hot days, and dressing in layers to be able to remove clothing as temperatures begin to rise.

Frostbite can occur when tissues freeze. Avoid severe weather and pay attention to covering your extremities, such as your fingers, nose, ears, face, and toes when temperatures are below zero degrees. Hunters in the woods in bitter conditions should be mindful of frostbite and the symptoms: tingling or prickly feeling of your fingers or extremities left unprotected; skin will turn an off-white color; you could experience a loss of feeling in the affected area. If you begin to experience frostbite, drink hot fluids, get to a warm shelter and warm the affected area, but do not rub the area, as it can damage the tissue. Never use hot water as a treatment, which could cause burns. If possible, seek medical attention immediately.

In cold weather survival, you need to build a shelter, stay dry, avoid contact with cold surfaces, limit your physical activity, and wear layered clothing. Thermal foil blankets will maintain a temperature of 60 to 65 degrees *F* inside the wrap, even if the outside temperature goes below 0 degrees *F*. It is highly recommended that at least one foil wrap blanket be included in every survival kit, and it is a good idea for every hunter to have one with them in their backpack in the event of an emergency. I also recommend that every backpack have at least one length of rope and one length or spool of twine. Rope and twine always come in handy, and I consider them as a standard item for survival. In an emergency you can use them to help support a shelter, make a snare, or support a splint. Remember to stay calm, use your ability for survival, and you will do okay.

Chapter Twenty-Seven

Attitude and Ethics on Hunting

Whitetail deer hunting is a sport that we have today due to the concerned efforts of many people we seldom think of when we discuss hunting, watch hunting shows on TV, or talk to fellow sportsmen while at home or in the field. You rarely hear about them while you are in a gun shop, attending a sports conference or at an outdoor expo, but they are always working hard to protect your interests and guard against those who would take away your right to enjoy the sport you are being introduced to or have learned to love. They work while you sleep and while you are in the comfort of you own home in front of a warm fire or watching TV. They are out in the field making sure the whitetail deer remain safe as all the animals under their protection and keep wildlife for you to see and enjoy.

However, unlike other guardians in your world, they receive no praise, no pat on the back, and are viewed as the enemy to some. Actually they are, but for you and me who are both hunters, sportsmen and sportswomen, they are your strongest allies, friends, and will always be there to help or to assist you if asked. They are the silent guardians of wildlife; they are the Conservation Officers. Together with other officials, biologists, forestry agents, corporative extension personnel, wildlife management teams, watershed agents, and a host of other participants, your sport lives today by their labor.

Their concerns are about carrying capacity, which is the number of animals the habitat can support. They study disease, parasites, starvation, pollution, accidents, predators, poachers, if the conditions are balanced or if there will be a surplus. They look into the habitat animals need to survive, food and water, how a drought or flood is affecting wildlife and what is needed to support the balance. They look into ecosystems that are adjacent to one another to make sure neither is adversely affected and assist to support one corridor or the other. They are in the field during the changing seasons to see that conditions never lead to threaten or endanger wildlife population.

Respect fences and posted property.

The average citizen or hunter usually will see them only during hunting season, possibly at a game check, or when driving by to see their empty vehicle while they are in the woods, and may never stop to think all that is being done for their benefit. It is all the people, combined with the conservation officers, who are keeping your passion and love of the outdoors alive and protected. They are keeping the woods that you enjoy walking through pristine so you and your family can walk and observe nature at its finest and not have to worry if the woods will be there for future generations to enjoy. They are keeping your lakes, streams, rivers, and ponds clean and useable. They are making sure the fish are there for you to enjoy and the waterways are open. They are the untold heroes of the outdoors. So when you take your boat out, load your campers or trucks to enjoy the outdoors, plan for a hunting trip or simply want to walk among nature, it is them who make it all possible for it to be there for you to enjoy. Let us not forget, all that made it all come together for you and others.

Most do it not because it is their job, but like you, their love for the outdoors has driven them to be the guardians that they are. So when you see agents working in the field, know all that they do and are doing for you.

Conservation is an important part of hunting.

If an agent is in the field and catches a poacher, he is doing it for the person who wants to see wildlife or the birdwatcher. He is there working for the camper who wants to be one with nature, the photographer in the outdoors, the painter by a stream or a pond who wants to capture nature on a canvas. He is working to help the hunter, the archer, the angler, the sportsman or sportswoman. He is working for your children and for their children to make sure their dreams come true and for future generations to come.

When you are hunting and see a young or immature doe or buck, your attitude about nature and your ideas about conservation can and will make a difference. Should you pass on the shot and allow this deer to mature and possibly have youngsters of her own, or do you really need to take a youngster, which will give you maybe twenty or twenty-five pounds of meat as opposed to waiting and harvest an animal that will give you seventy-pounds of venison? Only you will be able to make up your own mind, and you will have to make that choice one day if you become a hunter. The question you will have to decide the answer to is what type of hunter and what type of sportsman or sportswoman will you become. Will your desire outweigh the needs of wildlife? How will your attitude about conservation develop, and where will you draw the line? Will you be an ethical person in the outdoors? Will you be the inspiration and the guiding light that others will want to emulate? These are the questions you will have to answer for yourself. If you learn only one thing about the outdoors, learn who is there to protect you, your family, and future generation as your guardian for what your sport is all about.

What footprints will you leave upon the ground where you walk? Will you be an observer and be a help in the process, leaving a small footprint that is noticeable but not seen, or will your imprint be seen and felt by later generations to correct?

Attitude and ethics, no matter how slight or how strong, can and do make differences in the outdoors. Yours can be developed, added to, changed or corrected in your time, and your ideas are needed by all the animals in the woods, one of which is the whitetail deer.

Chapter Twenty-Eight

Information About Venison

Whitetail deer is one of the most hunted animals in all of North America, but venison, which is the meat of a deer, is one of the meats most commonly prepared incorrectly. Out of the many hunters who take a deer each season, about 80% of them do not know how to process a deer correctly or how to prepare the meat for the dinner table. Unlike what many people believe, venison does not have to have a strong, gamey taste. Venison does have its own taste, but it can be prepared in a number of ways to delight the most imperative of palates. The American Indians lived primarily on venison and knew the secrets of preparing this meat to perfection. While living in South Dakota, I had several friends who were of the Sioux nation, and I was able to learn several recipes that I will share with you, which you cannot find in any cookbook.

When was the last time you heard some say, "I don't like to eat venison because it tastes too gamey"? Too many good hunters do not know how to prepare venison or think they can cook it like a piece of beef—just add some seasoning and it will turn out fine. Then there are the hunters who have been eating venison for years, and are under the misconception that it should have a gamey taste. Over the years, they have cooked venison the same way, think everyone else should like it because they have become accustomed to the flavor, and feel everyone should enjoy it prepared as they cook it.

Venison prepared properly should melt in your mouth with every bite. It should be both delicious to the taste, nutritious in its properties, and wanted by everyone who has tasted a venison dinner cooked the way venison was meant to be cooked.

I have had venison prepared for me at different places I have stayed while hunting. Some were exceptional dinners, while others bothered my stomach for two days afterwards and tasted like an old boot that was cooked and seasoned.

Preparation is the secret, but the first step in the process is to shoot a deer and have the deer drop immediately or within a few steps. That is the number one key to having venison that does not have a strong, gamey taste. Many hunters who take small, immature deer say the meat tastes fantastic from a young deer that weighs every bit of forty pounds that they hit with a high-powered rifle and drops instantly from the shock of the bullet. Had they shot a 150-pound deer that dropped the same way, the meat would be equally as good and tender.

Another important thing that needs to be done is to skin your deer as soon as possible, and then get the carcass cooled down as soon as you can after the deer is dead. Hanging a deer to age is okay, but how many butchers that you know of will hang a cow to age with the hide on? None! But people who think that all meat should age have never seen meat hanging, or they would know that the hide has to be removed quickly. Yet when you see deer hanging and people say, "I am letting the meat age," most of the time it has not been skinned. You need to get a deer skinned to allow the meat to age, or the tissues between the hide and the meat will allow fluid from the skin to soak into the meat, giving the meat a strong, gamey taste. That is the second important key step when processing your deer, the removal of the deer's hide, known as skinning your deer.

Indians knew this, and as soon as a deer was killed, it was skinned. In western television shows you see deer hanging in Indian camps not skinned, but that is television and not what was reality. Farmers know this also, and when you see deer hanging in barns or meat lockers, they are skinned and often wrapped. If you do these two key steps, you will reduce the gamey taste of a deer by 40%.

Field dressing improperly has spoiled more deer meat than you can imagine. All hunters know that a deer has to be field dressed, but I would venture to say that out of every ten hunters who field dress a deer, at least four are doing it incorrectly. There are less than six cuts with your knife to properly field dress a deer, but I have seen hunters hack away at a deer for twenty-five minutes and open more organs before I could stop them.

I will never forget the time I drove to a diner to get a cup of coffee in Livingston Manor, New York. It was a nice diner I stopped at. I saw a nice doe on top of a vehicle and went over to look at it. The proud hunter was standing next to his vehicle and I congratulated him on taking a good size doe. I looked at the deer, and he had a stick propped up to air out the cavity. As I looked at the deer, I saw the heart and part of the liver was still inside the deer. I asked the hunter if he field dressed the deer, and he proudly said yes, and it was the second deer he had ever shot. I said he took a fine deer but that he missed taking out the heart and part of the liver. He told me that he read how to field dress a deer but was not too clear about doing it. I told him that if he took the deer off his vehicle, I would finish field dressing the deer for him.

He took the deer down, and we dragged the deer to the side and close to a nearby stream. I asked him if he had a large plastic bag, and I put on a pair of shoulder-length field dressing gloves I took from my truck and borrowed his knife. Well, his knife was a dull as a butter knife, so I got mine out. He went inside the diner and got a plastic bag; when he returned I began to show him where to start, because the anal vent had not been removed. I cut around the vent tube and tied it off; even though he had cut the vent from the inside, some of it was still inside. I showed him that he needed to cut the outside first around the vent, then tie it off and pull it out whole from the inside. I saw that he had severed the urine sac as the meat had a urine smell to it already. I told him where the urine sac was located and to avoid it the next time he field dressed a deer. I then reached inside the doe's neck and severed the windpipe, the heart, and then went lower to remove the liver. The hunter was from Babylon, Long Island, in New York. He was up hunting for the week and was on his way back home when he stopped at the diner. I told him when he got back home to hang the deer and be sure to clean out the cavity thoroughly.

I cannot begin to tell you how many hunters have a general idea about field dressing but actually do not know the proper way to do it because no one took the time to show them how to do it properly. Field dressing poorly can spoil your deer meat and cause it to have a strong, gamey taste.

If after you shoot your deer, the temperature is above 40 degrees, you need to skin the deer immediately and not let it hang. Warm weather can ruin deer meat that is hanging, especially if the deer is not skinned, as the meat will start to develop an odor, which will pass on when cooked as a strong, gamey taste. If you wait, time will cause your venison to have a stronger taste and even spoil the meat if left too long. Skinning a deer quickly is an important step in the process of eliminating the gamey taste associated with venison.

A good sportsman helps others.

In my home state of Missouri, I sometimes take advantage of the early bow-hunting season, which on some days can be 70-degree weather. After I shoot a deer in warm weather, I will field dress the deer and within an hour, I have the deer skinned, quartered, and refrigerated. This is an absolute must to preserve the meat.

Venison is not hard to prepare if it is harvested correctly, and the correct preparation has been done in the beginning. Proper field dressing will reduce the gamey taste of a deer by as much as 25%.

If you have shot the deer and it dropped immediately or within a few steps, field dressed it right away, then skinned the deer and not allowed it to hang with the hide on it, and then cooled the meat quickly, you have reduced the gamey taste by as much as 90%.

All that is left is preparing the meat properly and to cook it with one of the recipes I will give you. If you do this and follow my recipes, you will never again hear, "I don't like to eat venison because it tastes too gamey," from someone you prepared a venison dish for. All they will have to do is try what I will show you, and even the most adamant will like the dish you prepare if you follow my recipes.

I am fortunate enough to be married to a special kind of woman who enjoys hunting and cooking the venison we both bring home. This is important, because I hope she will get to the point where I don't have to hunt, and I can sit back and dream of past hunts, think of the memories, and then awaken to find a venison dish prepared and on the table. Then I can dream of the twelve and fourteen-pointers I passed up, and.... Okay, back to reality....

I am married to a special woman who does hunt with me and does prepare venison when we both want the great tasting flavor of it, which happens to be on a regular basis.

Other than elk, venison is often the meat of choice, as venison has about ¼ the fat of beef and about ½ the fat of ham. Per pound, venison has 40% less calories and about 15% more protein than beef, ham, or salmon. Think about that if you want to cut down on your fat intake and are counting calories but do not want to lessen your intake of protein. Venison, the dish of kings and nobility, can be the best meal you prepare if done correctly

Did you know that doctors recommend venison to people, as it is higher in protein than most meats you can buy in a supermarket? If you go to a restaurant in mid-town Manhattan, New York, and order a venison steak, you will get a piece of meat about the size of a fillet mignon and spend an average of $60 for it. I remember eating at Windows of the World, which was a restaurant at the top of the Twin Towers in New York City many years ago. The venison was delicious, with a taste that was beyond any doubt prepared superbly, but the portion could have been a bit larger. When I bite into a steak, I generally prefer it to be still on my plate after the fifth bite. However, venison prepared correctly is a true feast. Now I know what you are thinking, the venison came from a farm where they raise deer for the dinner table. That is true, but it still had to be prepared by someone, nevertheless.

Cooking venison is also a key to having it taste great, but the preparation is at least 60% of the whole process.

I have eaten steak that was prepared and tasted like a burnt piece of a boot, so knowing how to cook is part of it. However, cooking venison does not have to be a hard process. If you can follow simple recipes, you can cook delicious venison that your entire family will enjoy. The only problem you will have, as your family will totally enjoy the flavor, is getting one or two deer each season. However, if you read my book to this point that should no longer be a problem. Your next problem will be getting a freezer large enough to store the two deer you will have after you have harvested them and then processed the meat to the cuts your family enjoys the most. If you are like me, you will have two four-foot freezers and one six-foot box freezer. Well, maybe not like me, but you will buy another freezer.

Chapter Twenty-Nine

Recipes

These recipes I have selected I have personally prepared and are my favorites. Each recipe is a good way to prepare venison, during the year after hunting season, and I know you will enjoy all of them. Try each one, as I know you and your family and friends will enjoy venison dishes made this way.

Recipe Index:

Measurements

A pinch ....⅛ teaspoon or less
3 teaspoons...............1 tablespoon
4 tablespoons ....¼ cup
8 tablespoons ....½ cup
12 tablespoons ....¾ cup
16 tablespoons ....1 cup
2 cups ....1 pint
4 cups ....1 quart
4 quarts ....1 gallon
8 quarts ....1 peck
16 ounces..................1 pound
32 ounces..................1 quart
1 ounce liquid ....2 tablespoons
8 ounces liquid.........1 cup

Use standard measuring spoons and cups.
All measurements are to be level.

Fixes and Ideas for the Cook

Acidic foods — Sometimes a tomato-based sauce/gravy will become too acidic. Add baking soda, one tablespoon at a time, to the sauce. I use sugar as a sweeter alternative to cut the acid.

Burnt food on pots and pans — Allow the pan to cool on its own. Remove as much of the food as possible. Fill with hot water and add two capfuls of liquid fabric softener and one capful of liquid dish detergent, and let it stand for a few hours. You will have a much easier time removing the burnt food. Then wash thoroughly.

Lumpy gravy or sauce — Use a blender, food processor or simply strain.

Soup, sauce, gravy too thin — Add 1 tablespoon of flour to hot soup, sauce, or gravy. Whisk well to avoid lumps while the mixture is boiling. Repeat if necessary.

Stew or soup is greasy — Lay a cold lettuce leaf over the hot stew for about 10 seconds and then remove. Repeat if necessary to absorb more grease.

Venison Ground Meat — I always grind with pork at a 1 to 3 ratio.

Venison Grilling Guide

Steak Cuts

1-inch thick steak............Grill Time Per Side
Rare..............................7 to 9 minutes
Medium.......................10 to 13 minutes
Well Done...................14 to 19 minutes

2-inch thick steak............Grill Time Per Side
Rare..............................15 to 17 minutes
Medium.......................20 to 25 minutes
Well Done...................30 to 40 minutes

Strip Cuts

½ - ¾ inch thick...............Grill Time Per Side
Rare..............................3 to 5 minutes
Medium.......................7 to 9 minutes
Well Done...................10 to 12 minutes

Venison Burgers on the Grill

Use 75% venison and 25% ground beef *or* use 80% venison and 20% ground pork

For a charcoal grill (uncovered)
Rare..............................6 to 10 minutes
Medium.......................12 to 13 minutes
Well Done...................15 to 19 minutes

Venison Grilling Tips

Fresh herbs will improve the flavor of the meat, but I generally like to use Season Salt and a good barbeque seasoning on both sides when I grill venison burgers. Make each burger large enough to allow for some shrinkage, and watch the burgers disappear on your dinner table.

1. VENISON CHOWDER

(An all-time favorite)

Ingredients:

2 lbs. of venison cut into small 1-inch pieces
5 medium potatoes
½ minced medium onion
1 large can of chicken broth
2 tablespoons of butter or margarine
1 ½ cups of milk
1 can (10¾ oz.) cream of mushroom soup
1 can (14 oz.) of cream style corn
1 tsp. of salt
⅛ tsp. of black pepper
⅛ tsp. of cayenne pepper

Preparation:

1. Place the venison cubes in a crock pot; add chicken broth to cover and cook on high for 4 hours before you begin this recipe. You want the venison to be cooked and tender first.
2. Cover unpeeled potatoes with salted water and cook with the cover on a pot until tender.
3. Remove potato skins, then cut potatoes into small chunks.
4. In a large skillet or 2-quart saucepan, melt butter. Sauté onions for 5 minutes.
5. Add milk, cooked venison, cream of mushroom soup and potatoes.
6. Cook over medium low heat about 20 minutes and stir occasionally.
7. Add cream style corn, salt, and peppers.
8. Bring to a boil, then reduce the heat and simmer for 20 minutes and season with more salt or black pepper to taste.

This recipe will serve 4 people when completed and can be a main meal if served with warm garlic bread, or can be an added extra when served with a venison roast or steak.

2. Venison A La Mintz

(One of my favorites)

Ingredients for Marinade:

1 package of venison steaks cut 6-inches long (6 steaks) *or* venison cutlets from the 6 steaks making 12 to 14 cutlets.
1 cup of milk
1 egg
4 or 5 shakes of Paprika
¼ teaspoon salt
½ teaspoon pepper
½ teaspoon garlic powder
¼ teaspoon onion salt
4 shakes of Worcestershire sauce
2 shakes of Soy Sauce

Mix together thoroughly and soak the meat completely in this marinade for 1¾ - 2 hours covered in the refrigerator.

Preparation:

2 medium size onions sliced long
1 can of sliced mushrooms

1. Drain the marinade off the meat.
2. Pre-heat a large frying pan to medium-high.
3. Cook the onions until brown then remove and set aside.
4. Add generous amounts of butter into the hot frying pan with 4 to 5 shakes of teriyaki sauce.
5. Coat the meat with egg and then roll the meat in flour.
6. Cook the meat by turning it every minute. The meat will cook in 4 to 5 minutes. Be careful when you turn the meat not to lose the coating. Do not overcook the meat, as you will next place it in the oven.
7. Place the cooked meat into a long Pyrex style-cooking dish. Cover the meat with cooked onions and mushrooms, and then cover the dish with tin foil and place into the oven at 350 degrees and cook for thirty minutes.

This dish will feed 4 to 6 people, and will be the best tasting venison dish you have ever prepared for your family or friends. This is the perfect venison dish for those who say they do not like the taste of venison.

3. MARY'S VENISON MEAT PIE

(One of my favorites)

Ingredients:

2 lbs. of venison and 2 lbs. of pork ground together
4 medium onions
2 tablespoons cooking oil
12 medium potatoes cooked and mashed with milk and butter
1 teaspoon allspice
½ teaspoon pepper
½ teaspoon cinnamon
4 ready-made crusts, tops & bottoms
Salt to taste

Preparation: *(This will make 2 pies; cut recipe in ½ for 1 pie)*

1. Take the potatoes, peel them, and cook in boiling water.
2. Once potatoes are cooked, mash them while adding pepper; and add milk and butter to taste.
3. Chop the onions.
4. Place the chopped onions and ground meat mixture in a pan.
5. Cook onions and meat until both are brown in butter.
6. In a large pan, mix mashed potatoes, cooked meat, onions, and spices.
7. Fill the bottom piecrust with this mixture, and add the top crust and make two slices in the top of the piecrust.
8. Bake at 350 degrees until crust is nicely browned, usually about 50 minutes.

If you plan to freeze one pie, bake that one only ½ hour and take it out to cool, then cover and freeze.

When you are ready to eat the frozen venison pie, remove it from the freezer to thaw, but first add butter to the top. Then bake the venison pie until the top is lightly browned and heated completely.

I usually make 2 pies and freeze one.

This is a meal in itself, and one medium-size pie will feed 4 to 6 people, but if you have 6 people, make 2 pies and you will be surprised how quickly it disappears.

Note: If you want to spice up your mashed potatoes, add a can of brown gravy and another ½ teaspoon of cinnamon, and stir it into the mashed potatoes and see the smiles.

4. Bob's Venison Meatloaf

(My own recipe)

Ingredients:

2 lbs. of venison ground meat
1 medium onion
2 tablespoons garlic powder
1 medium size can of Italian style breadcrumbs
½ cup Parmesan cheese
½ teaspoon parsley
1 egg
1 tablespoon Italian seasoning
½ tablespoon oregano
¼ teaspoon basil
1 pinch of salt
2 pinches of black pepper
¼ cup of water

Preparation:

1. Take the 2 lbs. of ground venison and put it in a large mixing bowl.
2. Shake in the whole medium size can of Italian breadcrumbs and mix thoroughly.
3. Then add the Parmesan cheese and mix again.
4. Add the egg and the ¼ cup of water and mix.
5. Take the one onion, cut and mince it into small pieces, then add it to the mixture.
6. Then add all the remaining ingredients and mix thoroughly.

Set your oven to 350 degrees. Take a cooking pan and coat the bottom of it with a non-stick spray. Take the meat out of the bowl and place on a cutting board and form the meatloaf. Once the meatloaf is formed, put it in a cooking pan and wait until the oven has reached 350 degrees, then put the meatloaf in the oven to cook for 1 hour or until the top is brown.

This can be served with cut and cooked potatoes mixed with green peas for an excellent dinner dish. This dish will feed 6 to 8 people.

5. VENISON CHILI

(One of my favorites)

Ingredients:

2 lbs. of venison ground meat
2 cans of dark kidney beans
1 can of split mushrooms
1 medium onion
1 jar of tomato & basil Italian sauce
2 tablespoons Italian seasoning
1 tablespoon oregano
2 tablespoons garlic powder
1 pinch of salt
1 teaspoon black pepper
1 package of mild chili seasoning
2 cups of rice

Preparation:

1. Take the onion and cut it into small chunks.
2. Take the 2 lbs. of venison and put it in a large frying pan.
3. Cook the venison and onions until they are brown.
4. Add the tomato sauce and simmer.
5. Add the chili seasoning, stir to blend, and then add all the other ingredients and stir.
6. Cook the chili for 20 minutes with all the ingredients and taste.
7. If you desire the chili to be hotter, add chili powder to your desired taste.
8. While the chili is cooking, boil water in a pot and make the rice. Let the rice stand for 5 minutes after it is cooked, then serve.

This chili dish will take approximately 40 minutes from start to finish to prepare and will feed 6 people. It is generally served over rice and is a meal in itself or with rice. You can serve the chili with shredded American cheese over the top of the chili. If serving the chili alone, I recommend you add Italian bread to the table, as it will go well with the chili.

6. *MARY & BOB'S VENISON STEW*

(Our own recipe)

Ingredients:

2-3 lbs. of venison stew meat
4 medium potatoes
2 medium onions
4 carrots
1 can of whole kernel corn
2 cloves of garlic
1 jar of Italian sauce with basil
2 tablespoons oregano
1 tablespoon Italian seasoning
1 pinch of basil
1 pinch of salt
1 tablespoon black pepper

Preparation:

1. Take the venison, put it on a cutting board, and trim off most of the fat.
2. Place the venison into a crock pot.
3. Wash and peel the potatoes, and then cut them into medium sized pieces or wedges about one inch square, then put them into the crock pot.
4. Peel and cut the onions into small pieces and put them into the crock pot.
5. Clean the 4 carrots and cut them to be ½ wide; put the carrots into the crock pot.
6. Place the jar of Italian sauce and one jar of water into the crock pot and stir.
7. Open the can of whole kernel corn, drain, and then put it into the crock pot and stir.
8. Cut up the 2 cloves of garlic into small pieces, wait 15 minutes and then put the garlic into the crock pot and stir.
9. Put all seasoning into the crock pot and stir thoroughly until all seasoning is blended.
10. Put the crock pot setting to high and stir every hour. Cook for 6 hours, and then put the crock pot setting to low for 1½ hours, stirring every ½ hr. after you put the crock pot to the low setting.

This recipe will take an average of 7½ to 8 hours to complete. Serve with Parmesan cheese and Italian bread and watch the smiles as your family with love this Italian-style venison dish. You can serve this dish as is or over rice. Serves 6 people comfortably.

7. VENISON SAUSAGE & PEPPERS

(My own recipe)

Ingredients:

2-3 lbs. of venison sausage Italian style
4 bell peppers (1 green, 2 red and 1 yellow)
2 medium yellow onions
2 cups virgin olive oil
4 cloves of garlic
3 tablespoons Italian seasoning
½ teaspoon basil
1 teaspoon oregano
2 pinches of salt
1 teaspoon black pepper
1-2 loafs of Italian bread

Preparation:

1. Wash the bell peppers and cut lengthwise so the peppers are ½ wide and long and set aside.
2. Take and peel the onions and cut them so they are long and ½ wide as well, and set them to the side.
3. Cut the 4 cloves of garlic thin and set aside for 10 minutes.
4. Take the venison sausage and brown it in a large frying pan until the venison sausage is ½ to ¾ cooked.
5. Once the sausage is ½ to ¾ cooked, remove the sausages and cut them to be ¾ wide and put them back into the frying pan.
6. Add the peppers and the onions to the pan and the 2 cups of the virgin olive oil and stir.
7. Add the garlic and then all the spices and stir and cover to allow it to cook, stirring occasionally so the sausage and peppers and onions do not stick to the pan. Once the peppers and onions start to cook, lower the heat to med-low and keep an eye on it.
8. As this is, cooking cut the Italian bread into 5-inch pieces and put it on separate plates.
9. When the sausage, peppers, and onions are done, place them on the Italian bread to serve.

This is a meal all in itself and is the Italian-style way of cooking and serving venison sausage and peppers. From start to finish, this meal will take less than 45 minutes to prepare and will serve 4 to 6 people if you have enough Italian bread. Be sure to put the oil sauce on the bread with the sausage and peppers, as it should soak into the bread when served. You should put Parmesan cheese on top as you serve it.

8. Venison Swiss Style Steak

(Mouth watering)

Ingredients:

6 venison steaks
1 green bell pepper
1 medium yellow onion
1 jar of tomato sauce (with basil)
½ tablespoon thyme
½ tablespoon savory
1 teaspoon marjoram
¾ cup red wine
½ cup hot water with chicken bullion cube dissolved
4 tablespoons bacon fat
1 pinch of salt
½ teaspoon black pepper
Butter as needed

Preparation:

1. Peel the onions, then chop them and set them aside.
2. Take the green pepper, clean it, chop it and set it aside.
3. Put the bacon fat and 4 tablespoons of butter in a frying pan and get the butter to melt and mix with the bacon fat.
4. Salt and pepper each side of the steaks and set to one side.
5. Cover each side of the steaks with flour, pressing the flour into the meat on both sides.
6. Sauté each side of the steak in a pan that has the bacon fat and melted butter.
7. When the second side is brown, turn the stovetop to medium and add the onions and peppers.
8. When the onions and peppers are soft, add the wine, tomato sauce, herbs, and cover.
9. Check occasionally, but the steaks should be done in 1½ hours. Check with a fork, as the fork should go in easy when the steaks are cooked.
10. Turn the steaks twice in the process, and watch it as the flour will make the sauce heavy, and you do not want to lose or peel the coating off. If the sauce becomes too heavy, add a little bit of the bullion water, but only if you want a thinner sauce.

This is a delicious recipe and a great way to cook venison that will give the venison a delicious wine sauce flavor. You can serve this with rice or stuffing with Italian bread. This dish will feed an average of 4 to 5 people, and is a meal you will remember.

9. Crock Pot Venison Pot Roast

(For connoisseurs)

Ingredients:

3½-4 lb. venison roast
2 medium onions
1 can sliced mushrooms
1 large can of College Inn chicken broth
4 cups apple cider
2 carrots
3 cloves of garlic
½ teaspoon celery salt
½ teaspoon spicy mustard

Preparation:

1. Peel and chop the two onions and set aside.
2. Peel and chop the carrots into ¾-inch pieces and set aside.
3. Take the three cloves of garlic, cut into thin slices, and set aside for 15 minutes.
4. Now trim the venison roast, remove any excess fat, and put it into a crock pot.
5. Mix the apple cider and College Inn broth to cover the roast.
6. Add the garlic, onions, mushrooms, and carrots.
7. Put the celery salt and mustard, and stir so all ingredients come together.
8. Cover, set dial to high and cook for six hours.

Check every hour and stir lightly. After 6 hours, set the dial to low and cook an additional hour on low. You can serve this dish with wild rice, stuffing, or potato slices cooked in the oven with green peas.

I like to serve this dish with garlic bread, oven-cooked potatoes and peas, and stuffing. This dish will feed 6 to 8 people. The apple cider gives the venison a distinctive taste. Use all the apple cider and only add to it to cover the roast.

10. Bob's Venison Meat Balls

(My own recipe)

Ingredients:

2 lbs. of venison ground meat that has been mixed with pork
1 medium can of Italian breadcrumbs
1 cup grated parmesan cheese
2 tablespoons parsley
2 tablespoons Italian seasoning
2 tablespoons oregano
½ teaspoon basil
2 pinches of salt
2 tablespoons garlic powder
1 egg
¼ cup water

Preparation:

1. Take the ground venison and put it into a large mixing bowl.
2. Add the Italian bread crumbs.
3. Add one egg and mix by hand.
4. Add the cup of Parmesan cheese and mix again.
5. Add all the other ingredients and mix by hand thoroughly.
6. After it is completely mixed, roll the meatballs into the size of golf balls until they are tight with no cracks in the meat.
7. Put Canola oil in a large frying pan about 1-inch high.
8. Heat the oil, place the meatballs in and fry them until they are brown, then set them aside to cool.

They can be eaten as is or you can put them in homemade spaghetti gravy to cook for about three hours more, so the gravy is absorbed into the meat. Do not roll the meatballs and put them in gravy before you cook them to make them brown, as the meatballs will fall apart if not browned. You can serve them with stuffing or wild rice as is.

11. VENISON STIR FRY

(All-time favorite)

Ingredients:

1½-2 lbs. of venison cut into strips
1 medium size bottle of teriyaki sauce
3 shakes of Worcestershire sauce
1 package of stir-fry vegetables
2 medium onions
½ lb. butter
4 large cloves of garlic
2 pinches of pepper
4 good shakes of seasoned salt
2 cups of rice

Preparation:

1. Peel and cut an onion into long strips and set aside.
2. Peel and cut in thin slices the cloves of garlic and set aside for 15 min.
3. Put the strips of venison in a large frying pan, cover with teriyaki sauce and cook lightly, then drain the sauce and leave the venison in the frying pan.
4. Add the onions and the garlic and more teriyaki sauce and begin to cook again.
5. Add the Worcestershire sauce (3 shakes).
6. Add four good shakes of seasoned salt.
7. Then add the butter and allow for melting.
8. Add all other seasonings and the package of stir-fry vegetables; stir, mix, and cook on medium-low covered for 10 minutes.
9. While this is cooking, boil water and make the rice.

When the vegetables are cooked, shut the heat and serve over rice. Add some sauce to each plate when serving. I usually serve this with bread also. This meal will feed 6 people and can be used as a lunch or dinner meal.

12. Bland's Ozark-Style Fried Venison

(All-time favorite)

Ingredients:

2 lbs. of ¼-inch sliced tenderloins
2 cups milk
2 eggs
2 cups self-rising flour
1 tablespoon seasoned salt
½ teaspoon black pepper
½ teaspoon table salt
¼ teaspoon garlic salt
1 cup of cooking oil

Preparation:

1. Preheat skillet with oil (prefer large cast-iron skillet) to 250 degrees.
2. While skillet is heating, combine two cups of milk, with the two eggs and whip together.
3. In another bowl combine flour, seasoned salt, pepper, table salt, garlic salt, and stir well.
4. Once the oil is hot, put your meat in the milk and egg mixture, then roll the meat into the flour until it is covered well and put it into the hot oil to cook.
5. *Note:* The oil has to be really hot when you put the covered meat into it for the coating to stay on the meat.
6. Cook the meat until it is light brown, approximately 1 minute each, to be most tender. *Do not overcook.*

This is a really good family meal, which I have had the pleasure to eat several times at the house of the designer of this recipe. This meal will feed 6 people and is a great lunch or dinner meal.

A Hunter's Dream Meal

Fried tenderloins
Fried potatoes with onions
Biscuits and gravy
Molasses or honey butter with biscuits

13. Steve's Venison Stew

(Great family meal)

Ingredients:

2 lbs. venison stew meat
6 tablespoons flour
1½ teaspoons salt
1 teaspoon of dried thyme
¼ teaspoon pepper
Vegetable oil
1 small onion, minced
6 carrots, cut in half
12 oz. package of frozen peas
1 tablespoon Worcestershire sauce
2 tablespoons tomato paste
¼ cup sweet (red) vermouth

Preparation:

1. Mix together the flour, salt, thyme and pepper.
2. Coat stew meat well in flour; save extra flour mixture.
3. In Dutch oven or large pot, brown meat in batches in the hot oil, then put the browned meat aside.
4. Sauté minced onion in same oil for 1-2 minutes.
5. Add 1-2 tablespoons of reserved flour and brown, stirring constantly about 1 minute.
6. Add beef broth, Worcestershire sauce, tomato paste, and vermouth. Stir well, bring to simmer on low heat.
7. Add meat and simmer on low heat at least two hours, three is better. Stir as need to prevent sticking. If mixture gets too thick, you can add some water.
8. Add sliced onions, and carrots, then stew 45 minutes.
9. Add frozen peas, stir in, and then cook another 15 minutes.

This meal can be served over noodles, and I find it to be better when served the following day. This recipe we generally have the night before opening day of deer season. It is a meal that will serve 6 to 8 people and is a great venison stew that your whole family will enjoy.

14. BOB'S VENISON PARMESAN

(My own recipe)

Ingredients:

2-3 lbs. of sliced ½-inch thick venison cutlets
2 cups of Parmesan cheese
1 package of whole milk mozzarella
2 tablespoons of parsley
2 eggs
1 small can of Italian Style breadcrumbs
2 tablespoons of Italian seasoning
2 tablespoons of garlic
2 cups of vegetable oil.
1 medium size pot of homemade Italian gravy
(homemade spaghetti sauce for non-Italians)

Preparation:

1. Take the whole can of Italian Style breadcrumbs and put in a mixing bowl.
2. Add 2 tablespoons of parsley, 2 tablespoons of Italian seasoning, 2 tablespoons of powdered garlic, 2 tablespoons of parsley and mix with the Italian style breadcrumbs.
3. Take the 2 eggs and scramble them in another dish.
4. Take the venison cutlets and dip them into the eggs and then Italian style breadcrumb mix you made.
5. Cook them in HOT vegetable oil in a frying pan until they are brown and then set them aside. *Do not overcook.*
6. Take the Italian gravy and put a thin coat on the bottom of your Pyrex deep dish, or deep aluminum-cooking pan.
7. Put a layer of the cooked venison cutlets into the Pyrex dish, then cover with the Italian gravy.
8. Sprinkle a good amount of mozzarella over the cutlets and then sprinkle some parmesan cheese on top.
9. Put another layer of venison cutlets on top, put some Italian gravy on them to cover them, then add mozzarella over them, and sprinkle parmesan cheese over them again.
10. Repeat the process until you reach the top and then cover with Italian gravy, cheese, and sprinkle the parsley over them.
11. Cover with aluminum foil and put into a pre heated over.
12. Cook at 350 degrees 45 minutes, until all mozzarella cheese is melted. Take out of the oven and let sit for 15 minutes before you serve.

This is an excellent way to prepare venison cutlets Italian style that all will enjoy. I generally serve them with pasta or macaroni and cheese. This meal will feed 6 to 8 people, and you will see the smiles on their face.

15. BOB'S HOT VENISON CASSEROLE

(My own recipe)

Ingredients:

2 lbs. venison ground meat
1 lb. Italian rigatoni noodles
1 jar Italian sauce with basil
1 can sliced mushrooms
1 yellow onion
1 green bell pepper
1 can whole kernel corn
4 garlic cloves
1 cup Parmesan cheese
4 tablespoons Virgin olive oil

Preparation:

1. Take the yellow onion, peel it, chop it up in small pieces, and set aside.
2. Take the green pepper, clean it, chop it into small pieces, and set aside.
3. Take the garlic cloves, slice them thin, and set for 15 minutes.
4. Take a frying pan, put the Virgin olive oil in it, then add the venison ground meat, and cook with the garlic slices, chopped onions, chopped peppers, and mushrooms.
5. Once they are cooked, add the jar of Italian sauce, the drained can of whole kernel corn, and simmer for 15 minutes on med-low.
6. While this is simmering, cook the Rigatoni in a separate pot, and then drain.
7. Put the cooked rigatoni into a large serving dish, and put the cooked venison, onions, peppers, mushrooms, and corn in with the pasta. Stir and serve with the parmesan cheese over it.

This is a great dinner dish and will serve an average of 6 to 8 people. I generally serve this dish with garlic bread or Italian bread. This is a simple casserole dish to prepare and will sure to be a favorite for your family.

16. Venison with Red Beans and Rice

Ingredients:

1½-2 lbs. of venison ground meat
1 medium yellow onion
1 medium green bell pepper
1 reg. size can kidney beans
1 package (6.8 oz.) Mexican rice mix with seasoning
1-2 tomatoes

Preparation:

1. Peel the onion and dice it, then set it aside.
2. Clean the green bell pepper and dice it, then set it aside.
3. Take the tomatoes and clean them and dice them, and then set them aside, as you will be adding them last.
4. Get the can of kidney beans, open it and drain it, and then set it aside for the moment.
5. Brown the venison ground meat with the diced onions and the diced green pepper. I always use venison ground meat that has been mixed with pork on a 1 to 3 ratio.
6. Stir in the beans, then add the rice mix and seasoning, then add the water according the package directions. You do not have to add oil or butter. Bring to a boil, then reduce the heat and cook to the package directions for the Mexican rice.
7. Once the rice is cooked, top the dish with the diced tomatoes and serve.

This is a great recipe and a different way to serve venison ground meat from all other recipes. Your family will love the taste of venison prepared this way. This dish will serve an average of 4 to 5 people. If you are serving more people, adjust by adding more of each of the ingredients and 2 packages of the Mexican rice mix. This is a simple and delicious recipe that only takes 30 to 45 minutes to prepare.

17. Venison Roast with Yorkshire Pudding

Ingredients:

1 venison hind roast approx. 6-7 lbs.
1 teaspoon black pepper
3 teaspoons dried thyme
1 pinch of salt
8 cloves of garlic
1 cup flour
1 cup milk
2 eggs
2 tablespoons butter
2 tablespoons chives
6 tablespoons melted butter

Preparation:

1. Mince your garlic and combine with two teaspoons of thyme, pepper, salt, and rub and press onto the venison roast.
2. Heat your oven to 350 degrees in a shallow roasting pan and cook for two hours or until your meat thermometer registers 140 degrees.
3. While your venison roast is cooking, and 1½ hours before it is done, prepare the Yorkshire pudding.

Yorkshire Pudding Recipe:

1. Combine the chives, 1 teaspoon of thyme, salt, and flour into a mixing bowl.
2. In a separate bowl, add the milk and eggs and mix together, and then add the flour mixture. Whisk together until the mixture is smooth, and then refrigerate for 1 hour.
3. After the venison roast is removed from the oven, set the oven to 450 degrees.
4. Coat muffin cups with butter on the sides and bottom, then fill them half-way with the Yorkshire mix from the refrigerator.
5. Bake them in the 450 degree oven for 15 minutes or until they look golden brown on top. Serve right from the oven with your venison roast.

This is a great way to add excitement to your venison roast dinner. You can also serve wild rice to add more flavor to your dish. This recipe will serve 6 to 7 people comfortably, and watch the smiles.

18. Tangy Venison Steaks with Mushroom Sauce

Ingredients:

2 venison steaks, cut 1-inch thick
1 can sliced mushrooms
1 pinch of salt
1 tablespoon seasoned salt
1 teaspoon dried thyme
3 tablespoons butter
¾ cup balsamic vinegar
1 medium yellow onion
2 teaspoons pepper

Preparation:

1. Peel and slice onion into long pieces and set aside.
2. Heat a large skillet, then add the venison steaks and cook to medium rare, or how you prefer them. *Do not overcook.* As you cook each side, sprinkle with seasoned salt.
3. Remove after they are cooked; pepper each side and set aside.
4. Cook the onions until they are brown; add a pinch of salt and set them aside.
5. Add mushrooms to the frying pan, then the thyme and cook over medium heat a few minutes until the mushrooms are warm, then add the balsamic vinegar and the butter, then cook together with the onions you set aside. Cook about 5 or 6 minutes.

Serve the steaks with this mushroom and onion combination that will be a bit tangy, but it is a great way to serve venison steaks. This recipe will take about 45 minutes to prepare and can be served with stuffing, or mashed potatoes or wild rice. You will enjoy this new taste to venison steaks.

19. Venison BBQ Sandwiches

(A very nice surprise)

Ingredients:

1 venison roast, 4-5 lbs.
1 large can of beef broth
2 cups barbeque sauce
2 teaspoons oil
2 tablespoons garlic
1 teaspoon seasoned salt
Rolls or Buns

Preparation:

1. Cover venison with oil, black pepper and seasoned salt, and rub the pepper and salt into the venison.
2. Put the venison into a crock pot, then add the beef broth, garlic, and cover.
3. Set the crock pot to high and cook for four hours or until the venison roast tears with a fork easily.
4. Remove the venison roast, allow to cool slightly, and then shred the meat with a fork.
5. Put the shredded venison into a saucepan, add the barbeque sauce, oil, and cook over medium heat for 10 minutes. Add liquid as needed to keep the venison moist.

This is a tasty way to serve venison as a lunch or dinner meal. As a dinner meal, you can serve this with stuffing or a rice dish. I prefer macaroni and cheese with this myself. It takes about 4½ hours total to prepare with cooking the venison in a crock pot first. This meal will feed 6 people and is a good way of serving venison to newcomers or youngsters for the first time.

Once the venison is prepared, it will take about 30 minutes to prepare this dish, then watch the smiles.

20. Shredded Venison with Onions and Peppers

Ingredients:

1 venison roast 5-6 lbs.
1 large can of chicken broth
6 cloves of garlic
2 medium yellow onions
2 bell peppers
4 tablespoons oil
1 teaspoon pepper
1 tablespoon seasoned salt
2 teaspoons Italian seasoning
1 teaspoon basil
1 can of beef gravy

Preparation:

1. Put the venison roast into a crock pot with the chicken broth and garlic you sliced and cook for four hours or until the venison can be shredded with a fork.
2. Peel and cut the onions into long pieces, and set them aside.
3. Clean and cut the bell peppers into long pieces and set them aside.
4. After the venison is cool, shred the venison and place into a frying pan with oil, onions, and peppers with all seasonings; cook for 15 minutes over medium heat and covered to soften the onions and peppers.
5. Stir in beef gravy and cook for 10 more minutes.

Serve this dish over a bed of cooked brown rice or over cooked egg noodles. I also put Parmesan cheese on the table for those, like me, who like Parmesan cheese. Italian bread is also good with this venison dish. This dish will feed 6 people, and watch the smiles.

21. Venison Curry

(My personal favorite)

Ingredients:

2 lbs. of venison stew meat cut into 1½-inch cubes
3 medium yellow onions
2 pinches salt
3 pinches pepper
2 teaspoons curry powder
2 teaspoons thyme
4 tablespoons AP flour
4 tablespoons butter
3 pinches of parsley
2 pinches of Italian seasoning
1 quart chicken broth

Preparation:

1. Peel and slice the onions and set them aside.
2. Trim off the excess fat off the venison stew meat.
3. In a heavy covered pot or Dutch oven, put the venison stew meat with one quart of chicken broth.
4. Add the sliced onions, thyme and parsley and allow to simmer for 1½ hours, skimming off the scum-like substance that comes to the top of the pot for the first 30 minutes.
5. Remove the meat, strain the liquid and set the liquid aside for later.
6. In a small skillet, melt the butter and slowly add the flour and curry powder once the flour mixes completely.
7. Cook this over low heat and stir continuously for three minutes while adding the broth you set aside.
8. Add the salt, pepper, and venison and cook until the sauce thickens. Be sure to stir so as not to burn the sauce. Do not raise the heat. Once the sauce thickens, the dish is ready to serve.

If you want to try this, it is an excellent and different way to serve venison, providing you like a curry dish, which is a little spicy but not too spicy. I generally serve this dish over rice, but you can serve it with cooked egg noodles, as I have tried both. Remember to cook the venison in chicken broth, as it will give the venison a taste all will enjoy and it reduces any gamey taste. Serve this to those who say venison is too gamey for them and watch them smile at the taste of the dish you prepared. This dish will serve 6 people. If you like a spicier dish, add a teaspoon more curry powder and pepper the next time you serve this dish, but try this recipe first, as I know you will like it.

22. Venison Shish Kebab

(A great summer dish)

Ingredients:

2 lbs. of venison cut into 1½-inch cubes
Several small onions
2 bell peppers
4 large fresh mushrooms
1 can of chuck pineapple
2 pinches of salt
4 pinches of pepper
1 cup sweet cooking sherry
1 tablespoon vegetable oil
¼ teaspoon oregano
½ teaspoon Italian seasoning
2 firm tomatoes

Preparation:

1. Trim most of the fat off the venison and set aside.
2. In a square-shaped marinade bowl with a lid or a mixing bowl with a lid, place the venison, sherry, milk, oil, oregano, Italian seasoning, salt and pepper, and then allow marinating overnight in the refrigerator. Mix well and turn several times so all the meat is marinated.
3. Take the onions and cut into chunks, or if you have small onions, set them in a dish to the side.
4. Cut the bell peppers into 2-inch slices and set to the side.
5. Open the can of pineapples and set to the side.
6. Take a metal skewer and put on a piece of meat from the marinade. Put on a pineapple chunk, then an onion and then a piece of pepper, followed by a piece of tomato. Repeat in this way until the skewer is full and all are snug together. Then set in a dish.
7. Make other skewers the same way, be sure not to put two pieces of meat together on the skewer, so all vegetables are eaten and not just the meat.
8. Cook over charcoal and cook for 4-5 minutes, each side until medium rare. *Do not overcook.*

This is a great summer recipe over the grill, and the charcoal will give the meat a delicious taste. You can use barbeque sauce, but I do not recommend it with the vegetables. The marinade will give the venison a great taste. You can serve this with wild rice, stuffing, or any summer barbeque dish. This recipe will serve 8 people comfortably.

23. Venison Marsala

(My own recipe)

Ingredients:

2 lbs. of venison cutlets, cut thin
1 cup of parmesan cheese, grated.
2 tablespoons vegetable oil
2 cloves of garlic
Flour to thicken
½ cup chicken broth
¾ cup Marsala wine
6 tablespoons butter
1 pinch of salt
2 pinches of pepper

Preparation:

1. Peel and slice the garlic cloves thin and set aside for 15 minutes.
2. Melt the butter and oil with the garlic slices in a skillet.
3. Dip the meat in Parmesan cheese and coat both sides of the venison cutlets thoroughly.
4. Brown both sides of the venison and set on a warm plate.
5. Turn up the heat, add the chicken broth, salt and pepper, and cook for one minute.
6. Add the wine and then cook for another two minutes while mixing it all together. Add some flour to thicken the sauce.
7. Serve the thickened sauce over the venison cutlets.

This is a great way to serve venison cutlets, and the combination with the Marsala wine will give the venison a delicious new taste. Any alcohol in the wine will burn off while cooking, but the great flavor will remain in the meat, giving it a mouthwatering taste that both young and old will totally enjoy. I generally serve this dish with spaghetti cooked with garlic and oil as a side dish. You can do the same, but if you do not like spaghetti with garlic and oil, try this.

Cook enough spaghetti for your group, and in a separate pan, melt one stick of butter and add some spinach. Mix the melted butter and cooked spinach with the drained spaghetti and add some Parmesan cheese and serve the spaghetti this way, as it is delicious also. This recipe will serve 6 people.

24. Bob's Venison Salad

(My own recipe)

Ingredients:

1 lb. of venison ground meat
¾ cup mayonnaise
1 stick of butter
1 teaspoon sugar
1 tablespoon seasoned salt
1 pinch of pepper
2 stalks of celery
4 tablespoons heavy cream
1 head of lettuce
Salt to taste
1 hard-boiled and chopped egg

Preparation:

1. Take the celery, clean it and chop it into small fine pieces, then set it aside.
2. In a skillet, cook the venison ground meat that has already been mixed with pork in a 3 to 1 ratio over low heat. Cook it in the butter, while adding the seasoned salt, salt, sugar, and pepper until the meat is cooked and brown, and then set aside to cool. *Do not overcook.*
3. In a mixing bowl, add the cooled and cooked venison and the celery.
4. In another bowl, mix the mayonnaise and cream thoroughly with the chopped egg. Pour it over the cooked venison and celery and mix completely.
5. Arrange a bed of lettuce leaves and put the venison salad on top.

This is a good lunch meal and a new way to serve venison. I have served this over toast and even had it in a toasted sandwich, and it is a delicious way to serve venison. This recipe will serve 4 people comfortably and has a nice taste to it.

25. Venison Polish Sausage and Sauerkraut

This recipe calls for Polish Sausage that has been made of 90% venison and 10% pork fat.

Ingredients:

2 sticks of Venison Polish Sausage
4 tablespoons seasoned salt
2 tablespoons black pepper
1 can of Sauerkraut
4 potatoes
3 medium yellow onions

Preparation:

1. Take the potatoes, peel them and slice them into thin slices, then set them aside.
2. Clean and peel the onions, slice them into long slices and set them aside.
3. Take the Venison Polish Sausages, slice them into ½-inch slices, and set to the side.
4. Take a skillet, put the venison slices and a drained can of sauerkraut in it and cook over medium heat while adding the seasoned salt and pepper.
5. While this is cooking, take another skillet and cook the potatoes and onions in oil until the potatoes and tender and lightly brown.

After the venison polish sausage is cooked with the sauerkraut, serve with the cooked potatoes and onions. I generally serve this with garlic bread, and it is a fantastic meal. This recipe will serve 6 people.

I recommend all hunters to have a portion of their meat taken to a butcher to have Venison Polish Sausage made for them. It is a fantastic way to have venison processed and should not be overlooked. If you try it once, you will always have venison processed this way. I usually have 40-50 lbs. of venison processed into Polish Sausage each year. The ratio that works the best is 90% venison and 10% pork fat.

Appendix

This appendix contains copies of the official score charts used as the Office Scoring System for North American Big Game Trophies. The Boone and Crockett Club's score charts for typical and non-typical whitetail deer reproduced in this book are with the express written permission of the Boone and Crockett Club, 250 Station Drive, Missoula, MT 59801. To learn more about the Club and the many activities it is involved in, please visit their web site at www.booneandcrockettclub.com or call (406) 542-1888.

The Pope & Young Club score carts for typical and non-typical whitetail deer are reproduced in this book with the express written permission of both the Boone and Crockett Club and the Pope & Young Club, 273 Mill Creek Road, P.O. Box 548, Chatfield, MN 55923. If you wish to learn more about the Pope & Young Club and their activities, please visit their website located at www.pope-young.org or call (507) 867-4144.

The Boone and Crockett Club, which is one of the most famous of *Fair Chase* Clubs, was founded by wildlife's greatest champion and protector, Theodore Roosevelt, in 1887. It was his vision to establish a coalition of dedicated sportsmen and conservationists to address issues concerning hunting, wildlife and wildlife habitat. Today, the Boone and Crockett Club is the leading club that carries on the vision of the future by keeping big game records, supports conservation research, education and formulated the code of conduct and ethics for sportsmen and conservationists, which later became law. Their activities are numerous and as a hunter, you should become familiar with this club, what it stands for and the activities in which it takes part. I recommend you become a member of this club today. Please visit their website and see all that this prestigious club can offer you.

The Pope & Young Club is one of North America's prominent and leading bow hunting and conservation organizations, named in honor of bow hunters Dr. Saxon Pope and Arthur Young, whose exploits during the early part of the 20th Century drew national attention to his highly challenging form of hunting. As a bow hunter of today, you owe it to yourself to visit their website and learn about a club that exemplifies the sport you love. Please visit their website and plan a trip to their museum. Their website is filled with information you should be familiar with and aware. See all this club has to offer you as a member.

Boone and Crockett Club Official Scoring Charts

Records of
North American
Big Game

250 Station Drive
Missoula, MT 59801
(406) 542-1888

BOONE AND CROCKETT CLUB®

OFFICIAL SCORING SYSTEM FOR NORTH AMERICAN BIG GAME TROPHIES

MINIMUM SCORES	AWARDS	ALL-TIME
whitetail	160	170
Coues'	100	110

TYPICAL
WHITETAIL AND COUES' DEER

KIND OF DEER (check one)
☐ whitetail
☐ Coues'

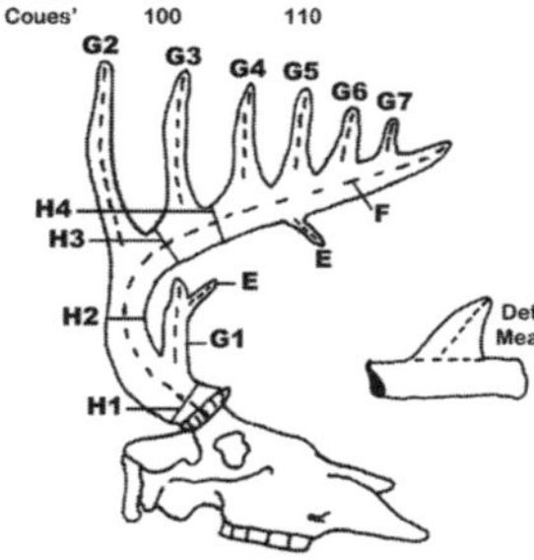

Detail of Point Measurement

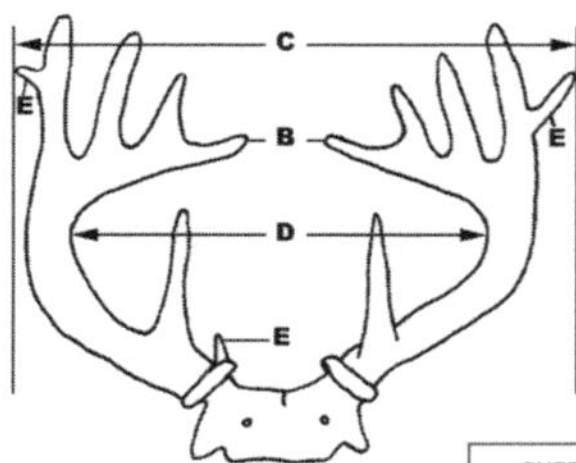

	Abnormal Points Right Antler	Abnormal Points Left Antler
SUBTOTALS		
TOTAL TO E		

SEE OTHER SIDE FOR INSTRUCTIONS				COLUMN 1	COLUMN 2	COLUMN 3	COLUMN 4
A. No. Points on Right Antler		No. Points on Left Antler		Spread Credit	Right Antler	Left Antler	Difference
B. Tip to Tip Spread		C. Greatest Spread					
D. Inside Spread of Main Beams		SPREAD CREDIT MAY EQUAL BUT NOT EXCEED LONGER MAIN BEAM					
E. Total of Lengths of Abnormal Points							
F. Length of Main Beam							
G-1. Length of First Point							
G-2. Length of Second Point							
G-3. Length of Third Point							
G-4. Length of Fourth Point, If Present							
G-5. Length of Fifth Point, If Present							
G-6. Length of Sixth Point, If Present							
G-7. Length of Seventh Point, If Present							
H-1. Circumference at Smallest Place Between Burr and First Point							
H-2. Circumference at Smallest Place Between First and Second Points							
H-3. Circumference at Smallest Place Between Second and Third Points							
H-4. Circumference at Smallest Place Between Third and Fourth Points							
			TOTALS				

ADD	Column 1		Exact Locality Where Killed:
	Column 2		Date Killed: Hunter:
	Column 3		Trophy Owner: Telephone #:
	Subtotal		Trophy Owner's Address:
	SUBTRACT Column 4		Trophy Owner's E-mail: Guide's Name:
	FINAL SCORE		Remarks: (Mention Any Abnormalities or Unique Qualities) OM I.D. Number

Boone and Crockett Club Official Scoring Charts continued

I, ______________________ (PRINT NAME), certify that I have measured this trophy on ______________ (MM/DD/YYYY)

at ______________________ (STREET ADDRESS) ______________ (CITY) ______________ (STATE/PROVINCE)

and that these measurements and data are, to the best of my knowledge and belief, made in accordance with the instructions given.

Witness: ______________________ Signature: ______________________ (B&C OFFICIAL MEASURER) I.D. Number [| | |]

INSTRUCTIONS FOR MEASURING TYPICAL WHITETAIL AND COUES' DEER

All measurements must be made with a 1/4-inch wide flexible steel tape to the nearest one-eighth of an inch. (Note: A flexible steel cable can be used to measure points and main beams only.) Enter fractional figures in eighths, without reduction. Official measurements cannot be taken until the antlers have air dried for at least 60 days after the animal was killed.

A. Number of Points on Each Antler: To be counted a point, the projection must be at least one inch long, with the length exceeding width at one inch or more of length. All points are measured from tip of point to nearest edge of beam as illustrated. Beam tip is counted as a point but not measured as a point. **Point totals do not add into the final score.**

B. Tip to Tip Spread is measured between tips of main beams. **Tip to tip spread does not add into the final score.**

C. Greatest Spread is measured between perpendiculars at a right angle to the center line of the skull at widest part, whether across main beams or points. **Greatest spread does not add into the final score.**

D. Inside Spread of Main Beams is measured at a right angle to the center line of the skull at widest point between main beams. Enter this measurement again as the Spread Credit if it is less than or equal to the length of the longer main beam; if greater, enter longer main beam length for Spread Credit.

E. Total of Lengths of all Abnormal Points: Abnormal Points are those non-typical in location (such as points originating from a point or from bottom or sides of main beam) or extra points beyond the normal pattern of points. Measure in usual manner and enter in appropriate blanks.

F. Length of Main Beam is measured from the center of the lowest outside edge of burr over the outer side to the most distant point of the main beam. The point of beginning is that point on the burr where the center line along the outer side of the beam intersects the burr, then following generally the line of the illustration.

G-1-2-3-4-5-6-7. Length of Normal Points: Normal points project from the top of the main beam. They are measured from nearest edge of main beam over outer curve to tip. Lay the tape along the outer curve of the beam so that the top edge of the tape coincides with the top edge of the beam on both sides of the point to determine the baseline for point measurements. Record point lengths in appropriate blanks.

H-1-2-3-4. Circumferences are taken as detailed in illustration for each measurement. If brow point is missing, take H-1 and H-2 at smallest place between burr and G-2. If G-4 is missing, take H-4 halfway between G-3 and tip of main beam.

MATERIALS RELEASE FORM FOR ALL NON-HUNTER-TAKEN TROPHIES

I certify by my signature that the information I have provided on this form is accurate and correct. I also understand that all my entry materials, including photographs, as well as any additional photographs taken by Boone and Crockett (our representatives or agents) during Awards Programs or Judges Panels, or likenesses rendered from these photographs become the property of the Boone and Crockett Club and may be used to promote the Club, and its records-keeping activities.

Date: ______________ Signature of Trophy Owner: ______________________

ENTRY AFFIDAVIT FOR ALL HUNTER-TAKEN TROPHIES

For the purpose of entry into the Boone and Crockett Club's® records, North American big game harvested by the use of the following methods or under the following conditions are ineligible:

I. Spotting or herding game from the air, followed by landing in its vicinity for the purpose of pursuit and shooting;
II. Herding or chasing with the aid of any motorized equipment;
III. Use of electronic communication devices to guide hunters to game, artificial lighting, electronic light intensifying devices (night vision optics), sights with built-in electronic range-finding capabilities, thermal imaging equipment, electronic game calls or cameras/timers/motion tracking devices that transmit images and other information to the hunter;
IV. Confined by artificial barriers, including escape-proof fenced enclosures;
V. Transplanted for the purpose of commercial shooting;
VI. By the use of traps or pharmaceuticals;
VII. While swimming, helpless in deep snow, or helpless in any other natural or artificial medium;
VIII. On another hunter's license;
IX. Not in full compliance with the game laws or regulations of the federal government or of any state, province, territory, or tribal council on reservations or tribal lands;

I certify that the trophy scored on this chart was not taken in violation of the conditions listed above. In signing this statement, I understand that if the information provided on this entry is found to be misrepresented or fraudulent in any respect, it will not be accepted into the Awards Program and 1) all of my prior entries are subject to deletion from future editions of **Records of North American Big Game** 2) future entries may not be accepted. I also certify by my signature that the information I have provided on this form is accurate and correct. I also understand that all my entry materials, including photographs, as well as any additional photographs taken by Boone and Crockett (our representatives or agents) during Awards Programs or Judges Panels, or likenesses rendered from these photographs become the property of the Boone and Crockett Club and may be used to promote the Club, and its records-keeping activities.

FAIR CHASE, as defined by the Boone and Crockett Club®, is the ethical, sportsmanlike and lawful pursuit and taking of any free-ranging wild, native North American big game animal in a manner that does not give the hunter an improper advantage over such game animals.

The Boone and Crockett Club® may exclude the entry of any animal that it deems to have been taken in an unethical manner or under conditions deemed inappropriate by the Club.

Date: ______________ Signature of Hunter: ______________________
(SIGNATURE MUST BE WITNESSED BY AN OFFICIAL MEASURER OR A NOTARY PUBLIC.)

Date: ______________ Signature of Notary or Official Measurer: ______________________

Boone and Crockett Club Official Scoring Charts continued

Records of North American Big Game

250 Station Drive
Missoula, MT 59801
(406) 542-1888

BOONE AND CROCKETT CLUB®

OFFICIAL SCORING SYSTEM FOR NORTH AMERICAN BIG GAME TROPHIES

NON-TYPICAL WHITETAIL AND COUES' DEER

MINIMUM SCORES	AWARDS	ALL-TIME
whitetail	185	195
Coues'	105	120

KIND OF DEER (check one)
☐ whitetail
☐ Coues'

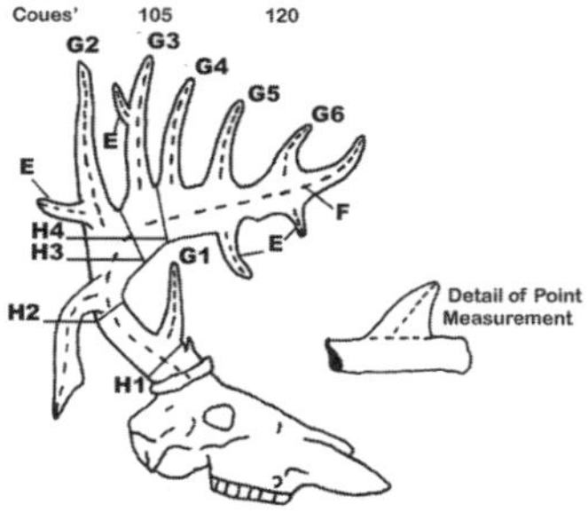

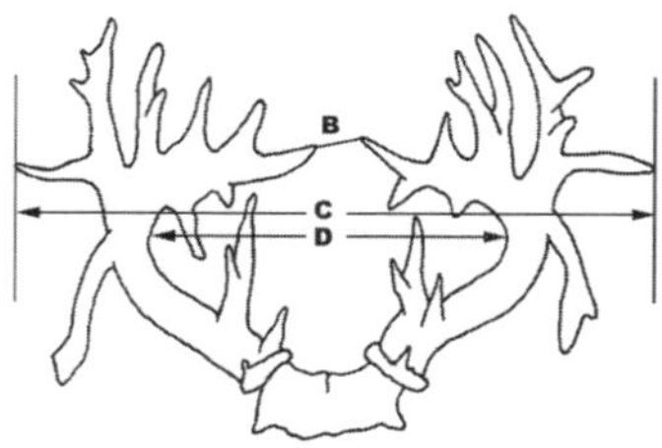

Abnormal Points	
Right Antler	Left Antler
SUBTOTALS		
E. TOTAL		

SEE OTHER SIDE FOR INSTRUCTIONS				COLUMN 1	COLUMN 2	COLUMN 3	COLUMN 4
A. No. Points on Right Antler		No. Points on Left Antler		Spread Credit	Right Antler	Left Antler	Difference
B. Tip to Tip Spread		C. Greatest Spread					
D. Inside Spread of Main Beams		SPREAD CREDIT MAY EQUAL BUT NOT EXCEED LONGER MAIN BEAM					
F. Length of Main Beam							
G-1. Length of First Point							
G-2. Length of Second Point							
G-3. Length of Third Point							
G-4. Length of Fourth Point, If Present							
G-5. Length of Fifth Point, If Present							
G-6. Length of Sixth Point, If Present							
G-7. Length of Seventh Point, If Present							
H-1. Circumference at Smallest Place Between Burr and First Point							
H-2. Circumference at Smallest Place Between First and Second Points							
H-3. Circumference at Smallest Place Between Second and Third Points							
H-4. Circumference at Smallest Place Between Third and Fourth Points							
TOTALS							

ADD	Column 1		Exact Locality Where Killed:
	Column 2		Date Killed: Hunter:
	Column 3		Trophy Owner: Telephone #:
	Subtotal		Trophy Owner's Address:
	SUBTRACT Column 4		Trophy Owner's E-mail: Guide's Name:
	Subtotal		Remarks: (Mention Any Abnormalities or Unique Qualities)
	ADD Line E Total		
	FINAL SCORE		OM I.D. Number

Boone and Crockett Club Official Scoring Charts continued

I, ______________________________ (PRINT NAME), certify that I have measured this trophy on ______________ (MM/DD/YYYY)

at ______________________________ (STREET ADDRESS) ______________ (CITY) ______________ (STATE/PROVINCE)

and that these measurements and data are, to the best of my knowledge and belief, made in accordance with the instructions given.

Witness: ______________________ Signature: ______________________ (B&C OFFICIAL MEASURER) I.D. Number [| | |]

INSTRUCTIONS FOR MEASURING NON-TYPICAL WHITETAIL AND COUES' DEER

All measurements must be made with a 1/4-inch wide flexible steel tape to the nearest one-eighth of an inch. (Note: A flexible steel cable can be used to measure points and main beams only.) Enter fractional figures in eighths, without reduction. Official measurements cannot be taken until the antlers have air dried for at least 60 days after the animal was killed.

A. Number of Points on Each Antler: To be counted a point, the projection must be at least one inch long, with the length exceeding width at one inch or more of length. All points are measured from tip of point to nearest edge of beam as illustrated. Beam tip is counted as a point but not measured as a point. **Point totals do not add into the final score.**

B. Tip to Tip Spread is measured between tips of main beams. **Tip to tip spread does not add into the final score.**

C. Greatest Spread is measured between perpendiculars at a right angle to the center line of the skull at widest part, whether across main beams or points. **Greatest spread does not add into the final score.**

D. Inside Spread of Main Beams is measured at a right angle to the center line of the skull at widest point between main beams. Enter this measurement again as the Spread Credit if it is less than or equal to the length of the longer main beam; if greater, enter longer main beam length for Spread Credit.

E. Total of Lengths of all Abnormal Points: Abnormal Points are those non-typical in location (such as points originating from a point or from bottom or sides of main beam) or extra points beyond the normal pattern of points. Measure in usual manner and enter in appropriate blanks.

F. Length of Main Beam is measured from the center of the lowest outside edge of burr over the outer side to the most distant point of the main beam. The point of beginning is that point on the burr where the center line along the outer side of the beam intersects the burr, then following generally the line of the illustration.

G-1-2-3-4-5-6-7. Length of Normal Points: Normal points project from the top of the main beam. They are measured from nearest edge of main beam over outer curve to tip. Lay the tape along the outer curve of the beam so that the top edge of the tape coincides with the top edge of the beam on both sides of the point to determine the baseline for point measurement. Record point lengths in appropriate blanks.

H-1-2-3-4. Circumferences are taken as detailed in illustration for each measurement. If brow point is missing, take H-1 and H-2 at smallest place between burr and G-2. If G-4 is missing, take H-4 halfway between G-3 and tip of main beam.

MATERIALS RELEASE FORM FOR ALL NON-HUNTER-TAKEN TROPHIES

I certify by my signature that the information I have provided on this form is accurate and correct. I also understand that all my entry materials, including photographs, as well as any additional photographs taken by Boone and Crockett (our representatives or agents) during Awards Programs or Judges Panels, or likenesses rendered from these photographs become the property of the Boone and Crockett Club and may be used to promote the Club, and its records-keeping activities.

Date: ______________ Signature of Trophy Owner: ______________________________

ENTRY AFFIDAVIT FOR ALL HUNTER-TAKEN TROPHIES

For the purpose of entry into the Boone and Crockett Club's® records, North American big game harvested by the use of the following methods or under the following conditions are ineligible:

I. Spotting or herding game from the air, followed by landing in its vicinity for the purpose of pursuit and shooting;
II. Herding or chasing with the aid of any motorized equipment;
III. Use of electronic communication devices to guide hunters to game, artificial lighting, electronic light intensifying devices (night vision optics), sights with built-in electronic range-finding capabilities, thermal imaging equipment, electronic game calls or cameras/timers/motion tracking devices that transmit images and other information to the hunter;
IV. Confined by artificial barriers, including escape-proof fenced enclosures;
V. Transplanted for the purpose of commercial shooting;
VI. By the use of traps or pharmaceuticals;
VII. While swimming, helpless in deep snow, or helpless in any other natural or artificial medium;
VIII. On another hunter's license;
IX. Not in full compliance with the game laws or regulations of the federal government or of any state, province, territory, or tribal council on reservations or tribal lands;

I certify that the trophy scored on this chart was not taken in violation of the conditions listed above. In signing this statement, I understand that if the information provided on this entry is found to be misrepresented or fraudulent in any respect, it will not be accepted into the Awards Program and 1) all of my prior entries are subject to deletion from future editions of **Records of North American Big Game** 2) future entries may not be accepted. I also certify by my signature that the information I have provided on this form is accurate and correct. I also understand that all my entry materials, including photographs, as well as any additional photographs taken by Boone and Crockett (our representatives or agents) during Awards Programs or Judges Panels, or likenesses rendered from these photographs become the property of the Boone and Crockett Club and may be used to promote the Club, and its records-keeping activities.

FAIR CHASE, as defined by the Boone and Crockett Club®, is the ethical, sportsmanlike and lawful pursuit and taking of any free-ranging wild, native North American big game animal in a manner that does not give the hunter an improper advantage over such game animals.

The Boone and Crockett Club® may exclude the entry of any animal that it deems to have been taken in an unethical manner or under conditions deemed inappropriate by the Club.

Date: ______________ Signature of Hunter: ______________________________

(SIGNATURE MUST BE WITNESSED BY AN OFFICIAL MEASURER OR A NOTARY PUBLIC.)

Date: ______________ Signature of Notary or Official Measurer: ______________________________

Pope & Young Club Official Scoring Charts

POPE & YOUNG CLUB

Official Scoring System for Bowhunting North American Big Game

MINIMUM SCORE
whitetail 125
Coues' 65

TYPICAL WHITETAIL AND COUES' DEER

KIND OF DEER (check one)
☐ whitetail
☐ Coues'

☐ **IN VELVET**

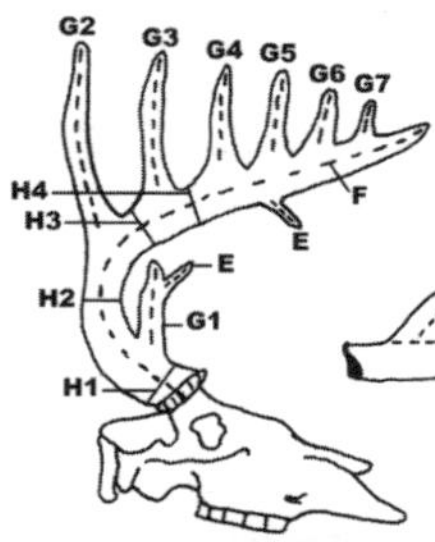

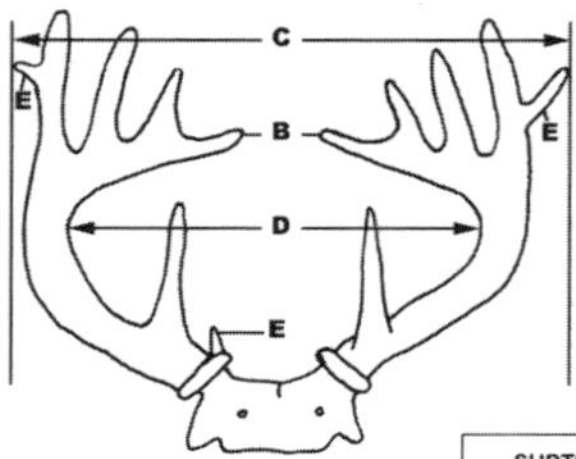

	Abnormal Points	
	Right Antler	Left Antler
SUBTOTALS		
TOTAL TO E		

SEE OTHER SIDE FOR INSTRUCTIONS				COLUMN 1	COLUMN 2	COLUMN 3	COLUMN 4
A. No. Points on Right Antler		No. Points on Left Antler		Spread Credit	Right Antler	Left Antler	Difference
B. Tip to Tip Spread		C. Greatest Spread					
D. Inside Spread of Main Beams		SPREAD CREDIT MAY EQUAL BUT NOT EXCEED LONGER MAIN BEAM					
E. Total of Lengths of Abnormal Points							
F. Length of Main Beam							
G-1. Length of First Point							
G-2. Length of Second Point							
G-3. Length of Third Point							
G-4. Length of Fourth Point, If Present							
G-5. Length of Fifth Point, If Present							
G-6. Length of Sixth Point, If Present							
G-7. Length of Seventh Point, If Present							
H-1. Circumference at Smallest Place Between Burr and First Point							
H-2. Circumference at Smallest Place Between First and Second Points							
H-3. Circumference at Smallest Place Between Second and Third Points							
H-4. Circumference at Smallest Place Between Third and Fourth Points or half way between Third Point and Beam Tip if Fourth Point is missing.							
			TOTALS				

ADD	Column 1		Location of Kill:	(County)	(State/Prov)
	Column 2		Date Killed:	Hunter:	
	Column 3		Hunter's Address:		
	Subtotal		City: State: Zip Code:	Telephone #: ( )	
	SUBTRACT Column 4		Guide's Name and Address:		
	FINAL SCORE		Remarks: (Mention Any Abnormalities or Unique Qualities)	OM I.D. Number	

Pope & Young Club Official Scoring Charts continued

I, ______________________________ (PRINT NAME), certify that I have measured this trophy on ____________ (MM/DD/YYYYY)

at ______________________________ (STREET ADDRESS) ____________ (CITY) ____________ (STATE/PROVINCE) ________ (ZIP CODE)

and that these measurements and data are, to the best of my knowledge and belief, made in accordance with the instructions given.

Witness: ______________________________ (TO MEASURER'S SIGNATURE) Signature: ______________________________ (P&Y OFFICIAL MEASURER)

______________________________ (ADDRESS)

____________ (CITY) ____________ (STATE/PROVINCE) ________ (ZIP)

BRIEF INSTRUCTIONS FOR MEASURING TYPICAL WHITETAIL AND COUES' DEER

Measurements must be made with a flexible steel tape or steel cable and recorded to the nearest one-eighth of an inch. To simplify addition, please enter fractional figures in eighths and in proper fractions. Refer to **P & Y Measurer's Manual** for a detailed description of measuring procedures.

A. Number of Points on each antler. To be counted a point, a projection must be at least one inch long AND, at some location at least one inch from the tip, the length of the projection must exceed its width. Beam tip is counted as a point but not measured as a point.

B. Tip to Tip Spread is measured between tips of main beams.

C. Greatest Spread is measured between perpendiculars at a right angle to the center line of the skull at widest part whether across main beams or points.

D. Inside Spread of Main Beam is measured at a right angle to the center line of the skull at widest point between main beams. Enter this measurement again in "Spread Credit" column if it is less than or equal to the length of longer main beam. If greater, enter longer main beam length for Spread Credit.

E. Total of Length of Abnormal Points. Abnormal points are generally considered to be those non-typical in location (such as points originating from a point or from bottom or sides of main beam). Sketch all abnormal points on antler illustration (front of form) showing location and length. Measure in usual manner and enter in appropriate blanks.

F. Length of Main Beam is measured from the center of the lowest outside edge of burr over outer curve to the most distant point of the main beam. Begin measuring at the location on the burr where the center line along the outer curve of the beam intersects the burr.

G-1-2-3-4-5-6-7. Length of Normal Points. Normal points project from the top of the main beam as shown in illustration. They are measured from the top edge of the main beam (baseline), over their outer curve, to their tip. To establish the appropriate baseline, lay a tape or (preferably) a cable on the top edge of the beam on each side of the point and draw a line under the cable to reflect the top edge of the beam as if the point was not present. Record point lengths in appropriate blanks.

H-1-2-3-4. Circumferences. Circumferences are taken at the smallest place between corresponding normal points, as illustrated. If first point is missing, take H-1 and H-2 at smallest place between burr and second point. If G-4 is missing, take H-4 halfway between the center of G-3 and tip of main beam. Circumference measurements must be taken with a steel tape (a cable cannot be used for these measurements).

ENTRY REQUIREMENTS

1. **Original scoring form** completed by an Official Measurer of the Pope & Young Club or the Boone & Crockett Club.
2. **Completed Fair Chase Affidavit.**
3. **Three photos of antlers, horns, or skull** (a view from the front side, a view from the left side and a view from the right side). A field photo is also requested, if possible.
4. **$35.00 recording fee** (made payable to the Pope and Young Club)

Drying Period: To be eligible for entry in the Pope & Young Records, a trophy must first have been stored under normal room temperature and humidity for at least 60 days after date of kill. No trophy will be considered which has been altered in any way from its natural state.

Pope & Young Club Official Scoring Charts continued

POPE & YOUNG CLUB

Official Scoring System for Bowhunting North American Big Game

MINIMUM SCORE

whitetail	155
Coues'	80

NON-TYPICAL WHITETAIL AND COUES' DEER

KIND OF DEER (check one)
☐ whitetail ☐ Coues'
☐ **IN VELVET**

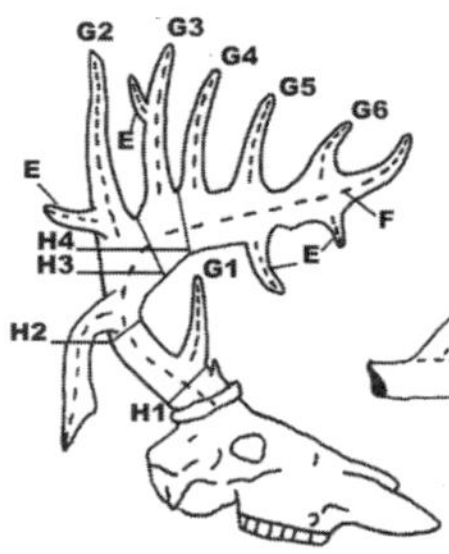

Detail of Point Measurement

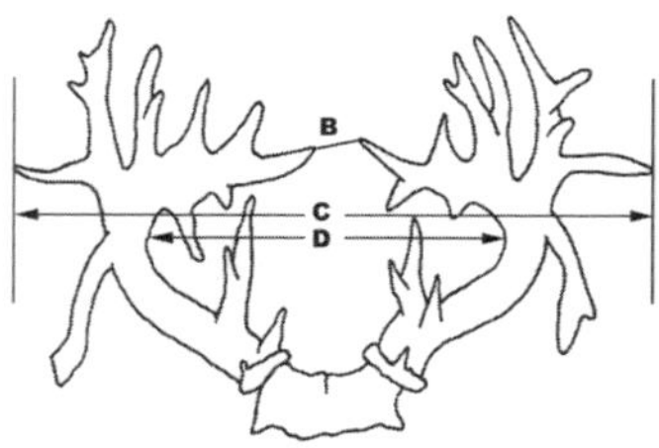

	Abnormal Points	
	Right Antler	Left Antler
SUBTOTALS		
E. TOTAL		

SEE OTHER SIDE FOR INSTRUCTIONS				COLUMN 1	COLUMN 2	COLUMN 3	COLUMN 4
A. No. Points on Right Antler		No. Points on Left Antler		Spread Credit	Right Antler	Left Antler	Difference
B. Tip to Tip Spread		C. Greatest Spread					
D. Inside Spread of Main Beams		SPREAD CREDIT MAY EQUAL BUT NOT EXCEED LONGER MAIN BEAM					
F. Length of Main Beam							
G-1. Length of First Point							
G-2. Length of Second Point							
G-3. Length of Third Point							
G-4. Length of Fourth Point, If Present							
G-5. Length of Fifth Point, If Present							
G-6. Length of Sixth Point, If Present							
G-7. Length of Seventh Point, If Present							
H-1. Circumference at Smallest Place Between Burr and First Point							
H-2. Circumference at Smallest Place Between First and Second Points							
H-3. Circumference at Smallest Place Between Second and Third Points							
H-4. Circumference at Smallest Place Between Third and Fourth Points or half way between Third Point and Beam Tip if Fourth Point is missing.							
			TOTALS				

ADD	Column 1		Location of Kill:	(County)	(State/Prov)
	Column 2		Date Killed:	Hunter:	
	Column 3		Hunter's Address:		
	Subtotal		City: State: Zip Code:	Telephone #: ( )	
	SUBTRACT Column 4		Guide's Name and Address:		
	Subtotal		Remarks: (Mention Any Abnormalities or Unique Qualities)		
	ADD Line E Total				
	FINAL SCORE			OM I.D. Number	

Pope & Young Club Official Scoring Charts continued

I, ______________________________ (PRINT NAME), certify that I have measured this trophy on __________ (MM/DD/YYYYY)

at ______________________________ (STREET ADDRESS) __________ (CITY) __________ (STATE/PROVINCE) __________ (ZIP CODE)

and that these measurements and data are, to the best of my knowledge and belief, made in accordance with the instructions given.

Witness: ______________________________ (TO MEASURER'S SIGNATURE) Signature: ______________________________ (P&Y OFFICIAL MEASURER)

______________________________ (ADDRESS)

__________ (CITY) __________ (STATE/PROVINCE) __________ (ZIP)

BRIEF INSTRUCTIONS FOR MEASURING NON-TYPICAL WHITETAIL AND COUES' DEER

Measurements must be made with a flexible steel tape or steel cable and recorded to the nearest one-eighth of an inch. To simplify addition, please enter fractional figures in eighths and in proper fractions. Refer to **P & Y Measurer's Manual** for a detailed description of measuring procedures.

A. Number of Points on each antler. To be counted a point, a projection must be at least one inch long AND, at some location at least one inch from the tip, the length of the projection must exceed its width. Beam tip is counted as a point but not measured as a point.

B. Tip to Tip Spread is measured between tips of main beams.

C. Greatest Spread is measured between perpendiculars at a right angle to the center line of the skull at widest part whether across main beams or points.

D. Inside Spread of Main Beam is measured at a right angle to the center line of the skull at widest point between main beams. Enter this measurement again in "Spread Credit" column if it is less than or equal to the length of longer main beam. If greater, enter longer main beam length for Spread Credit.

E. Total of Length of Abnormal Points. Abnormal points are generally considered to be those non-typical in location (such as points originating from a point or from bottom or sides of main beam). Measure in usual manner and enter in appropriate blanks.

F. Length of Main Beam is measured from the center of the lowest outside edge of burr over outer curve to the most distant point of the main beam. Begin measuring at the location on the burr where the center line along the outer curve of the beam intersects the burr.

G-1-2-3-4-5-6-7. Length of Normal Points. Normal points project from the top of the main beam as shown in illustration. They are measured from the top edge of the main beam (baseline), over their outer curve, to their tip. To establish the appropriate baseline, lay a tape or (preferably) a cable on the top edge of the beam on each side of the point and draw a line under the cable to reflect the top edge of the beam as if the point was not present. Record point lengths in appropriate blanks.

H-1-2-3-4. Circumferences. Circumferences are taken at the smallest place between corresponding normal points, as illustrated. If first point is missing, take H-1 and H-2 at smallest place between burr and second point. If G-4 is missing, take H-4 halfway between the center of G-3 and tip of main beam. Circumference measurements must be taken with a steel tape (a cable cannot be used for these measurements).

ENTRY REQUIREMENTS

1. **Original scoring form** completed by an Official Measurer of the Pope & Young Club or the Boone & Crockett Club.
2. **Completed Fair Chase Affidavit.**
3. **Three photos of antlers, horns, or skull** (a view from the front side, a view from the left side and a view from the right side). A field photo is also requested, if possible.
4. **$35.00 recording fee** (made payable to the Pope and Young Club)

Drying Period: To be eligible for entry in the Pope & Young Records, a trophy must first have been stored under normal room temperature and humidity for at least 60 days after date of kill. No trophy will be considered which has been altered in any way from its natural state.

Acknowledgments

Mark Sanders

Mark Sanders is an Instructor in English and Philosophy at Three Rivers Community College in Poplar Bluff, Missouri. In addition to teaching writing, literature, religion, mythology, philosophy and ethics, he also serves as Director of Creative Design Services, where he creates many of the designs for the college's printed materials and advertisements.

Mr. Sanders is a graduate of the University of Missouri School of Journalism, where he received extensive training in writing, editing, reporting and graphic design. He graduated summa cum laude in 1990. He also received his MA in English/Creative Writing at Mizzou, where he was a William Gregory Fellowship recipient. While in graduate school, Mr. Sanders was editor of *Stir*, the student creative writing magazine, which was the student-run outlet for creative fiction, poetry and art for more than ten years.

Terry Staton

During his freelance art career, Terry Staton has developed his talent that is used in creating artwork that has sold all across the United States. From illustrations, to canvas oil paintings, to murals that have towered some twenty feet and spanned forty feet or more, and now even to include photography. Mr. Staton has met the challenge and created eye-catching works of art. With attention to detail and the ability to create a sense of perspective, Mr. Staton has catered to young and old viewers alike.

Mr. Staton continues to create masterpieces in all kinds of art mediums, and strives to produce something that will stir the emotions of what the public likes to see in art. It's not complicated, nor is it the kind of art that leaves the viewer stumped as to what is represented. Mr. Staton continues to work in new areas of art with computer graphics, 3D sculpting and leaded glass. Commissions come from around the world, and he welcomes any challenge for any new work.

Larry Ditto

Larry Ditto is a full time nature photographer residing in McAllen, Texas. He leads a number of photography tours and workshops each year. A schedule can be found on his website at www.larryditto.com. Larry's work has appeared in *Sports Afield, Field & Stream, Gray's Sporting Journal*, and *National Geographic* Books; he is a frequent contributor to *National Wildlife, Texas Parks & Wildlife, Texas Highways, Birders World, Bird Watcher's Digest* and other magazines, books and calendars.

About the Author

Born in an Italian neighborhood in the heart of New York, Bob grew up in the South Bronx. Bob first developed his interest in writing at a Bronx school that Hollywood portrayed as the toughest school in the country in the movie "The Blackboard Jungle." Attending Pace University for a year, he taught martial arts, formed the Pace Athletic Club, and edited the college newspaper. Bob then volunteered for both the U.S. Army and the U.S. Air Force, serving his country in combat in the Vietnam War.

His interest in the outdoors was inspired by his father, Frank J. Amendola, general manager for *Reader's Digest* who also had a unique talent for writing. Bob was known for writing short stories about hunting and the outdoors before attempting to write a book about hunting whitetail deer. This effort came to an abrupt halt when a family member asked, "Who would want to buy a book about hunting written by you?" Throwing a half-written manuscript away in the wake of that rejection, Bob stopped writing until he became older and was encouraged by friends, who saw his special talent as a writer, as a marksman with both firearms and bows, and his exceptional abilities as an outdoorsman and hunter.

After years spent gaining an acute and intense comprehension of all facets of hunting, Bob turned to teaching, conducting hunting seminars and archery exhibitions that astonished his audience with his archery skills. Once again, the desire arose to write a complete and comprehensive book about whitetail deer hunting. The result of that dream is *Today's Deer Hunting Handbook: The Complete Illustrated Guide for New and Experienced Hunters.*

Bob wrote this book to give every new and novice hunter the knowledge and information of an experienced, professional hunter. Bob's skills and experience will also fine-tune the senses of any hunter and enable experienced hunters to harvest quality whitetail deer consistently, making their hunts more memorable and enjoyable, by proven methods that Bob uses on a regular basis to achieve consistent results.

Bob is currently attending Three Rivers College and is a full-time student majoring in both English and History. He is a member of two prestigious Honor Societies both for academics and English; Phi Theta Kappa and Sigma Kappa Delta. Attending Three Rivers College has enabled Bob through the help of Dr. Devin Stephenson, Mark Sanders, and many other staff and faculty, to excel and move forward through their encouragement and inspiration. Bob is currently working on his third book concerning bow-hunting, which will be completed in 2014, that will enable both novice and experienced hunters alike to produce both consistent and memorable results. Bob may be contacted at www.bobamendola.com.

Hunting Record

Date of Kill	Weapon Type

Hunting Locations

Index